Purrrfecting Your Bond

A PRACTICAL & SPIRITUAL GUIDE TO CREATE A LASTING, LOVING RELATIONSHIP WITH YOUR KITTY

JESSICA MOCKETT

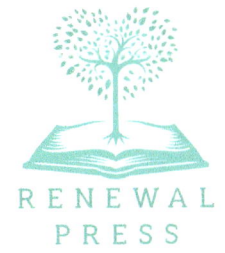

RENEWAL PRESS

Cover and interior design by Megan Sheer. Cover photo by Jessica Mockett.

All photos taken by Jessica Mockett or under license or with permission of the photographer unless otherwise indicated.

Illustrations by Anna K. Mockett.

ISBN 979-8-218-45424-1

Disclaimer: The author's opinions expressed herein are based on her personal experience, observations, and her research and readings on the subject matter. The author's opinions may not be universally applicable to all people in all circumstances. The events, places, and conversations in this book are the recollections of author that have been recreated from memory and/or supplemented and/or condensed. Names or genders of several individuals have been changed to maintain anonymity and to protect their privacy. The information presented in this book regarding the care of humans is in no way intended as medical advice or as a substitute for medical or other counseling. The information should be used in conjunction with the guidance and care of your physician. In addition, the information presented in this book regarding the medical care of cats is in no way intended as veterinary and/or behavioral advice or as a substitute for veterinary and/or behavioral review. The information presented in this book should be used in conjunction with the advice of your veterinarian. Do not rely upon any information to replace consultations or advice provided by qualified health care professionals. The publisher and author disclaim liability for any negative or other medical or other outcomes to humans and felines that may occur as a result of acting on or not acting on anything set forth in this publication.

All registered and unregistered trademarks mentioned in this book are the property of their respective owners.

For more information, go to the author's website at www.jessicamockett.com

For the kitties in my life whom I have helped and loved.
I thank them for all they taught me.

Contents

Introduction

WHO AM I?

I have loved and been involved with cats my whole life. During a difficult time in my mid-thirties, I found cat rescue work. It was truly a God-sent activity that helped me not be self-focused and depressed.

After a decade of involvement in cat rescue and over 15,000 volunteer hours logged—personally fostering nearly one hundred cats (mostly fragile neonates or critical-health-needs kittens) and helping hundreds of additional animals via working numerous adoption events and operating in rescue leadership—I now have a wealth of knowledge about best-care practices for felines. Furthermore, I have witnessed how many cat owners make situations harder for themselves and their furry friends because of misunderstandings about the nature of cats and unhealthy beliefs and practices in how they care for the cats (and even themselves). I began consulting with cat owners a few years ago, stumbling into it really. Since then, I've earned many certifications and credentials for feline behavior and training. I tell people at adoption events that rescue work has taught me much about cats. Every new cat situation, whether fostering, mentoring, managing, healing, consulting, or teaching, I learn something new.

Much of my success working with cats—and guardians—comes from my desire to approach feline care in a spiritual, intuitive, and holistic way. In this book you will discover that I genuinely seek angelic assistance, use prayer, and listen to spiritual promptings to help many of the cats I have encountered. I have successfully used holistic techniques like energetic muscle testing, nutritional supplementation, crystal supports, and vibrational frequency treatments with cats while still advocating routine and sound veterinary care.

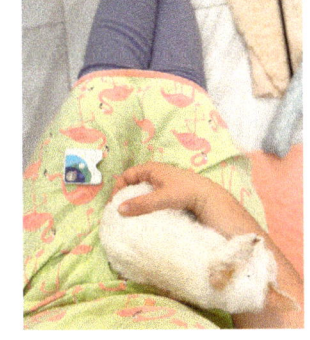

❀ *Using frequency healing device with foster Hero.*

1

❀ Above: *My grandmother, Rochelle (center) with her sisters. Benny and Sweet on the end hold kitties. Circa early 1920s.*

❀ Far left: *My mother with her cat growing up, Sugar. Early 1950s.*

❀ Left: *Me with my kitty growing up, Pepé. 1996.*

Along with my feline-care certifications, I am certified as a practitioner of three energy healing modalities—The Belief Code®, The Body Code™, and The Emotion Code® created by Dr. Bradley Nelson. These alternative healing practices, which together comprise a comprehensive method of energetic balancing, have allowed me to help many human and animal clients since 2016.

Born in the late 70s in Florida, the youngest of a large family, I was drawn to cats as a little girl. It's in my blood. We have a family legacy, written in our DNA, of cat ladies, going back at least four generations.

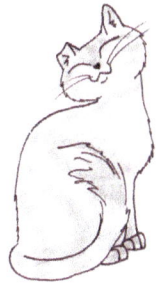

As a little one, I collected a plethora of stuffed cats. Our family adopted a kitten when I was about four years old. I loved her, but she was truly my mother's cat. *My* first cat came when I was about ten years old. My sister Marcy found a shorthaired orange tabby in the church parking lot. He was starving, so Marcy brought him home. We already had a family cat, and my father groused about a second cat, demanding we find it a home as soon as possible.

Because this kitten had starved, his system was very stinky as he began to eat again. We didn't know how to reintroduce food to an animal that had starved; we just gave him lots to eat. He passed gas so often, we nicknamed him Pepé Le Pew. Still, he quickly became my best friend. At that time I struggled with severe depression from a deep trauma (likely a form of PTSD). I needed a friend. My mother knew this and talked my father into letting me keep the kitty. I carted him off to bed every night, and he purred under the covers until I fell asleep. He then moved to the foot of my bed where he stayed all night, every night. His companionship was a healing salve.

Two years into our relationship, Pepé became ill with a urinary blockage. My parents paid for a corrective procedure, but months later couldn't pay for another he needed. The vet recommended euthanasia because Pepé hadn't been able to pee for days. My preteen-self begged God in prayer to save my kitty. I sat weeping alone next to my very sick furry friend and bargained with God. I told Him I'd read the whole book of scriptures if He would heal my cat, my only friend. Moments later a gush of urine came from Pepé as he lay there. I was so elated; I sang songs as I cleaned up the mess.

Pepé was healed that day. He never again had a urinary block. My little buddy taught me my first important lessons in God, prayer, and miracles. That day, I truly became converted to knowing God is there. For me, it was no coincidence, but a clear miracle. Of course, I no longer bargain with God when I ask for needed or wanted help, but I know that God accepted that tactic from a young girl desperate to be heard. I was known; I was loved, and so was my little orange tabby cat.

❀ *Me with my Pepé and our other cat Puddy when I was about eleven years old.*

3

Now all these years later, who am I? What has my life journey to this point revealed about me?

Describing yourself to strangers and doing it justly can prove difficult. Women especially can suffer from the common "not good enough" complex, and I am often one of them. I truly feel it is a weakness of mine to use the right words in interviews to convey who I am and what I am capable of. With that context, please know that the rest of this paragraph is not coming from a place of ego, but from a place of trying to do better at recognizing what strengths I do have. At my core I am a spiritually focused being, emotionally sensitive and somewhat empathic, an intuitive healer, and strong-willed for what is good or just. I am opinionated and share my thoughts in clear ways (usually), and I have the capacity to speak openly about hard things. I am compassionate and giving toward women, children, and animals—a protector of anyone more vulnerable than myself. Beauty and nature rejuvenate me, I am very feminine in my tastes, I have a creative brain able to see something in my mind then create it in reality, and I long to contribute to building a better future for myself and others. Though still an intrinsically flawed human, I value these traits in myself and strive to increase their capacity.

A great deal of this book really deals with our personal healing and wellness and using them as vehicles to better understand our pet cats. Having witnessed how frequently owners misunderstand and mistreat cats, how often they abandon, euthanize, or surrender cats because of behavioral concerns that could be resolved, I am dedicated to using all of my experience in healing the wounds that cause rifts in human-feline relationships. As such, my approach will be holistic, giving you a bit more to ponder than other cat behavioral books currently available. I will present cat care not only from a physical and mental (scientific methodologies) perspective but also combine with these the emotional, spiritual, and alternative healing practices that will greatly enhance your feline understanding and bonding.

I will use everything I have learned in more than a decade of serving cats in a variety of circumstances to help teach the key principles of building a healthy cat-human relationship. This book is not perfect, but I hope *purrrfect*! No doubt, a few imperfections will be contained herein; certainly another feline consultant or behaviorist would treat a circumstance differently.

MY CAT FAMILY

Stella, my first cat as an adult, was a loving and gentle, little, black-and-white shorthair. I will mention her a few times throughout this book. She taught me a hard lesson of loss when ignoring spiritual prompts.

As I will mention them throughout this work, I will include an introduction to my current cat family. I have six forever cats. I adopted the two eldest prior to getting involved in rescue work and the remaining four are what rescue workers jokingly refer to as "foster failures," meaning I failed to adopt them out because I kept them for myself.

Gigi & Prim

Gigi, a short-haired blue, ticked tabby, and her biological sister Prim, a medium-haired chocolate lynx point, were about twelve to fourteen weeks old when I adopted them. Gigi and Prim recently turned twelve. Gigi suffers from arthritis but still has daily zoomies at 10 pm. She is a gentle spirit, an "old soul." Prim, officially Primrose, is true to her name: a beautiful kitty, well-mannered, gently shy, and very sweet. My big scaredy cat, Prim really wishes I never began fostering and kept so many other cats.

Trixie & Beaux

Nine years old, my next fur babies are biological siblings as well. They originally came to me as four-week-old orphaned foster kittens with two other siblings. A handsome long-haired black-and-white kitty, Beaux is such a cuddler, hence his name. Trixie, a black-and-white shorthair like Stella, has a quirky personality. She is one of my miracle fosters who survived serious illness as a kitten. I struggle the most with her. She tries the limits of my patience each day because of her relentless need to lounge on top of my shoulders.

Honey

At six years old, Honey is a gorgeous long-haired cat with a rarer amber, ticked tabby coat. She came to me as a bottle baby with a few siblings when she was about five to seven days old. She is extremely affectionate and confident with people. However, I do a lot more cat parenting with her in the mix because she ruffles everyone else's fur.

❀ Sweet Stella snuggling me at night.

❀ My serious Gigi girl.

❀ Beautiful Beaux at Christmas time.

❀ Fluffy Honey on the deck.

❀ Prim enjoys the new plants and sun on the deck.

❀ Trixie loves the snow.

❀ Handsome Skippy boy.

Skippyjon

I received Skippyjon, my final furever friend, when he was about three weeks old. He is a beautiful, sleek, short-haired chocolate seal point going on four years old. I worked hard to keep him alive as a kitten because he had panleukopenia (distemper). To this day he snuggles up to me like a human baby, flipping over on his back in my arms and looking lovingly into my eyes with his baby blues while he purrs.

This is my cat family whom I will reference throughout this book. I am grateful for my fur babies who have taught me a myriad of lessons in love and "parenting." They have given me additional opportunities to witness miracles and tender mercies from God.

WHY ADD SPIRITUALITY TO THE CARE OF CATS?

It's honestly who I am. I genuinely turn to God, Christ, Angels, and Spirit all the time for help in caring for my forever and foster cats. I have gotten push back from family, editors, other authors, and marketers saying I can't mix the topic of spirituality with the practical care and behavioral concerns of felines. "Audiences won't appreciate it." "It's confusing." "Where's the market for this message?"

I admit to feeling scared there won't be an audience. Writing a book involves a lot of work and investment, to then have no one pick it up and read it. Still, I have pushed that fear aside and pressed forward because I think there are many more spiritually-minded people out there than not. I think there *is* room for my message because there isn't currently a similar message available. Publishers want new authors to follow a formula of previous authors who had some success on the topic because it produces less risk. But then where can new ideas and perspectives fit in? Sometimes, someone has to be bold enough to break the mold.

7

HIGHER POWER: 77%   MORE OPEN TO GOD: 44%   SPIRITUAL BELIEFS: 80%

Those of us who feel spiritually motivated should be encouraged because we are in no way alone. In October 2022, a Barna survey of 2,000 U.S. adults (statistically speaking, a thousand respondents is typically considered a significant enough response for valid results), three out of four (74%) want to grow spiritually. Additionally, the same proportion (77%) believe in a Higher Power. Nearly half (44%) are more open to God today than before the pandemic, and 80% of Americans believe in a spiritual or supernatural dimension to this world (AKA Angels or spirits).

Anecdotally, spiritually sensitive, open minded, and emotionally intelligent people are more often drawn to cats as pets. I hope this helps make the case for a spiritually driven cat-care book!

I want this book to evoke inclusivity. I don't want any potential reader to feel they don't belong inside the words because they think or feel differently. However, I also believe as audiences, we need to allow authors to be vulnerable and authentic to themselves. If their lives are filled with God, Spirit, Buddha, Allah, Mother Earth, or the metaphysical, they should feel free to express it. A *New York Times* best-selling author of numerous self-help books felt she wasn't truly free to discuss her belief in Angels until her eighth book. I admit I avoided using the name of Christ in my initial draft of this work. I worried that if I expressed my belief in Him, this book would be auto-categorized as "Christian," meant only for Christian audiences. I don't want that, because many spiritual people who do not see Christ as their Savior still need a good book on how to apply spiritual principles in caring for their cats. We need to find, as a culture, a more balanced way to allow authors to be authentic and still include those in our readership who do not share all our beliefs. I think the key is this: as authors we do our best expressing our beliefs in loving ways, and as readers we do our best to use a loving filter to examine the words written. Then readers of other religions or belief systems from the author can still gain value from the words and happily apply the writer's ideas into their own lives.

I personally enjoy reading many uplifting books written by people of all kinds of religious or spiritual backgrounds. I learn and grow from them even if not every word aligns with my own beliefs. I am now capable of calmly pondering other perspectives instead of getting distressed that it might contradict my own. I am grateful to have changed.

Sometimes an unfamiliar message, especially when it challenges our current spiritual perspectives, won't resonate with us simply because we are not ready to hear the new idea. Our willingness level may result from inexperience, pride, or faulty negative beliefs about ourselves or the world, but as we grow and have more life experiences it is possible to come back to that same idea and feel differently. In my twenties I used to roll my eyes at people who talked about Angels showing up for them, guffawed at folks who thought of crystals as anything more than mute rocks, and thought people who spoke about their Near-Death Experiences (NDE) were frauds. And I considered myself a spiritual person back then! Twenty years later, I love to talk about Angels, I value my crystals as a beautiful, comforting, and supportive healing tool, and I voluntarily read NDE books, moved by many of them. My point is that if something I write here in this book doesn't jive with you, hold on to it in some way and maybe down the road it might align better with your life and beliefs.

All this setup allows me to express that I hope you are eager to discover how to use your faith and spirituality, combined with practical tips and scientific methods, to improve the life of your feline friend (as well as improve your own life)!

HOW TO USE THIS BOOK

This book contains a lot of ideas and information. Tackling every single idea at once is not possible, nor reasonable. I want this book to serve as a companion to you for years to come, for the lifetime of your feline friends. Focus now on the concepts most pertinent to healing the situation with your kitty. When it comes to healing yourself, select two to four ideas to test out. For addressing a behavioral concern with your cat, consider many ideas. Start with the most important need for creating change, then add others in order of priority as you are able to. If you hit on the most important ones, behavior will improve. If you need help with either healing yourself or healing your kitty, please involve professional help. Go to an energy healer, hire a cat behavior consultant, go to the vet, or see a therapist. I am here for you, too, should you want to work with me. You can reach me at www.jessicamockett.com.

You likely picked up this book because your kitty currently struggles with a behavioral concern. Feel free to skip ahead to one of the chapters that addresses kitty's needs. Please head to the chapters in Part 2 which will be most meaningful for this support. If we are frazzled and angry about kitty's negative behavior, it will be harder to look inward and contemplate how changing ourselves will help the situation. However, if we can make some quick adjustments and see progress, the relief will engender hope, patience, and a willingness to give the situation more reflection. Jump right in. Get some basics addressed to begin behavior change, then come back to read the full book. I want to help you create a genuinely loving and lasting bond with your cat.

If you picked up this book because you really want to create a loving bond and understand your kitty better, wow, I love it. Proactive kitty parenting is awesome. You will be fine reading the book from cover to cover, but if you want to skip around you can. You will likely find the most content for your consideration in Parts 3 and 4. Should your kitty ever struggle in the future, you now have a great resource.

If you chose this guide because you are thinking of getting a pet cat but want to have greater awareness of their needs prior to adopting—amazeballs! Your future cat will thank you for taking the time to understand their nature, communication methods, and necessities. Part 2 of the book will give you a leg up on avoiding major issues, and Part 4 will help you care for your kitty to the best of your ability.

If you picked up this book because you are interested in how your kitty relationship can help you grow spiritually, I'm so grateful. We each have many opportunities in life to progress spiritually, and a pet cat, especially one that is struggling, can really allow a spiritually-minded person to stretch. Your cat *can be* a spiritual path or awakening if you are willing to look at how meeting their needs requires you to change for the better. Any relationship can bring this kind of opportunity if we choose to allow it. For that, read Parts 1 and 3, but truly this whole book is designed to help you grow.

Being a better cat guardian, deepening your care of them using spiritual tools and personal development, is a journey. This guidebook can help you along on that journey—to become more successful in communicating with cats, more aligned and in tune with Spirit, more at peace with yourself, your kitty, and your life.

The biggest concepts I hope you walk away with, once you have read the whole book are these:

- Lasting relationships are a journey. Set a healthy pace and put in the effort needed to have the road lead you, over time, into a better relationship with your cats.

- We will not be perfect. But in the context of our cat relationships we strive for "purrrfection" by doing our best to provide a safe, healthy, happy life for kitty.

- Spiritual growth is vital. Seek it. Want it.

- **BOND**—everything we do for our cats can be boiled down into this acronym "**B**e **O**bservant, **N**urturing, **D**edicated."

- Lap cats are not rare—however, we have to be the guardian cats love and trust to earn their lap time and snuggles.

- Think of cat care holistically—address emotional, spiritual, mental, and physical needs of kitty and do so with an abundance of alternative and spiritual tools available to you.

HOW THIS BOOK APPLIES SPIRITUAL TOOLS TO CAT GUARDIANSHIP

The most important point of this book is to help us see where and how we might improve on an emotional, spiritual, mental, and even physical level so that we can become healthier all around. Healthier individuals are able to practice more patience, compassion, and empathy or sympathy to other's needs, including kitty's. Prior to starting my own healing journey, I was loving to my cat Stella, but more uptight, more rigid in what I would or wouldn't do for her. More self-centered in our relationship, I lost my patience more readily over messes or items she chewed. When she became gravely ill because of my defiance to Spirit, lack of education, and slowness of observation, I selfishly dragged out her pain because of my own fear of death and sadness at her potential loss.

Numerous times, I have seen similar mistakes from cat owners during my interactions with them because of their cat behavioral concerns. Their choices for kitty often come from a place of wounded child energy (which we will discuss briefly in this book), from anger, the strange anthropomorphizing of how the cat is retaliatory or vindictive, the unwillingness to bend or change and/or to see how they themselves are causing harm. These all stem from that place of unresolved trauma, trapped negative energies, self-protective and self-focused living, and a deficit of spiritual thoughts and perspectives.

Shift away some of that pain, smooth the way to connection to Spirit, and gain more self-worth through understanding and personal enrichment, and as a result we become a drastically more effective cat guardian. Our relationship with kitty can finally become healthier.

I hope you will see the efficacy of utilizing Spirit and those associated skills and holistic approaches to your own wellness, to help enhance the care you can give to your kitty. I find them invaluable.

PART 1

Why Life with Cats Isn't Always Perfect

❀ *Sweet, but shy and fearful foster, Brownie.*

CHAPTER 1

Is Your Cat Happy?

When you adopted your cat did you ever think you might wind up in a bad relationship? Most of us envisioned lots of snuggling, laughing, playing, and generally enjoying the cuteness of our furry friend, and if we were *really* lucky, capturing a funny video or two. We didn't foresee urine dripping down our wall, stinky litterboxes, scratches on our hands, losing our favorite chair to claw-shredding, or constantly saying, "No, no!"

Some people naturally relate to cats *and* adopt a gem of a cat and thus have no struggles. They live the cat-human dream, but if it were always rosy, then why have so many people given up on their cats? Every year, around 3.2-3.4 million cats enter US shelters and rescues. From 2015-2020 these shelters euthanized about a third of those cats. In 2020, with the covid pandemic, pet adoption boomed. However, with inflation costs and unemployment rates, cat surrenders spiked in 2021, 2022, and 2023 because of this financial duress. In 2023 the number of cats euthanized went up 15% compared to 2022. Additionally, though not documented thoroughly, owners of cats frequently request "convenience euthanasia" from veterinarians because of behavioral concerns. Between 93-98% of vets in the US and Britain have received this request. The term euthanasia means "Good Death," but there is nothing good about an unnecessary death. Still other people move and leave cats behind or dump cats far from home.

While millions of cats are abandoned or euthanized, millions more live together in a struggle with their humans. That may be where you are at right now. Guardians love their cats or want to do right by them, but the cat causes upheaval, stress, or anxiety in the home from their misunderstood behaviors.

How does this happen? Let's set up a quick generalized scenario. We will dive a bit deeper on the hows and whys later on page 35.

SETTING THE SCENE

Mary has a demanding family life, but she wanted the kids to have a pet. Plus, she wouldn't mind getting some sweet furry snuggles, so she adopted a super cute, lively, funny kitten. However, she didn't realize that the kitten, twelve weeks old when she brought him home, still needed continuing socialization with humans. With her stressful life, she didn't consider that the cat could or should be trained or that her children needed to learn to respect boundaries with kitty so that he would be unharmed in the home. Busy working her job, driving kids around to activities, folding laundry, and getting dinner on the table, Mary didn't notice that the kitty started to withdraw because he didn't feel safe with all the noise, commotion, and kids grabbing at him.

After some time the kitten-cuteness wore off, and Mary finds that when she plays with the cat, he bites and claws harder than he used to. The kids frequently get bad scratches. The cat hides most of the day and races around at night when everyone is sleeping (or trying to sleep). Now, Mary discovers that kitty has scratched up her new couch. With everything she has going on, the litterbox often gets forgotten, and about two years into her cat relationship, kitty starts peeing outside the box. He never snuggles her, he loathes the kids, and now she is rethinking the whole thing.

What went wrong? Most people adopting cats over dogs think they are choosing an "easy" animal to live with, but the relationship, like any, still requires work to make it healthy and strong.

It is because of broken-down communication and deflated expectations between humans and their felines that every year, millions of cats face abandonment, homelessness, and even death. Millions more live in stress and frustration with their humans who are trying to keep their commitment to kitty, but do not enjoy her.

The biggest cause in this all-too-common situation stems from lack of owner education. Cat experts and cat advocates like me constantly try to reach people with our messages of hope and plans of action that will mend cat-human bonds. Thank you for picking up this book and being willing to learn!

Let's start with assessing your current relationship with kitty.

Quiz: How Healthy is Your Cat Relationship?

Select one answer for each. Choose the one most true for you and your cat. Be honest with yourself. No one will know your answers unless you share them. Track each letter on a piece of paper and then score your answers. The **Answer Key** is on page 369.

1. **How frequently do you yell at your cat?**

    a. Never.

    b. A few times a month.

    c. At least one or two times a week.

    d. Almost every day.

2. Do you find yourself complaining about your cat to others?

a. I gripe every day—under my breath, to the cat, my spouse, friends, and even sometimes co-workers.

b. I don't complain to anyone really, but I think about my frustration in my mind a fair amount.

c. I complain about the cat to the cat more than anything.

d. I don't really have any complaints.

3. Have you ever used corporal punishments with your cat like spanking, slapping, nose bopping, shoving, flicking, or kicking?

a. I have once or twice over the years when my patience was really thin.

b. Is it a problem to use corporal punishment? It was how I was raised, so yeah, all the time.

c. I lose it a few times a month and punish the cat physically.

d. I don't think I have ever intentionally punished the cat this way.

4. Do you use punishments like water spraying, yelling, hand clapping, scolding?

a. Yes, all the time.

b. Yes, sometimes.

c. No, because it doesn't make a difference.

d. No, I never thought of treating my cat like that.

5. Does your cat spend the day mostly hiding away from everyone?

a. Yes.

b. No.

6. Does your cat lash out at you when being picked up, petted, or played with?

a. Yes, occasionally.

b. Yes, but this just recently started. She used to be fine.

c. Yes, all the time.

d. No, never.

7. Does your cat follow you around the house from room to room?

    a. Yes.

    b. No.

8. Does your cat ever seek you out for snuggles, petting, or lap sitting?

    a. Yes, frequently.

    b. Yes, occasionally.

    c. No, never.

9. Is your cat curious, exploring, playful?

    a. Yes, very much so.

    b. Sometimes.

    c. No, never. She mostly hides or stays out of reach.

10. Was your cat fully socialized during the critical period of age two weeks to nine weeks with humans prior to adopting her?

    a. Yes.

    b. No.

    c. Unsure.

11. Do you have behavioral concerns with litterbox, spraying, aggression, destroying furniture/home, yowling, fear of people, or overgrooming?

    a. Yes, a few issues and they bother me a great deal.

    b. Yes, a few issues but I'm not overly concerned by them.

    c. Yes, we have one of those issues, and it's really bad.

    d. Yes, we have one of those issues, but it's only mildly concerning.

    e. No, our cat doesn't have any major behavioral concerns.

12. Is your cat spayed/neutered and vaccinated?

    a. Yes, both.

    b. Vaccinated, but not fixed.

    c. Fixed, but not vaccinated.

    d. Neither have been done.

13. When did you last go to the veterinarian with kitty?

a. Within the last 6 months.

b. Within the last 12 months.

c. About 1-2 years ago.

d. Over two years ago.

e. Never been to the vet.

14. Do you ever swear at the cat?

a. Yes, all the time.

b. Yes, but rarely.

c. No, never.

15. Did you give kitty a negative sounding name or nicknames?

a. Yes, it's hysterical.

b. Yes, she earned them.

c. No, she has a cute name and positive nicknames.

16. Do you love your cat?

a. Ugh, I don't know. I used to before things got hard.

b. Yes, but it isn't easy to love her because she causes so much stress.

c. Yes, I totally love her, issues and all!

d. No, I never really liked the cat.

Scoring Results

If you received a 16-24: Sounds Like a Pretty Strong Relationship! I am pleased for both you and your furever baby. You seem to be patient and calm. If you want to improve upon your relationship or have some behaviors you want to address, this book can help.

If you received a 25-35: Your Kitty Relationship is *Okay*. Being bewildered by the cat's behavior and losing your patience every now and then is completely normal. Though normal, it isn't super healthy or ideal for either you or kitty. This book will help you identify what is pertinent to understand and change to strengthen your bond.

If you received a 36-48: The Relationship is Not Going Well. I'm sorry you feel discouraged, overwhelmed, confused, or frustrated by your cat. Getting along with a cat isn't always as easy as you may have hoped. They can seem "wild" in their behaviors, but you can learn to help kitty become happier and safer in your home. This book will improve your dynamics when you practice the skills laid out for you.

If you received a 49-60: There is Concern for Kitty's Welfare and Your Happiness. Unfortunately, the relationship appears a bit toxic for both of you. It can be repaired with the right effort and tools and this book will provide those to you. It is likely important for you to do some inner healing and centering so that you can experience more peace for *yourself*. This book not only helps you see how your reactions and old wounds impact your life together but also guides you in how to healthily interact with your cat.

No matter your score, you picked up this book because you want help and desire to have a more loving relationship with kitty. Wherever you are on this journey of life with your cat, you can mend the bond and maybe even wind up with a snuggle bug. Seriously, a lap cat is possible!

THIS BOOK IS ABOUT THE JOURNEY

Some ideas in this book may hit home in a challenging way. It is not intended to berate anyone who is struggling. I want to help shed light on the processes of healing yourself *and* kitty and the joy of connecting in real ways with your feline friend.

Becoming a more spiritual and emotionally healthy person is a lifelong journey. Amazingly, pets, and maybe especially cats, prove great catalysts (no pun intended) for helping us recognize what needs to change within us.

In this book, we will look at both ourselves and our cats. How can we change, grow, heal? What does kitty's behavior say to us about how she feels and what needs she is crying to have met? Let's go into this with a lifelong, growing-together, journey mindset. Your kitty could live with you as long as twenty years, so make them predominately wonderful, joyful years.

The title of this book is a cute play on words, but I also wanted to convey a deeper meaning. First, we won't be perfect. None of us will get it right 100% of the time for the rest of our lives. But we should seek to become more perfect by letting go of what isn't serving us, what is holding us back, and what is harming ourselves or others. With kitties, we are striving toward *purrrfection*—creating a home where contented purring happens daily.

Creating healthy and lasting bonds takes work. No relationship stays in tip-top shape without effort. There are ups and downs, good times and not so good times. For me, and throughout this book, the word "bond" has additional purpose. To create a good bond with your cats, I want you to **Be Observant, Nurturing, Dedicated—BOND**. All of my instructions pretty much boil down to this with your kitty.

BUSTING THE LAP CAT MYTH

When volunteering at rescue adoption events, I often hear people confess to longing for a "lap cat," as if it is a rare, golden unicorn among cats to find one that wants to sit on you and cuddle you. A "lap cat" is actually *not* a rare cat problem, but more of a rare human problem. Trust me, all cats up for adoption yearn just as much for humans on whose laps they *want* to sit and snuggle.

As shared in the introduction, I have many kitties. We do not have a perfect home, but what I do have are six well-bonded, loving cats that seek to sit in my lap numerous times daily. In fact, I have the opposite problem of many cat owners; I do not have the ability to hold and snuggle them all to their hearts' content each day.

Many Saturday afternoons of my life were spent at cat adoptions where I met and screened hundreds of potential adopters. As they browsed the choices at events or came to my home to meet my fosters, they often spoke about their past cats and current cats or told me about their childhood experiences with cats. From these conversations, I learned that a strong overall belief persists that cats are aloof, unfriendly, independent, prefer isolation, and are prone to drastic mood swings and, therefore, do not need or want human interaction often or at all.

I try to help prospective adopters understand that this is an incorrect belief. Do I acknowledge they base this belief on real-life experiences? Absolutely. They observed genuinely

✿ *Gigi on me. Honey next to me. Hard-to-reach laptop while writing this book.*

unpleasant behavior from that particular cat, a cat likely mistrusting of her environment or people, a cat insecure and afraid, a cat hiding to try to keep more stability in her world. However, this is not true pet cat behavior when healthy, happy, and feeling safe.

Happy cats love and trust their humans. They want to be near you—in the room with you, follow you around the house, stick their paws under the bathroom door, sit with you, and snuggle you. Cats that feel safe love socializing. They *need* interaction, affection, and your company.

With this book, I hope to facilitate changing the ongoing false belief that cats are indifferent, mean, or moody. This work will help more cats live with less-rare humans who know how to give cats the care they need to build trust, safety, love, and strong relationship bonds. Part of this care includes embracing the spiritual side of our nature and utilizing the unseen, but real power available to us for the healing and protection of ourselves and our furry friends. Let us keep as many cats as

possible from abandonment and instead make it easier for laps around the world be full of snuggly kitties. (Look on page 231 for step-by-step instructions for creating a "lap cat.")

RECOGNIZING HAPPY, HEALTHY CATS

How do you get a snuggly cat? Make sure you start with having a happy cat! How do you know if kitty is happy? Let's go over some of the most common and meaningful signs that show you are on a good track, but if you see only few of these signs or none of them, kitty-cat needs you to make some adjustments to her care.

Signs of a happy & well-taken-care-of cat are when she regularly:

- Follows you from room to room because she likes you and wants to be social with you.

- Rubs your legs, hands, and face with her own body and head, claiming you as hers.

- Puts her bum in your face when sitting on your lap or when you are lying down. She's inviting you to sniff her—a very friendly gesture in cat culture. Don't worry; you don't have to follow through with sniffing. Just say "thank you" and offer a pet.

- Marks her territory in polite ways by rubbing her face on furniture and wall corners. This releases pheromones from her scent glands.

Trixie particularly likes to put her bum near my face. (Photo credit Rachel Beecher)

- Seeks to sit in your lap or snuggle beside you on a regular basis. She kneads you when settling in for snuggles.

- Sleeps with her belly exposed or rolls around on the floor in front of you, exposing her belly and showing you how cute she is. (Note: this is not usually an invitation to touch her belly.)

- Is curious and frisky and wants to play with you. She has bursts of energy or does things that are humorous.

- Walks through the house with her tail confidently up, either totally straight or with a hook at the end.

- Allows you to touch her and hold her. She may even permit or ask you to pick her up, nestling into your body.

- Hops onto your back when you lean over or wants to ride on your shoulders.

- Grooms you, most likely your hair, face, hands, or feet.

- Shows you affection with head bonks, extended paw touches, love bites, soft blinks, kneading, and purring.

- Misses you when you are gone and gets excited when you return home, greeting you at the door.

- Likes sleeping with you on your bed.

- Spends a lot of time sitting or sleeping in your scent-heavy places like your bed, pillow, and favorite spot on the couch. She may sit on your used underwear or nuzzle the shoes you barely took off.

- Brings you gifts of "dead prey." There is no scientific proof that these are "gifts" because cats don't share food with other cats except their kittens. However, I see the "dead prey," which could also be toys dragged to you or placed on your bed, as a friendly offering, a sharing. Or a "notice me and praise me" opportunity for the cat.

- Becomes excited about and chatters over birds and bugs she sees out the window or in the house.

- Is relaxed with calm body language most of the time. Examples are softening or closing her eyes, lying stretched out, sleeping with her back to you, having ears forward, and purring. Additionally, she sits relaxed while she eats.

- Gets along with the other cats or pets in the house relatively well.

- Uses her litterbox with no problems.

- Talks to you with a variety of different meows.

🐾 *Gigi often captures a yarn skein "rat," meows triumphantly to announce her catch so I'll praise her, then drags and plops it on my bed.*

A HAPPY CAT MAY STILL OCCASIONALLY STRUGGLE

Even when you are doing a great job overall as a cat guardian, life has its ups and downs and changes inevitably occur. Your happy and healthy kitty may still have occasional struggles.

Often new people or situations will throw a cat off her game to varying degrees. Cats are very habitual by nature. Rearranging your living room furniture may spook the cat for a few days. If you have guests over, kitty may hide most or all the time while these strangers invade her home. Construction noises may send her diving under the bed.

This is all acceptable. A cat totally unfazed by new situations or people is rare. Because they are truly as much prey as predators, cats must exercise caution with the "new" to survive.

Like any human, your cat may have an off day. She may not feel her best. She may feel worried about an unseen stressor. Circumstances may cause moments of temper or annoyance with other animals or with you. Redirected aggression is discussed on page 133, but for example, a cat has just quarreled with a fellow cat-mate or gotten spooked by thunder, so she hisses or bites if you try to touch her in that moment. It isn't about you, but the outside trigger.

Otherwise happy cats will potentially pick up on any stress in your home, and this may lead to new concerning behaviors you haven't seen before. For example, if her owners begin arguing a lot, kitty may start urinating outside the box. If her owner is going through a divorce, experiencing work-related anxiety, recently lost a loved one, or the like, the cat can absorb some of the unhappy energy, and it will absolutely impact her. For example, recently, I was laid off from a job I had for many years. At first life improved for me emotionally to be done with a job I didn't love and to focus on this book. However, my anxiety and fear increased substantially as financial realities hit. One of the cats started isolating herself in the basement storage room to yowl. Nothing else in her life had changed; she was negatively impacted by *my* intense feelings of stress.

❀ *Skippy after a stressful morning.*

Lastly, your happy cat will inevitably experience sicknesses. Over the course of her life with you kitty will likely have several illnesses. These may range from a mild cold with some sneezing to conjunctivitis in the eyes to a bad bout with a calicivirus strain. Your cat may pick up a parasite, have a rash, or get repeated ear infections. Kitty may have cancer or get a broken leg. Make sure you do your part in caring for her when she does get ill.

PURRRITO WRAP UP

When we adopted from the rescue or picked up our kitty from a breeder, we excitedly looked forward to that bundle of furry joy. However, life happens to all of us, and we make mistakes. Sometimes our little cat gets lost in the shuffle of daily existence. Now we've gauged our current relationship with the quiz and have a good idea of where we are starting from. No matter the current situation, things can and will get better. This is a life-long journey with kitty, so adopt a mindset of patient dedication through this process of healing yourself and helping kitty. Remember that any relationship will take effort, and with our cats everything we should do adds up to the word BOND. Be observant, nurturing, and dedicated.

We now know that lap cats are not mythical like unicorns. Most well-adjusted cats that feel safe in their homes will be loving and snuggly. If your kitty does not currently feel safe and snuggly, it is possible to attain that in the future. Having gone over the big list of ways to recognize a happy cat, you can look out for improvements. Reassure yourself that if your kitty displays some or all of those behaviors, you have a good start to the relationship. If not there yet, you can anticipate marking those items off the list as they blossom along with the relationship. Not every day will unfold purrrfectly, and even cats have hard days or off days. Take the long view, and embrace looking back to see the progress as this can be very encouraging.

CHAPTER 2

Accidentally Creating an Aloof or Unhappy Cat

Relationships can be hard. Communication is always key, but imagine if you don't speak the same language or come from the same cultural background. Getting into a relationship with a cat is a lot like this. They do not speak our language and what is polite and reasonable in their culture is *not* in ours. Exactly like in a human relationship, if we refuse to learn, change, grow, compromise, and give of ourselves to meet kitty's needs, it isn't likely to last long.

It's a bit of a running joke in our culture during a breakup to tell the other person, "It's not you; it's me," when we frequently think the opposite. In our cat relationships, because their abilities to communicate will never be in our language, it really is *us* and not them if the relationship struggles. We didn't bother to learn their language or to understand their culture. In other words, we didn't meet their needs.

I don't want you to even consider breaking up with your cat. There are already too many kitties abandoned (or worse) by owners who once said they would love them forever. This book is here to help you become the relationship partner (guardian) the cat needs in order to become the loving pet you always wanted.

With that aim in mind, to be clear about how to get it right later in this book, we do need to spend a bit of time on how it can go wrong.

After reviewing in the first chapter what a happy cat looks like, it is important for us to now discuss how to recognize an unhappy, afraid, or struggling cat. Likely you picked up this book because you are already aware that your relationship with kitty should be better. Your Chapter 1 quiz results will lend a hand in helping you to know just how difficult circumstances are for the cat and for you. Let's get to the signs of a stressed-out kitty.

SIGNS YOUR CAT IS UNHAPPY

Hiding — The biggest gauge for the happiness and comfort level of the cat in your home is how much he hides. Does he remain out of reach most of the day hidden under a bed, in the back of a closet, or tucked behind the furnace or another impossible to reach spot? I typically see this extreme hiding behavior with feral cats, tremendously stressed cats, abused cats, and with cats who cannot handle the behavior of the children in the home.

Remaining separate from you and the family says that kitty does not trust the environment. This behavior could have happened right from the start or slowly over several weeks or months. If the cat used to participate in family life and suddenly begins hiding and it's barely been a day or two, find him immediately and make sure he isn't seriously ill. Cats will often hide in the home when really sick or when they are preparing to die.

Hiding and Refusing Food/Water — Again, hiding often signals illness, so first ensure kitty isn't sick. However, what I want to focus on here is when the cat is not ill, but terrified—so scared, in fact, they cannot leave their hiding spot to perform basic needs like eating, drinking, or eliminating. These kinds of intensely afraid cats only dare to come out when the house has been silent and dark for some time. Then they sneak out to do their business, eat, and quickly resume their concealment.

When cortisol and adrenaline pump through the cat at max levels all the time, this creates health problems. If you have a cat in this condition of fear, confine him to one room with two or three safe hiding spots. As you work on building the relationship in a healthy direction, you will need to cater to kitty's needs to make sure that the cat has adequate nutrition, hydration, and elimination. Try not to touch kitty when in this state of intense stress, as unfortunately, we can worsen the relationship with the cat, even when our intention is to soothe and help.

Story Example: When Touch Makes It Worse

Years ago, I fostered an older feral kitten with the intent to tame her, but she did not want me to touch her. Sadly, because she was ill the first week of our relationship, I needed to hold her by the scruff, wrap her in a towel, or corner her in a kennel to get her to take antibiotics and put in eye meds. This was a terrible way to start off trust building with a wild animal, but I had no choice. I worked with her for three months, and she did warm up. If I laid down on my tummy, she'd sit on

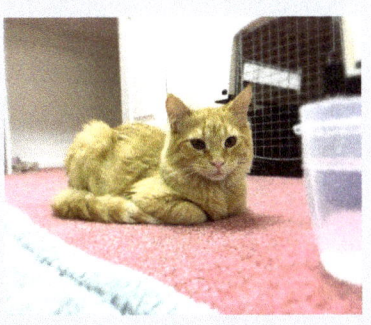

❀ *The little feral kitten I tried to tame years ago.*

my bum or back. If I got out a toy, she would play right on my lap, but she still wouldn't permit my hand to touch her directly and she would run and hide if I stood up. I passed her on to another more experienced foster to continue the taming process in hopes she could help kitty build more trust with humans.

Aggressive Toward People — We will dedicate a whole chapter later in the book to the topic of aggression. I bring it up here because if you have a cat hissing, growling, swatting, attacking, biting, or scratching at you, it means you have a very unhappy kitty. Now, feral cats will almost always behave this way and unless you know the correct approach to taming, the cat will most likely remain aggressive toward people. If your cat isn't feral though, e.g. you adopted him as a kitten and he was social at first but over the months or years turned angry and/or fearful *or* you adopted an adult cat that came with baggage from a previous home, likely he can be reconditioned, and trust can form.

Side Note: Feral vs. Stray Cats

Some people lump all homeless cats under the "feral" label. This isn't the case. A feral cat is one that did not have any exposure to humans during the most important weeks of social development as a kitten, between two to nine weeks old. These cats grew up outside and are *wild*. They see humans as a threat to their survival and fear them. With cats, a stray, yet tamed mama cat can birth a litter of kittens outside, and without any consistent human engagement, they will revert to being feral in that single generation. Some ferals become semi-feral with continued positive human contact, but still retain some fear of people.

Homeless cats that are friendly toward humans are strays. They were raised around humans during that critical period of socialization as a kitten. Often, people who do not fix their queens get tired of dealing with homing kittens and will drive them somewhere and dump them off when weaned. For any kitten that survives this ordeal, and most do not, they become the more friendly *strays*. Strays likewise include those cats intentionally or unintentionally left behind when a family moves.

I do not advise that you take on any feral cats by trying to bring them into your home as a pet. I commend your kindheartedness, but the best help you can offer them is:

- Get them Trapped, Neutered, and Returned (TNR) back into the wild.
- Put out food for them regularly.
- Offer some kind of safe shelter in winter if you reside in a cold area.

🐾 *Feeding feral cats.*

Do not pilfer young feral kittens from a mama cat. They need to stay with her until at least eight weeks old; twelve weeks is healthier. If you take in a wild kitten after eight weeks old, realize you must know how to tame kitty. Even if you know what to do, fully socializing wild kittens doesn't always succeed. If you are worried about the health or safety of a feral mama with young kittens, try to locate a cat rescue group willing to trap them all together and tame the kittens while wild mama continues to raise them.

Aggressive Toward Other Pets — Again, we will go over this more later, but if tension emerges between kitty and another pet in the household, you will likely hear growling, hissing, spitting, yowling, or more. You may experience chasing or actual fighting and the cat being bullied will likely begin to hide more. This conflict may trigger other behavioral concerns.

Story Example: Skippy & Prim

This happened in my multi-cat home. When Skippyjon reached about two years old and hit social maturity, he started behaving aggressively toward a few of the other cats. The cats all quickly put him in his place except Prim. Now, Prim runs and hides from him and meows fearfully whenever he approaches. It is very stressful for Prim. I am working on ways to help Skippy feel less of a need to dominate and ways for Prim to feel more confident, and my methods have reduced the number of spats. I will discuss what to do later on if this is happening in your home.

Slinking Around — If kitty walks around low to the ground, with tail down or tucked, ears and eyes on high alert, and appears to be slinking (while not in play or hunting mode) as he travels from place to place within the home, he feels unsafe. Also, if he darts quickly skirting widely around people or seeks to move through rooms by going under the furniture (e.g. dives under a couch, shoots under the armchair nearby, scoots quickly in the open space between the armchair and kitchen table), this body language tells you he

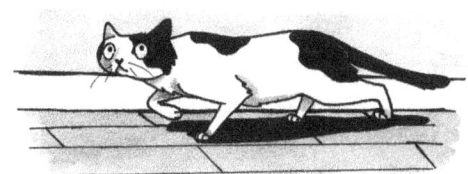

cannot relax while you or someone else is out and about in the house. Often, small children are the culprit for this type of learned behavior from kitty because when toddlers see the cat they squeal in delight and run to grab him.

Avoiding Certain People — Kitty may avoid a lone individual in the home. This could be a child or an adult. If the cat has experienced something truly negative or abusive from a person (or from a person who looked or sounded like them in a previous home), the cat might not come out if that individual is around. Quite possibly kitty may behave aggressively toward only that human.

Redirected Aggression — Sometimes called displaced aggression, this behavior occurs when the cat lashes out for no apparent cause. If another animal, noises such as thunder, or a child worries a cat and you happen by, the cat may direct their fear toward you. It might seem like kitty is "psycho," but that is rarely the case. Generally, a stressor triggered the cat, and the cause merely needs to be discovered and resolved.

Eliminating Outside Litterboxes — This behavior upsets most owners. Rarely though, does a cat stop using the box for no reason. Kitty's humans must ferret out the cause. It could be an illness now or that happened in the past that started the behavior. There are a lot of layers here to understand, and as such a whole chapter discusses this topic. If this is an ongoing problem, kitty has likely been unhappy about something for a while.

Urine Marking — Spraying or other types of scent marking with waste signals that kitty isn't happy about something. You can find more on this subject on page 111. Most fixed cats do not spray, especially if fixed prior to the onset of sexual maturity. However, a small percentage of cats past sexual maturity will spray after being neutered or spayed, with male cats the most likely to develop this trait. Typically, if you start to notice urine spray after the cat has reached social maturity (two to four years of age) then stress likely induced a response where they feel the need to claim territory or resources in the home in a more tangible way.

Apathy or Depression — If your cat is oversleeping and/or apathetic toward anything fun (exploring/playing/hunting) and they are not a geriatric cat (fifteen years+), then he might have high stress levels, depression, or illness. An undiscovered chronic health problem might be at the root.

Other Odd Behaviors — Stressed cats can display other behaviors to tell you they need help. These may be big or small deals to you. Look out for a cat that overgrooms; this creates bald spots on the fur and can even lead to irritated, inflamed, or bleeding skin. Cats may scoot their bums across the floor. They may over-vocalize. They may overeat or eat aggressively. They may have  a chewing issue or a problem with consuming non-food items. Kitties may overdo scratching, marking, and destroying things like carpet. They may continuously try to escape the home every time a door is opened. There are a lot of possibilities here.

HOW DID THIS HAPPEN?

If you see any signs from the above list, you will need to use this book to unravel why this happened. We are going to start looking at the possibilities in this section, with the assumption that the causes derive from the kitty's current environment. The next section of this chapter looks at possibilities for helping you decipher what baggage the cat may have brought with them from their previous life before coming to your home. Of course, problems could stem from a combination of a previous trauma *and* kitty reacting to his new home.

I will lay out the situations frankly and base them on real ones witnessed in my time working with cats and their owners. I hope you will not be upset by these but instead take the opportunity to reflect and recognize which, if any, of these scenarios (or some version of them) are playing out in your home.

Controlling — Sometimes people withhold (love, food, acceptance, permission) to passive-aggressively control others or forcefully control through punishments or fear. Some cat owners use control over their animals as a misguided way to get the cat to do what they want. It is not effective for building a loving and bonded relationship. Examples include confining the cat for long periods in a single room or a crate to teach him a lesson or withholding food to punish.

Yelling — Using an angry, loud, forceful voice with animals simply serves to break trust and create fear. Though often utilized to control the cat to get wanted behavior, this approach to "training" is totally ineffective. In the cat's mind, these outbursts have no relation to his own behavior, so you just come across as an aggressor, someone to fear and hide from or to attack to remain safe.

Corporal or Physical Punishments — This is a sure-fire way to create a rift between you and your pet. This includes spanking, slapping, hitting, throwing, and kicking. Also nose bopping, pushing noses into messes, throwing things at the cat in anger, flicking, or pushing. Additionally, more severe "punishments" like cigarette burns, starving, beating, or the use of any weapons against the animal would fall here, though I hope cats are rescued from homes where anyone goes to these intensely abusive extremes.

Sexual Abuse — This may seem like a shocking "what??" for most of us. But it happens. I have personally delt with a few cases. Children who struggle with understanding sexuality have been known to do abusive things to the cat's sex organs from a place of curiosity or meanness. Some kids and adults can be sexually stimulated by the animal and abuse it by masturbating while touching the cat. Most of these animal sexual abuse situations extend from pornography exposure or other sexual trauma the child or adult has already encountered— but this is a conversation for a whole other book. In short, pornography and sexual trauma can change one's natural arousal template and put ideas and desires into the mind and body that would never have been there otherwise. If you discover this happening in your home with your pet, I strongly suggest rehoming the pet immediately for his safety and wellbeing and help the child or spouse/partner seek therapeutic support for their abusive behaviors.

Another aspect to this matter involves cats watching people in the home have sexual encounters. Some animals remain unfazed, but others may find it distressing. I have seen a few situations like this where cats now act out behaviorally or get disturbed when they see partners touching. I would caution that if the sexual encounters you have are heavily lustful, aggressive, or violent, the energy of those events will upset the sensitive spirits of cats. These types of sex acts are more and more common with the easy exposure to violent pornography online and the acceptance of many couples by reenacting this content in their real lives. For cats' health, dismiss them from the room before sex and let them back in afterward. Moreover, for your own wellness, consider shifting your sexual relationship to one of mutual love, safety, and respect if that isn't currently the case.

Side Note: Abuse Hurts Everyone

The first four scenarios I've presented in this section are all forms of abuse toward kitty. Some aspects I mentioned might be less damaging and others very traumatizing to the cat. Please, if you are inclined to being abusive as a first response in situations where you feel out of control and want desperately to regain control no matter how you do it, choose today to heal and change. Find the professional help needed to uncover personal wounds and traumas often rooted in childhood experiences. I will suggest some healing options in the next chapter that may be useful to explore.

If the abuse toward kitty comes from someone else in the household, not you, and you cannot end or correct the abuse immediately, the right thing to do for the cat is find the first possible chance to safely surrender the animal to a friend, family member, shelter, or rescue. If possible, even when it's embarrassing, tell the individual or staff what kind of abuse the kitty endured to help them know how to rehabilitate the cat.

If you suffer from an abuser in your home, I am so sorry that is happening. No one should be controlled with violence or fear. Not you, not the children, not the pets. I hope you can find a way out of the situation as soon as possible. Sometimes it's more subtle abuse or differs from the abuse you experienced as a child, and you aren't sure if what you are encountering qualifies as abusive. You can be physically abused, emotionally abused, psychologically abused, sexually abused, or a combination of all. Generally, serious abusers tend to be narcissists, sociopaths, psychopaths, addicts, or someone dealing with severe PTSD. More subtle abuse can come from anyone with an abuse background, low self-esteem, and unresolved trauma. Read up on the term "gaslighting," as abusers have a knack for making it all seem like your fault.

You owe nothing to an abuser. Your responsibility right now is to yourself, and any innocent individuals involved (children and pets). The abuser is responsible for themselves and can endure any consequences they receive for their actions. Abusers live to isolate and control. Regain or discover your courage and strength. Ignore any shame telling you it's too awful to confide in someone else. Find a safe person to help you—someone at church, a women's shelter advocate, a lawyer, a trustworthy police officer, your parents, a good friend. Ask for their discretion and help. Pray for God and the Angels to orchestrate the right path out. I pray for you, too, with a heart that wants everyone to find a way to safety, healing, and hope.

Not Taking Care of Basic Needs — Sometimes owners do this in complete ignorance of any wrong-doing. The basic needs for your cat include healthy food, clean water, safe shelter, comfortable elimination, fun activity, and quality sleep. If you are not providing enough of any of these items, kitty may become stressed, and behavior may alter.

Story Example: No Clean or Safe Potty

I adopted out a sweet solid white kitten to a family. Months later they attended another adoption event and approached me to talk to me about the cat. One of the family members referred to the kitten using mean names, calling her a "turd" and "jerk" while relating that she wasn't using the litterbox but instead peeing on the bed and laundry. This kitten had zero litterbox concerns while in my care, so I asked the mother questions about the environment and litter situation. It turned out that they had five cats in the house and only a single litterbox that the kids scooped once a week! Distressed with this situation, the kitten started seeking more comfortable ways to eliminate. I urged them to get several more litterboxes and scoop daily. The mother expressed genuine surprise that their litter set up and cleaning schedule wasn't good enough.

✤ *Sweet Sugar, the kitty in this story while in my care.*

Children Tormenting — Please understand that I am in no way suggesting that children cannot have pet cats! What I am saying is that unsupervised children often create trauma for a cat. Occasionally children treat the cat abusively, causing great harm. More often though, children are excited by the kitty, chase the kitty to touch it, grab the kitty's tail and tug, squeal loudly or shrilly at the cat, capture the kitty and won't let it go, dress the kitty in doll clothes, or over-pet the kitty. Children who scream and yell or throw loud tantrums, even if nothing to do with the cat, can still send the cat into hiding. Older kids sometimes tease too much and roughhouse with the cat. These behaviors toward kitty can create stress, fear, and aggression in the relationship.

Story Example: Stress Response to Kids

My sister adopted two kittens, Stoney and Stella. She had four very young children, and like most kids, they loved animals and wanted to play with them. Stella couldn't cope. She eventually found hiding places in the home to isolate all day and overgroomed her fur to the point of creating bald patches. The other cat, who had a rarer personality, was completely chill with all the kids.

Ignoring Cat's Affection — You won't always have the time or ability to accept your cat's show of love. But if you constantly ignore the animal trying to connect with you—pushing him away or walking away when he seeks you out— he will learn to ignore you in return. You cannot expect to only connect to the cat when initiated by you. A lack of bond and trust may lead kitty to behave in undesirable ways.

Negativity — Negativity might impact kitty in several ways. The first would be a big one—giving kitty a negative name or nicknames that you say all the time. Please don't pick mean, rude, or villain names if they truly are negative in your mind. Sometimes it seems comical to give a "mean" name to a cat. Like my high school senior English teacher named her runt cat "Chainsaw" because she thought he needed a tough name when out and about in the neighborhood. However, I caution using these types of names especially if you feel anything other than humor, charm, and love when saying the name or nickname. If you ever say it with feelings of negativity toward the cat, then it isn't a good name for kitty. Names like Butch, Beast, Evil One, Satan, Villain, Bad Ass and the like are not good name choices. Likewise, monikers such as Jerkface, Menace, Hellion, Psycho, Bad Boy, or Naughty One don't help either. Why? Because names that incite anything negative within us translates to the cat. They may just live up to their namesake in ways we do not want.

Speaking negatively to or about the cat likewise harmfully impacts kitty. Our words have power. They create our situations. Our thoughts, feelings, words, *and not just* our actions create our reality. If we are facing a challenge with our cat, speaking about it in terms of "never-ending" or "no point" or "no way out" will make it that much harder to overcome. Cats understand much more of our language than we give them credit for. On top of that, they are incredible intuitive creatures. Some have such heightened senses, they truly understand your thoughts. For example, I have several that "know" *before I even get out medicine* that I plan to disseminate it. They will flee from me and hide out of reach. I must be super spontaneous with those cats by making a last second decision about picking them up to give them meds. If they can know what's on our minds before we actually put action to those thoughts, if we are thinking or saying how much the cat frustrates or annoys us, then we not only deepen the reality but likely hurt the cat's feelings.

Another aspect of this topic encompasses behaving rudely to the cat. This could occur in your speech like, "Ugh! Get out of my way stupid cat!" Or it could involve making fun of or laughing at the cat. It's key to understand the difference between mocking and sharing in a laugh. Laughing at kitty is okay if they do something charming or funny! However, picking on kitty, embarrassing kitty, or using sarcasm with kitty creates distrust between the cat and you. Cats are often smart and wise. They understand a lot—if not all the meanings of each word, surely the tone, inflection, and intention.

Getting Angry — Some flashes of anger or frustration will happen because you are human. Getting scratched or bitten is inevitable; therefore, managing your reactions and tolerance is necessary. When we get a deep scratch from our cat, in that very moment our brain is wired to get away from the pain, asap. We may push the cat away from us, run from the cat, yell, or cry. These are chemical reactions. It is possible to retrain your brain to move away from panicked, angry, or hurt reactions to more calm, controlled, and thoughtful reactions. It takes emotional healing, spiritual growth, patience with yourself, and practice. When a cat scratches me (and mine never scratch me intentionally) I keep my reaction fairly calm. But sometimes it really hurts, and the lizard brain pops out to protect me. I have on occasion pushed a cat away or cried out in pain. The point is, we can improve our reactions to keep these occurrences to a minimum.

Another area where we might feel anger or frustration occurs when the cat makes messes like barfing, scratching furniture, litterbox misses, or we get sick of shedding fur or tracked litter. By the time we discover these nuisances, the cat is so far removed from the action that yelling or punishing will *never* make any sense to him. Even if you catch him in the act, the anger merely serves to sever bonds and create more stress for the feline, which then spills over into inciting additional behaviors you don't like.

Keeping our cool is a progressive journey. We won't "arrive" without effort and time. Bear in mind, if our flashes of anger are intense or frightening to kitty, we damage our relationship. If in the minutes afterward, we punish or lash out at the cat, we harm our bond. If the cat is scratching us out of self-protection or fear, we have some changes to make in how we (or our child) interact with kitty.

Ignoring Kitty's Comfort — If we never offer little kindnesses or tiny luxuries to kitty, we are not trying to incorporate them into our lives. Treats, toys, scratchers, or catnip are *some* of the ways kitties need to be regarded in our homes.

Ignoring Medical Care — Cats hide illness well. I will remind you of this throughout the book. As cat guardians we must be on the lookout for changes in our cat and get him any needed medical attention promptly. Ignoring signs or changes in behavior and simply passing it off as "cats are jerks" will not help the situation. I will dive deeper into potential medical problems as causes in all three behavioral chapters of the book. If we commit to caring for a pet, it is our responsibility to meet his health needs to the best of our ability.

Any of these behaviors or situations in this section can singly or in combination cause a kitty to become stressed, hide, and potentially lash out or have other behavioral concerns. Reflect honestly on the above or pray to discover a cause not listed here. You could hire a professional cat behavior consultant like me for a more objective look at the environment.

DID KITTY COME WITH HIS OWN BAGGAGE?

You and your home may offer kitty a wonderful refuge, but the kitty you adopted may have brought some of his own baggage into the environment that can cause stress for everyone. Even kittens who had rough starts in life can have trauma. We can all inherit trauma from our parents and ancestors passed down in our genetics, humans and animals alike. That is why you might still have a shy or highly cautious cat in an otherwise safe and lovely home.

We cannot change the past for a cat, but we can certainly have compassion toward the animal now as we work out how to move forward. Hopefully, if you adopted a cat with behavioral concerns, the previous owner, shelter, or rescue disclosed those matters to you or at least as much as they were aware of. Sometimes the behavior resolves immediately upon moving into a new home because kitty finally has his needs met appropriately. Other times they may linger and potentially worsen.

Please don't give up. And I assume you aren't if you are reading this book! Take hope that kitty can heal at least to a degree to make the relationship healthier and home life happier.

You may not have the entire picture of the cat's history, but you can make some informed assumptions. If kitty runs or cowers from our feet, something in his past was traumatic that involved feet. It could be as toxic as a previous owner who repeatedly pushed or kicked kitty with their feet, *or* as simple as a human accidentally stepping on him once, and he worries about a repeat scenario. If men terrify kitty, a man in his previous home may have treated him unkindly *or* it could be kitty never lived with a man before. If he won't use your litterbox set up, maybe he has chronic outside the box elimination difficulties *or* maybe he doesn't like the litter you chose because it differs from the one he is used to. It is often best when we don't know the history to leave ourselves open to the idea, it could be x, y, or z that caused the behavior. Sometimes adopting the ugliest possible reasons in our minds as the "truth" can increase the behavioral problem. How? Because it lessens our belief it can actually be healed or resolved. We easily believe the cat can overcome a fear of feet if no more than an accident traumatized him, *but* we may accept a cat physically abused by feet will *always* be afraid of them. We wind up unintentionally blocking the possibility of healing.

These are some tips for helping a kitty you adopted that entered your life carrying a load of cares:

- Have a cat consultant come out to your home to aid you in deciphering your kitty's baggage, help you unpack it, and handle it.

- Use energy work to help kitty to remove the baggage. Cats have emotional and traumatic wounds like humans, and the removal can offer such relief. I prefer the energy modalities of Body Code and Belief Code, but you can do most energy modalities with cats, even Emotional Freedom Technique (EFT)® or tapping. If you are not skilled at this yourself, schedule a few sessions with a certified practitioner. Most energy work can be done remotely; kitty will not be stressed by it.

- Review the behavioral section of this book if you have a specific concern addressed there.

- Be patient with kitty and yourself. Change takes time.

PURRRITO WRAP UP

Not surprisingly, cats have individual opinions, personalities, and feelings which means it matters how we interact with them. Each situation and kitty is unique. We have to recognize what kitty is saying to us, especially if they are unhappy. Meeting the cat's needs is the basic first step in creating the bond we all desired at adoption. Our kitty may struggle with fear, anxiety, or stress which means he needs us to truly see, hear, and comfort him by making his world safer. Sometimes we adopt a kitty who has an abuse history or who has experienced trauma. When 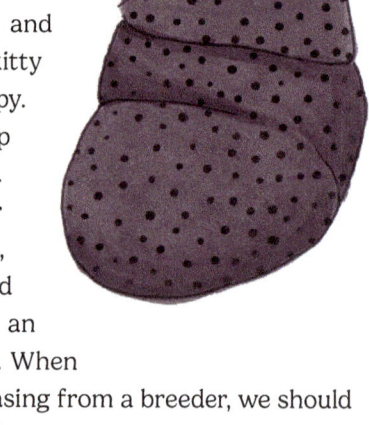 we commit to a cat at adoption or when purchasing from a breeder, we should take our commitment seriously. We pledge to do our best to love, protect, and care for kitty. Sometimes it takes self-reflection and becoming more aware of what is going on in our homes and lives.

While we will spend a great deal of time in this book discussing feline behavior tips, talking about training, and increasing our awareness of cat care, first let's take a sincere look at ourselves. Are we emotionally healthy? If so, great! However, many of us might feel we struggle right along with our kitties. For example, is there something within us that makes it hard to keep our commitment? If we allow it, our cat's problems can hold up a mirror for us to see ourselves more clearly. Take a deep breath. Accept where we are right now. This is a step in the process of building healthier bonds with our cats and with anyone else. Looking at ourselves takes courage, vulnerability, openness, and hope. Healing our hurts leads to more maturity in our souls which will impact all facets of our lives in beautiful and meaningful ways—including how we relate to our companion animal friends.

CHAPTER 3

Let the Healing Begin

I want you to have an adoring, loving, bonded relationship with your furry feline friend. Why is it harder than you anticipated to get along with your kitty, you wonder? By now, shouldn't our culture have gotten this domesticated feline cohabitation thing right? Certainly, a lot of progress has happened in the last twenty to thirty years as felines have finally garnered more time and space in the scientific research realm. Many great books have come out since 2000 to help cat owners understand why their cats may struggle with behavioral problems.

Books with scientifically proven and researched methodologies of cat care are absolutely useful. I have personally read many of them. With this available knowledge, I have wondered why more cat owners are not educating themselves? Or if they do find out good information on why their cat struggles, why then are they often unwilling to make necessary adjustments to heal the environment for kitty? I think it very likely that it boils down to a general brokenness in the cat-human relationship. Broken humans, worn out from stress, struggle to get to a place of peace and sanity for themselves. How can they possibly spend time and effort prioritizing a cat that just adds to their stress levels? Recently someone told me, that even though they knew their cat had many red flags for kidney disease, they felt too busy and overwhelmed to help the cat, needing to help themselves before they could consider the cat.

Our culture has many of us tied up in knots. We are busy! We are stressed! We are overwhelmed! We are so burdened by a hectic life and frequently strapped financially. Therefore, everything additional we take on, like a pet, needs to be easy, right? Or it just isn't worth it.

Another reason for the broken cat-human relationship is that many of us are emotionally wounded and mentally traumatized. Most humans have unresolved heartache and confusion from childhood. Much of that stems from various forms of abuse. Or we have broken or hardened hearts from adult experiences from feeling betrayed, abandoned by a partner, out of place in society, or just plain not good enough. Many people struggle with addictions that overtake their lives, and they have little left within them to handle challenges or upsets.

After working in cat rescue, I can attest to meeting many cat owners surrendering their kitties, for this reason: "It isn't easy, so I am done." I

❀ *A little snuggle bonding time with my Prim kitty.*

want to help more cats stay with their families. And not merely in an "it's better enough that I can tolerate this cat now" way, but in an "I love my furry friend, and I am glad she came into my life to help me grow," way. I know that if you open your heart and mind to this chapter and are willing to make positive shifts in your emotional and spiritual wellness, your physical environment and mental awareness will automatically improve, and all this will help you and your cat build a harmonious relationship.

A WILLINGNESS TO LEARN & CHANGE

People tend to blame a relationship problem on the other party. Something must be wrong with them, right? Swallowing our pride, looking deeply at ourselves and our flaws and failings, is not easy. It requires a quite painful dive inwards to sort out why we have become the way we are. But doing so always improves our wellness, self-love, and life.

In the case of your feline relationship, it might not be such a deep dive; it depends on the health of the current relationship. When I speak with cat owners or potential cat owners, few seem open to learning how to start the relationship out on the right foot or that they might be the one who needs to change to make improvements in an existing relationship. They display an element of pride or carelessness in their attitudes. Either "I totally already know everything about how to take care of a cat," or "Please, how hard can it be, really?" I can quickly see how this lack of knowledge will lead them astray. I visualize the future for that kitty, and the picture isn't always pretty. A little willingness to learn on the part of the human caregiver could make a whole world of difference in kitty's life and happiness.

I have great confidence in you because you picked up this book and have read this far. This demonstrates that you think there is more to understand about felines and how humans should interact with them. Since I grew up with a few cats, as a thirty-something woman adopting my first cat as an adult, I went in with that attitude of, "I've got this. It's easy." A few years later that poor kitty died because, in at least one area of cat care, I was completely ignorant. As I got into rescue work, again I felt a lot of confidence because I naturally love and accept cats' nature and get along well with them, yet I learned something new every time I fostered. To this day, even after more than a decade of experiences and formal education, I continue to learn new concepts.

❀ *Poppy, my longest foster kitty who lived with me for about six months. Did you know shorthaired black cats have one of the hardest times getting adopted?*

As you work through this book, I hope you do so with a desire to learn, with a heart ready to hear some potentially hard truths and a mind and soul willing to change to become an amazing cat guardian.

HOW OUR OLD TRAUMAS & WOUNDS INTERFERE

Human weaknesses and patterns of behavior can negatively impact how we live with and accept our feline friends. Be prepared to look inward for a minute either at yourself and/or at the other individuals living in your environment. We need to uncover some of the deeper issues that make us impatient, controlling, quick to anger, easily frustrated, fearful, unreliable, or other traits that lead to deteriorating the bonds of love with kitty.

You probably have heard the terminology "wounded inner child" at some point in your life. If not, the "inner child" term was first introduced by the world-famous psychiatrist Carl Jung. Over the decades, therapists have continued developing Jung's original work and now help clients address healing the wounds their inner child held on to and hasn't processed and released, thus impacting their adult lives in negative ways.

Why am I bringing this up? Well, because often our unhealthy or negative reactions to situations in our lives and with our cats are at least in part related to having a wounded inner child, who on a subconscious level, still dictates how we respond to challenges. We can start the healing process by gauging our own behavioral responses to tough situations and reflect on if we reacted with mature adult energy or if we responded with wounded child-like energy.

I am not a licensed therapist. The concepts I will address I learned over years of self-study and helping my own inner child to heal. To first identify, then correct, our own unhealthy behavior feels wonderful. It requires a fair amount of hope and patience with ourselves, because we humans tend to fall back into old patterns of thinking or behavior. This is why I love energy work. From my experience, it helps us leave behind those old ways of thinking and responding, faster than any other form of therapy.

A person approaching personal healing with a multi-faceted process more likely succeeds. When people combine scientific methods with alternative, holistic, and spiritual methods, they generally get substantial results. If they combine, say, appointments with a great cognitive behavioral therapist along with consistent Body Code and Belief Code sessions (energy work), at the same time focusing on better self-care habits like more rest, exercise, and healthy eating—and all while increasing their spiritual development via self-study or with a mentor—they board a *fast* and *solid* trajectory to personal healing.

When we only try out one method, it is rarely enough to create lasting healing. As much as I love energy work, for instance, it is not enough all on its own. I witnessed that those I helped with this tool who were not actively pursuing other forms of wellness, self-reflection, and development would quickly fall back into old patterns and create new trauma that sent them almost back to the beginning.

How can we identify if we struggle with reacting and responding from a place of wounded-child energy? Below is a list of common struggles that harm all relationships, including our feline bonds, that many or most humans grapple with now or at some point in their lives. These suggest unresolved childhood trauma and/or additional unresolved trauma experienced in adult life, and we may need professional help to overcome.

1. **Feeling easily hurt or offended and then quickly becoming defensive.** If someone says something unkind to us, do we immediately lash out with a harsh insult back? Do we cry or seek to hide? Do we get physically aggressive, like hitting or kicking as a response? Do we often feel belittled, disrespected, or rejected? This can point to unresolved childhood pain from a toxic relationship with a guardian or sibling where their words caused us to feel less-than.

2. **Struggling with one or more addictions with dangerous substances or behaviors.** This incorporates a huge range of possibilities from the least offensive to incredibly damaging to oneself and others. I cannot list the practically infinite options, but anything *we feel we must do to escape this reality* constitutes an addictive behavioral concern. Common but often less recognized addictions revolve around technology or media—binging on TV shows or movies, voraciously reading novels, playing games on phones, and scrolling for hours on social media. If we ever feel anxiety when we can't look at our phone or often pick it up for no valid reason, our brain is showing signs of addiction. Some addictions *seem* healthy, but when performed compulsively, they can harm us. These include workaholism, overachieving, perfectionism, excessivee restriction or control with food, over studying, and over exercising. Sometimes our addictions present emotionally, such as blaming, being a victim, or creating drama. Addictions to gambling, shopping, and gaming can lead to loss of time and money. Very dangerous addictions sometimes steer toward criminal actions such as obsessions with alcohol, drugs, pain meds, and sex. The drive to escape struggle often points to painful unresolved trauma.

3. **Mental illnesses going unaddressed or ignored.** Gratefully, our society continues to progress toward a place of more acceptance with obtaining help for mental illnesses. We would never expect someone with a physical illness to not seek help, so why put stigma behind seeking help for mental illness? If we feel shame in this regard, I hope we can let it go and seek the care we need. Depression, anxiety, suicidal ideation, and other complex mental ailments are often rooted in childhood trauma and pain.

4. **Needing control to feel safe.** Controlling comes in *many* forms. It can look like aggression, passive aggression, gaslighting, manipulation, over dramatizing, feigned apathy, disordered eating, forms of OCD, abusing, or self-harming (like cutting). Be on the lookout for any areas of weakness when it comes to control. Most everyone struggles with this on some level, wanting our worlds to be how we prefer and manipulating outcomes to get what we think we need. Sadly though, controlling never brings us real peace of mind and serves to hurt ourselves and those around us.

5. **Punishing others when hurt or angry.** This, too, is a form of control. Consequences are natural results of actions. Generally experiencing consequences are good for humans and cats alike. It helps us learn. For instance, a young cat constantly pesters an older cat because it wants to play. The older cat does not, so it hisses or swats the young cat in the face. These are normal behaviors in the cat world and helps teach the young cat to back off. With children, having prearranged and age-appropriate consequences to actions teaches them limits and boundaries. Punishments on the other hand are often used in the heat of the moment and can be very unhealthy reactions. This might look like slapping, hitting, squeezing angrily, pushing, beating, throwing, yelling, or other harming. It could also appear as withholding, such as refusing to show love.

6. **Overt selfishness and lying to get what we want.** These behaviors can reflect wounded inner child concerns. It might look like an attitude of living only for now, for this life, and not for a better one. Or it could be seen when caring first about getting our needs fulfilled and no one else ranks in our mind. Or when we lie to others to maintain having our needs and wants met.

7. **Being quick to feel impatience, frustration, or anger.** A short fuse often strongly indicates that past trauma interferes with our day-to-day life.

8. **Acting the victim in many situations and relying on blaming others to feel better about ourselves.** We may have genuinely been a victim to someone else's crime, abuse, neglect, or selfishness unwillingly inflicted upon us. That isn't what I am pinpointing

here. The victim energy I want to point out is more about not taking responsibility for our life and circumstances, seeing our part in failing relationships, owning up to our mistakes, and being able to apologize. We blame everyone else for why our life is hard. It can be difficult to face up to our part if our lives are not going well, and if we *cannot* do it, it is likely because of that traumatized child within.

9. **Judging others harshly.** When we are hard on others, this often indicates someone was hard on us in early childhood and/or that we are hard on ourselves, judging our own failings and flaws severely. This comes from shame-based living. When we expect everyone to behave and act as we deem correct, life gets very hard for others around us.

10. **Prideful attitudes.** Though pride comes in different forms, I am speaking of the negative pride that keeps us from learning new ideas, accepting that others may know more than we do, or asking for help when we need it. Pridefulness creates feelings of deep shame over our flaws or failures. Negative pride allows us to view ourselves as better than someone else, justifies hurting others for being different from ourselves, enforces the need to be the smartest, the best, the winner, or having the final word at the expense of others. This kind of false pride is often a mask for someone who has very low self-worth and may signify harm done in childhood.

11. **Thinking negatively all the time.** Some people relish being negative, sarcastic, or judgmental. They feel it makes them savvy and realistic, but in reality, to speak toxic words, think in worst-case-scenarios, and feel gloomy and unhappy all the time damages themselves and others. I am not advocating false feelings or invalidating negative emotions here, but I am concerned that as a culture we have made a mistake to promote, revere, or encourage negative energies. The inability to recognize our own negativity may similarly point to past unresolved trauma.

There are other manifestations of inner child trauma and traumatic experiences impacting people's lives, but I mention these because they seem more prevalent in situations where I am trying to mend really strained cat-human bonds. Identifying the ways we each struggle begins the healing process.

WOUNDED VS MATURE REACTIONS

Let's spend a moment illustrating scenarios that might help us see if we struggle with reacting from a place of wounded-child energy. I have seen the following interactions in real life, and they will serve to help us correct human-feline relations.

Scenario 1

A family owns an expensive leather couch purchased from a high-end store. The father in this home resents the financial loss when he discovers that the family cat has started sharpening claws there. This father gets angry and yells at his wife about it, placing blame on her for bringing the cat into the home in the first place. He insists she correct it immediately. The wife doesn't like the habit of the cat but isn't really bothered by it; plus, she doesn't appreciate how her husband treated her and becomes defensive. She doesn't know how to curb this feline behavior, so it continues. Later, the father catches the cat scratching the couch and in an uncontrolled moment of anger, aggressively kicks the cat across the room.

Pinpointing Unhealthy Responses in Scenario 1

- The father cares too much about money and investment because it creates anger within himself over a perceived loss.
- He places responsibility on someone else to fix the issue when he was the one upset by it.
- He blames someone else for his problem.
- This man tries to control others through intimidation and anger.
- The wife has a passive-aggressive response by choosing to do nothing to help because she is hurt.
- This man resorts to physically abusive reactions on a weaker creature.

Healthy Ways to Respond to Scenario 1

- Without getting angry, the father identifies that he would rather not have the cat scratch up nice furnishings.

- He has a calm and open discussion with his spouse and family on ways they might address the behavior.

- He makes sure that the directions chosen for curbing the behavior in kitty are viable, proven, and non-threatening.

- Since he is the party most interested in fixing the issue, he participates in or takes charge of retraining kitty.

- The family shows compassion and kindness to the cat for expressing a part of her true nature.

Scenario 2

Kitty gets into a barfing position and is about to throw up on the rug. A woman hurriedly approaches and angrily yells at the cat. The cat flees out of fear and stress from the woman's reaction so vomit is strewn all over the room as kitty runs away. She chases down the cat, grabs it, brings it back, shoves kitty's nose in the barf and scolds the cat for making a mess. She lets go, and the cat runs away again as the woman swears at kitty for being an "inconsiderate jerk."

Pinpointing Unhealthy Responses in Scenario 2

- She chose to startle the cat in a difficult moment. Not only was it unhelpful but could pose a choking hazard for kitty if scared enough and caught off guard. Her response did not prevent the natural bodily function of vomiting.

- She got angrier because she wasn't able to prevent the act of throwing up on the rug and she now has an even bigger mess to clean.

- She believes that the cat deserves to be punished, so it will learn not to barf again and therefore stop making her life harder.

- She punished the cat in an abusive way both physically and emotionally for a necessary bodily function.

- Swearing and using negativity to express herself did not help.

Healthy Ways to Respond to Scenario 2

- She should show concern when she hears kitty beginning to barf.

- To help save her rug, she could carefully move kitty onto the hard floor if there is time, or she could place a piece of paper or plastic bag in the spot kitty is about to throw up on.

- She could use gentle and kind words to sympathize with kitty.

- She will need to keep cool when kitty scoots a few feet away and gags again, as this is normal behavior.

- She should patiently clean up the mess and if needed find healthier solutions for preventing barfing in the future, like hairball prevention supplements and brushing fur frequently.

Scenario 3

A young mother with a toddler decides to adopt a kitten because her daughter gets excited by cats. She chooses a well-socialized and friendly kitten that behaves nicely with the young girl at the adoption event. However, once home, the toddler is very controlling with the kitty; grabbing her and not letting go, squeezing kitty and screaming, and chasing kitty and throwing loud fits when she gets away. The mother does nothing to teach or curb her child's behaviors toward the kitten. In this woman's mind, the kitten is akin to a toy she obtained for her child. This kitten, now terrified, resorts to an appropriate means of defending herself and begins to scratch the child every time she gets near her. The mother gets angry at the kitten for hurting her daughter and repeatedly punishes the cat by picking her up by the scruff, screaming at her, and throwing her away from the child.

Pinpointing Unhealthy Responses in Scenario 3

- The young mother thought it acceptable to adopt a real kitten to be a child's "toy."

- She did not proactively parent, teaching her child limitations in behaviors.

- She was enraged when the child experienced natural consequences with the kitten.

- She did not respect that another living being has feelings and fears.

- Lashing out at a tiny creature when her child is hurt constitutes physical abuse.

Healthy Ways to Respond to Scenario 3

- The mother should recognize that a toddler is not a fit pet owner.

- The woman should acknowledge that kitty has feelings and will adequately respond with what God gave her when threatened and scared.

- When choosing to adopt with a young child in the home, the mother should teach the child how to appropriately interact with the kitten.

- She should remain calm when a child gets scratched or bitten and help the child recognize why the cat responded that way.

- The mother should protect kitty from trauma and harm by helping the two youngsters create a healthy, loving relationship.

These situations are more intense than average, but I selected them to clarify the point. If you would never behave in these extremes, that is good, but how might you still struggle with some wounded child reactions in your feline relationship? Identifying weaknesses is the first step in redirecting one's responses into more "adult" energy. This mature energy is calm, compassionate, reasonable, open, gentle, and steady, and never out of control with anger. Adult energy is wiser and more deliberate. This type of energy thinks first and then chooses the right response. We are all capable of becoming this kind of individual with education, self-reflection, forgiveness, patience, healing, and persistence.

❀ Wild kitten energy versus calm adult cat.

BECOMING A BETTER CAT GUARDIAN

When our day-to-day interactions with our cats emanate from a place of wounded-child energy, we severely damage the relationship and bonding potential. The above scenarios came from real-life examples. The cats in all these homes were afraid or wary of the owner who treated them with such disdain. In fact, in the last scenario, the mother returned the kitten about a month later, claiming the kitten was "psycho." It took some gentle prodding to get the real story. The kitten was genuinely traumatized and now dreaded humans, whereas she had been a loving, trusting kitten before adoption. A gifted foster spent an additional six months with this cat to rehabilitate her. Even after treatment, she remained aloof and struggled finding a new forever home. The abuse permanently changed her personality. Animals are not unlike humans when they go through traumatic experiences.

We become better cat guardians when we stop reacting to them in immature, child-like ways. Does it seem odd that even as "grownups", some of our behaviors remain immature? Certainly, as adults we have greater capacity for responsibility than we did as children, but our reactions and behaviors in difficult circumstances—things that try our patience, create fear, increase stress, or cause pain—can tell us a lot about our emotional and spiritual maturity. Our cats long for us to be emotionally and spiritually adept, so they feel safer with us.

As a culture, we effectually put our physical care in the forefront—the extremely profitable medical industry, beauty industry, diet industry, fashion industry, sports industry, food industry, and sex industry are evidence of that. Culturally, we have begun to pay more attention to our emotional and mental needs by permitting people to receive support and care with far less shame, but we often don't make the needed connections of cause and effect. For instance, we don't take appropriate action in limiting technology or social media use when they are distinctly linked to depression, addiction, anxiety and more. Ironically, as a culture we put our spiritual needs on the backburner when in fact if we made our spiritual needs the main priority in our lives, our physical, mental, and emotional care would automatically leap forward. Our spiritual development helps us adopt greater-than-us views of this life. It helps us stay present, and when we focus less on the past or the future, we are freer to feel calm, peace, love, and compassion for ourselves and others. We don't need to control everything or everyone around us to feel safe. As a result, we often experience less stress, which means better immune function, less weight gain, more energy, better sleep, more clarity when faced with choices, and much more.

PURRRITO WRAP UP

We all have moments in our lives where we behave badly. We were triggered and our wounded child lashed out in an unhealthy way. This life journey encompasses forgiveness—of ourselves and others— so we can change and grow. Be gentle with yourself if this chapter helped to reveal any current weaknesses. I know that you have the power to heal and change when you sincerely desire it and move toward it.

Our personal spiritual and emotional development truly brings us closer to our cats! Silly? No. It will bring us closer to all living things. Life is full of ups and downs, times of peace and times of struggle. When we must face a challenge, how do we respond? When we respond with calm, peaceful maturity—wonderful. If we react in negative ways like seeking control or unhealthy escape, we likely are coming at the problem with our wounded inner-child in charge. We should identify if we struggle with any residual trauma in our lives and if so, seek out the help we need to recover. If we grow and change in positive ways, we become more open, loving, and easier to connect with. Our purrry friends can now reach our hearts and make that bond we truly desire. This journey you travel with your feline is one of many potential paths to help guide you to a place of peace, love, hope, and compassion.

CHAPTER 4

Spiritual & Holistic Tools Available to All

The last chapter may have been hard. I apologize if it was at all triggering. The intention is to help us all heal in any way needful, so our cats will benefit. Not only that, but also so we and everyone around us will benefit. I hope we feel a desire to grow in a spiritual direction, to step firmly on the path or to walk further down the path if we are already on it. When we become spiritually-minded beings, then we can encircle our cats into that love and light. I have not fully arrived myself. It is a journey. But I really appreciate looking back and saying, "Yeah, I've come a long way, and that feels really good to me." The tools I will present in this chapter all played a part in my healing journey. I pray they will support you as well.

If your cat is happy and doing well and you have not yet done any spiritual healing in your life, you can keep on as you are, *or* you could take the opportunity to increase your personal wellness and spiritual power to have an even stronger bond. Having a strong spiritual connection and a holistic approach to living will give you a great advantage into discovering unique and personally tailored ways to help your individual cat.

Side Note: FDA Approval?

I need to say that some of what I mention in this chapter is not FDA (Food and Drug Administration) approved for healing and wellness. What does that mean? It means that the US government has not given these methods their endorsement. Please do your own research on each approach I bring up that you want to explore. To get a clearer picture, you can research how other governments (especially Europe) approach some of these tools and their approved uses. Additionally, it's good to understand the FDA's overall agendas and corporate affiliations.

SOME OF THE BEST TOOLS TO EXPLORE

Relationships with Deity

I love God. My understanding of Him is still imperfect because of my finite state. My love is really strong at times and at others, weaker. I talk to God. I listen for His responses. I try to keep His laws and align with His will, but I do not always manage this perfectly. I fall at times. Yet my heart ultimately longs to be in His word, power, grace, and abundance. So, I keep trying. Seeking God, loving Him, trying to connect with and understand Him is how we form a relationship.

My specific beliefs lead me to try to draw closer to and emulate Christ as much as I can. I see Him as my path back to God. Not all readers will agree with this. And that is okay. You build your relationship with Deity in the ways that feel true and right for you at this time. As long as that relationship is healthy— meaning your faith and beliefs lead you toward genuine love and compassion for all living beings and not away—you are on a good path. I know as my love of God has grown, my levels of tolerance, acceptance, patience, and compassion have grown too. This has translated onto my furry friends, both for those in my home and around the globe.

There are many tools that will help support a relationship with God, bringing us closer together. Opportunities to hear, see, feel, and know what we need or can do to make our lives healthier and happier are all around us. I will try to be brief on describing these tools. You may already be totally familiar and comfortable with these, but bear with me as other readers may need support in incorporating them into their lives.

Prayer

This is one of my go-tos for support with my forever cats and fosters. Life has its challenges, and whereas you may have been on a strong course with your connection to Spirit, it can slip away from you without constant nourishment or when hardship hits. Prayer is one of the core practices to keep you closer to Spirit and God. At some points in my recent history, I readily accessed answers through prayer and at other times I permitted adversity to cut that connection. Generally, though, I find this resource hugely comforting and helpful.

Pattern for Formal Prayers

Just in case you are out of practice or have not done much praying, here is a general pattern for longer or more formal prayers. You can additionally have short communions with God like "Thank you for that help, God," "I love you, God," "God, I need your help!" or "God, please protect us." Of course, adapt the following suggestions as you need to for your own beliefs.

- I prefer, when I can, to pray out loud as it helps me stay focused.

- If I pray out loud, I first ask silently that God will protect my prayer—that I will be able to receive His help and guidance without interference of any evil or impure influence and that any such influences will be confounded and unable to understand or even hear my prayer.

- I begin my prayer by addressing God, typically saying, "Father in Heaven," "Father above," "Dear God," or "God in Heaven."

- I next offer gratitude for the things I have seen His hand in that day. I thank Him for my comforts, safety, health, capabilities. I express my love for Him, Christ, Angels, the Spirit—all beings helping me to receive guidance and support.

- Often, I ask forgiveness of any sins, shortcomings, weaknesses, or addictive behaviors. For me, this is important to show my contrition, awareness, and desire to better align with God's will.

- Then I begin to discuss my concerns at hand. With cats, I often ask for help in healing them, to know if I should be more concerned, to know how to help solve a problem, or with fosters, I ask for help in finding the best possible forever home. I ask for specific blessings or ask for help to be led to inspired thoughts or feelings.

🐾 For me, I close my prayer using the name of Jesus Christ—"I ask for these things in Jesus' name. Amen,"—but close your prayer in a way that works for your beliefs.

Revelation & Answers

A crucial tool as a companion to prayer is how to receive answers to our questions. It's best to figure out our primary and secondary (and even tertiary) methods in which we are most likely to receive answers. This is totally unique to each person. It can be very frustrating to pray when we feel like no answers are coming. This is in large part because many of us expect God to communicate directly to our hearts or minds with distinct clear words. While that is a viable possibility, it may not be the prominent method in which we receive individually. For a long time, this is what I expected for myself, and I assumed God didn't love me because I rarely got those "clear words spoken in my mind" messages.

What are some ways I have experienced or heard of for receiving answers to prayer? First, for me, if I am truly connected and have a pen and paper handy, I often begin to receive a gentle flow of words as I hold my pen at the ready. It takes practice, and if you don't keep it up, you have to retrain yourself again. The words are not my own; it isn't in my syntax. I often have phrases repeat until I get them written down before more will come.

When I am in good practice with receiving messages in this way, I have more success sensing my secondary form of receiving which is a *quiet* voice in my heart and mind. Often, I see words written out in my mind or images appear in my thoughts.

I also receive answers a third way by making a decision and then verbally and prayerfully put it into God's hands, e.g., "God, I have decided *x*. If this is right or if it matters in the grand scheme of things, I ask that you make it plain to me by making the path forward easy. If the path forward is not easy or it becomes difficult or impossible, I will accept that my decision was not in my highest good or in the highest good of others involved."

Story Example: Answer to a Prayer

As a kitten ready for adoption, I took Honey and her two sisters to a Saturday event. Honey was very popular because of how cute she was. A nice woman in her late 60s arrived with her daughter and grandkids. They adored Honey and pressured this woman into adopting her. The woman liked Honey but felt unsure if getting a kitten was right for her. Her husband had barely entered hospice care, putting her under a lot of stress. Coerced by her daughter's words that someone would quickly adopt Honey that day, this woman filled out paperwork and took her home.

The rest of that day I felt grumpy. When I left the event and got in my car, I cried. I didn't know why. I didn't connect it with Honey's adoption, because it had never entered my mind to keep her. Two days later, I still felt off. I got a phone call from the woman who adopted Honey, telling me that she lost the kitten, couldn't find her anywhere. I hurried over to her apartment, worried for my baby. As I walked in, I called out my standard, "Babies!" that I use for calling kittens to me, and Honey rushed out from her hiding place. The woman seemed relieved yet saddened. Honey was hiding from her but came to me immediately. She stated, "She loves you so much," in a disappointed way. I told the woman that Honey would grow to love and trust her over time. I felt heartsick leaving Honey and had a compulsion to grab the kitten and run. I resisted. She didn't belong to me. I got in my car and bawled all the way home. Now, to clarify, I had adopted out about fifty kittens at this point and had never reacted like this.

❀ *Honey on the left with her sisters Sugar and Sweetie at adoptions.*

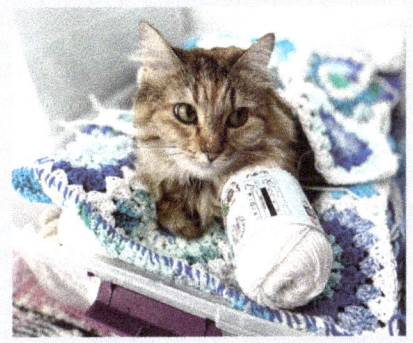

❀ *Honey, all grown up hanging out on one of my crochet projects.*

The next morning I continued to feel cranky and even a bit paranoid regarding work colleagues. However, as I took a moment to look deeper at my attitude, I realized that my great unease resulted from not having Honey in my life. I prayed to God, saying something like, "God, I don't know why I feel so strongly about this, but I am truly upset. If you think Honey should be my cat, then if that women decides not to keep her for any reason, I will adopt her."

Two hours later I received a phone message from Honey's adopter saying she decided keeping Honey wasn't a good idea and could she return her? For me, that was no coincidence but a direct answer from God that He too felt Honey should remain with me.

Additional ways one might receive answers to prayers include:

- In song or poetry.

- An article or post randomly in your news feed with the answer.

- Someone you talk to saying *the thing* you need to hear.

- In dreams, visions, or meditations.

- A flood of emotion like love.

- Feeling immense peace or a "burning" sensation in the chest area.

- A "stupor of thought" or your mind going blank in the midst of your prayer can mean God is saying "no."

God can communicate with you in other ways, too. Find joy in discovering. Ask God to lead you to understand how you can best hear Him.

Fasting

This tool can help us focus our intentions and prayers when we really need an answer, help, direction. One could fast in many ways, but often involves a sacrifice of not eating for a day or so. Fasting should not be overdone at the risk of your health, but a 24 hour fast every now and then actually benefits our digestive tracts. The act of not eating for a while is a humbling experience. The humility can work as a device to help us draw closer to God. If you cannot sacrifice by abstaining from food, then choose something else to sacrifice for a time. It could be TV, social media, or anything you like to do but can see how it might deter a stronger connection to Spirit.

Giving & Serving

Giving of our time, means, and talents brings us closer to God. God is a God of service. He wants us to serve, support, love, and care for one another. We most often give service to our family and pets, work colleagues, church community, or neighbors. This is as it should be. We should take care of those closest to us first and move outwards as we have time and ability. We offer our time but also sometimes our talents or money. If we can, we show up to volunteer for organizations that help make the world a better place. We can give money to charities and non-profits that puts the work in when we cannot. Showing kindness and concern for others always draws us closer to the power of love that is God.

Scriptures & Sermons

Dive into the texts and talks important to you for bringing you closer to Deity. Spending time learning in these ways about the God you love can help you become closer to Him. I try to read from scripture every day for ten to twenty minutes. I also listen to a ten-to-fifteen-minute sermon given by leaders of my religious faith on a daily basis. This small habit does a powerful job keeping my mind and heart focused on God.

Humility

This word can prove difficult to understand because it can represent many things and because our current culture defines it in several ways. We often see humility in a negative light. We might think of poverty, neglect, or lack of education when we think of humility. We might think of being humiliated which we associate with feeling embarrassed, hurt, ashamed, or foolish. So then what form of humility brings us closer to God? It is a feeling or understanding that we are no better than any other living person. We have a belief in a greater power than ourselves who leads and guides us and others. Good humility means we have no unhealthy pride in what we have accomplished because we know ultimately any praise goes back to the God we serve.

Universal Intelligence & Support

Whisperings of the Spirit & Promptings

In my religion we use the terms "whisperings" or "promptings" to convey how the Spirit of God operates in this world. It helps us understand that rarely will God send a message that is loud, shiny, over-the-top obvious. Why might that be? Because His greatest gift to us in this life is our agency. We need to *choose* to seek and listen for those quiet communications sent to help us. I have learned that the more we seek these words and feelings and then follow through with them, the more frequently they come. If we always ignore them, they often stop coming. This tool, these whisperings, are such a comfort while navigating this life and comes in handy as a pet parent.

Story Example: Kitty Getting Out of Danger

One morning a few days after my parents returned from a cross-country road trip where they had numerous car troubles, my dad went out into the garage and then came back inside while I worked in the kitchen. A few minutes later I felt prompted "Go out to the garage." I did and immediately saw that Honey had slipped into the garage while dad came in or out. She was licking up something from under his car. I got closer and noted the oily substance had dribbled from the motor. I brought Honey inside and asked my dad what might be dripping from his car. He said he'd had power steering fluid issues. I quickly Googled "cats and power steering fluid" and discovered it was toxic and potentially deadly. We immediately went to the vet. Gratefully the veterinarian thought she hadn't consumed enough to warrant stomach pumping, but the vet force-fed her charcoal to counteract the toxins.

What if I ignored that prompting? Honey would have gotten sick, and I likely wouldn't have put two and two together quickly enough to save her life. Toxins like this destroy a cat's kidneys or liver in a very short amount of time.

Have you ever had thoughts like this: You are driving home, but a notion pops into your mind like, "Take the backroads and not the freeway." You may have ignored it and taken the freeway, and everything turned out fine for you. *But* what if Spirit prompted you to take the backroads because, say, a stray kitten along the road needed saving? These thoughts that arise are typically spiritual promptings.

I have learned (mostly) not to ignore these promptings. Sometimes they are literally life or death warnings. I have decided to just follow the direction even if it seems silly. I never go wrong by following, but I have certainly gone *very* wrong by not doing so. I have had a few promptings I ignored that really haunt me. Once, in my late twenties, I pulled into a busy gas station and noticed an elderly woman sitting in the driver's seat at a pump and looking sad. I had a distinct prompt say, "Go and pump her gas." It was rainy, cold, and windy, and several other patrons, all men, filled their cars at the pumps, so I justified to myself, "If she needs her gas pumped, one of those men should do it." I drove off and regretted that ever since. What if I received that prompt because none of those men could hear the Spirit? What if the lady would have been fearful of a strange man approaching her, but not likely to fear a young woman? What if she felt sick or in pain? What if her husband had recently passed and he always filled the car with gas, and she didn't know how to do it?

How can we tell if the prompting we receive originates from our own mind or from Spirit? What I have learned is that when the idea comes from our own head, the format usually appears as a question, like "I wonder if I should take the backroads tonight?" or "That lady looks sad. I should probably help her out, right?" Whereas a spiritual prompting usually forms more like a command statement such as, "Go and pump her gas." or "Take the backroads tonight." If you have a kind thought or idea that isn't a prompting and springs from your own thinking process, follow through with it anyway and help someone out.

Side Note: "Hard Hearts"

I should mention that when you feel angry, defensive, judgmental, or negative, connecting to Spirit can prove difficult. Having a hardness about you, and in particular a hardening energy around your heart, keeps you from reaching God. For myself, I often use Emotion Code (energy work) to remove "heart wall" energies before I can truly connect. I likewise need to be in a place of generally feeling positive, hopeful, and receptive. If you don't have an energy releasing tool easily available to you, you can try other tools like tapping (EFT), crystals, meditation, or frequency healing to help you get to a more open and peaceful place of receiving.

Intuition

Your intuition is slightly different. It is more like an inner knowing, your "gut" feeling about something. Heeding your intuition takes courage and practice. Some folks will pooh-pooh you for saying something like, "It just didn't feel right for me," because these people tend to be driven more by logic. If you are a logical thinker, begin to give yourself permission to listen to your inner knowing. If your gut says you need to take your cat to the vet, even when you don't see a logical reason to do so, follow it. Don't be discouraged if the cat gets a clean bill of health, and you think thoughts like, "Clearly that was stupid and a waste of money!" You may never know the ripple effect your choices have. Maybe a person in the vet's lobby whom you chatted with felt lonely and needed to connect with someone that day.

The more you tune into your own guidance system, the more you will trust it. By the way, your instincts come from that part of you connected and listening to all life and energy. It is a life force that knows all. I consider it the creative power or light of Christ; you may consider it to be the Universal Intelligence or something else entirely.

With kitty, your intuition may tell you that your cat feels depressed, and it's best to extend extra attentiveness or gentleness for a few days. Your gut feelings my lead you to buy a new cat tree that helps reduce conflict among cats. Or you may feel like your indoor-outdoor cat should simply stay inside that day.

Angels

I don't consider myself an expert on Angels. I am not sure if they are all deceased humans, yet to be born humans, not human at all, or a combo of all three. Currently I'm leaning into the all-three possibility. I do not see Angels with my physical eyes like some individuals, though a handful of times in my life I felt the presence of specific people or animals who moved on from this life and I could "see" them in my mind's eye. We have a lot to learn about Angels. In fact, one of my personal journaling messages from God told me I needed to learn more about them, to understand their different roles and how to best ask for their help.

We can ask for Angels by name. I am not sure why, but I rarely permit myself to do this though I have certainly asked for Angelic support by their skills and interests. Specifically with cat care, I ask for help from Angels who love and understand cats or from Angels who are healers or for Angels who can comfort and communicate with the cats on a deeper, more spiritual level.

I ask most often for the Angels to watch over my cats before they go outdoors. The cats and I have a ritual where I open the front door to reveal the storm door. I put the cat's collar on as she waits at the door, then stroke her from head to tail several times and verbally ask that her shield be up (I visualize it too), that God and His Angels will watch over and protect her outside, that she will remain safe from harm, evil, and accident. I then tell the kitty she is loved and open the door. (More on page 78.)

My cats usually come home when called, but on occasion, they do not. When I ask for the Angels to send them home, I kid you not, within minutes the cat always arrives at the door, asking to come inside.

Some of the cats quarrel at night, especially on nights when I do not want to host any of the cats in my bedroom while I sleep. I ask for Angels to help me out by keeping them from fighting. I have found the majority of the time this support is honored. (I'm a light sleeper and wake up if I hear a cat spat.)

If I have foster kittens or any of my forever cats going under anesthesia for any procedures, I always ask that Angels attend my cats, to help support the vet and vet techs, that nothing will go amiss, and that their bodies will process the drugs successfully.

You could ask for numerous types of assistance when communicating with Angels. Nothing is too small to ask about if you want help or support. The Angels of God love us because they love Him.

Thoughts to ponder in regard to Angels:

- I believe that we should not "pray" to Angels. That is a communication method meant for God alone. However, we can "talk" to Angels to ask for help. You could also pray to God to ask Him to send Angels to help you and your kitty.

- I believe we have to ask specifically for their help. Because of our agency, rarely can they intervene (unless directed by God) on our behalf without our explicit request for help.

- I believe our communication with them is more effective if we speak out loud to them. Some sources say that they cannot hear us otherwise. I'm not entirely convinced of that, but if I am in a position where I cannot openly speak to my Angels and I need help, I pray to God to send Angels to my aid. That works just as well in my experience.

Signs

The Christian world often views "sign seeking" as sinful. When I talk about asking God for signs, this does not mean wanting Him to prove Himself to me. I already love and believe in Him. Seeking signs simply means finding a few additional ways that Spirit, Angels, or God can communicate with you that you are loved, watched over, and on the right path for your highest good. Certain signs are somewhat universal, like seeing a rainbow or a hummingbird when you feel lost or alone. I first learned this

technique from author Gabrielle Bernstein in her book *The Universe Has Your Back*, which I highly recommend. She advises that when you've decided on a sign, clear your mind, and then the first object that comes into your head is a good sign for you. It could be an animal, a flower, a book, a number, or some other object. You could have more than one sign of import or meaning to you. The book *Signs: The Secret Language of the Universe* by Laura Lynne Jackson is an uplifting and heartwarming read that I endorse as a way to help you learn more about how these symbols can help you connect to Spirit and bring you comfort.

Story Example: Sign to Know I was Making the Right Choice

I have a very cool experience to share with receiving a sign that I was doing the right thing.

I was fostering two older kittens that were surrendered back to me after being in an adopter's care for five months. They had a bit of a rough time in that home, at least for the month prior to being surrendered, and needed some rehabilitating. When I put them back up for adoption, they were almost a year old, and I wanted them to go together as a bonded pair. At adoptions, they received little attention.

Prior to this, I read *The Universe Has Your Back* and had come up with the "elephant" as my sign. Thus far, I hadn't really seen it on my path in a meaningful way.

A young married couple showed interest in my cats at an event but didn't complete the adoption. However, later in the week they called to say they wanted to adopt both cats. Nice military kids, they punctuated their speech with a lot of "yes ma'ams" in the process of filling out the adoption application. Frankly though, I worried about giving the cats to them because of the *many* red flags on their application—items that rescuers have learned from experience often lead to surrendering the animal. They were 1) very young, 2) getting transferred in a few months, 3) expecting their first baby, 4) had a large dog (these cats had no experience with dogs). I was torn, because I felt like they were good people but feared the environment wasn't stable enough for cats that had already been surrendered once. I eventually said yes to the adoption after an open conversation about not wanting the cats to be surrendered again, that their home needed to be a true forever home.

🐾 *Jelly (left) and Peanut Butter (right).*

I prayed to God and asked Him to help me know before the adoption was final if this was the right thing for the cats. I fretted because on paper the adoption didn't look sound. A few hours later the couple arrived at my home to pick up the cats, and I still hadn't gotten an answer. I actually scanned both of them for any elephant iconography in their clothing to no avail.

My elderly parents live in an apartment in my home, and my cat room is located in their space. My dad loves that we live near a US Air Force base and enjoys the fighter jet flyovers that shake the house. As the couple completed the adoption paperwork in my parents' apartment, my friendly, outgoing dad asked them about their various jobs on base. He then asked about a recent jet formation that he witnessed, and the young man said, "Oh you mean the elephant walk?" I was stunned. Of all the names for the formation! Both continued to talk with my father, and each said the word "elephant" several times. I had received my sign!

Openness & Hearing

This may almost seem obvious, but in order to find and maintain connection to the intelligence and unseen support all around us, we have to believe in it. We need to open ourselves to the possibilities. A great weakness of our current culture is to only "believe what we can see." Hoping, believing, trusting all play a part in allowing ourselves to accept the reality that Angels surround us, that Spirit will send signs or whisper to our hearts and minds, and that following your intuition is a strength, not a weakness. We need to not simply believe and trust but also make space for sensing and hearing those communications. Receiving requires a state of stillness. Interesting then, that in general our world is chaotic, busy, and noisy.

Journaling or "Channeling"

Therapeutically, journaling in and of itself promotes healing. Writing down experiences, feelings, thoughts and reflecting on them can make order out of discord. However, here I make mention of a different type of practice, one more spiritual in its intention and purpose. I mentioned above that this is a way to receive answers to prayer. I don't care for the term "channeling," but I use it here because it may be a term readers are more familiar with than what I refer to it as—personal revelation from God.

For "channeling" while journaling, I am talking about allowing a flow of information from Spirit or Angels to come through your mind and you write the words as they come. It is not allowing a spirit to take over your body; rather it is asking righteous Angels or God's Holy Spirit to convey the things that God would have you know and understand.

It often takes a pure heart, a clear mind, peaceful acceptance, and practice to truly receive messages in this way. For me, I second-guessed myself in the beginning of learning. I wrote messages or ideas that I scratched out because I wondered if it came from my own thoughts or from divine energy. Eventually, the voice became clearer, and I developed more trust. However, this skill isn't like riding a bicycle for most. Picking it up and putting it down for large gaps of time may require some "relearning." This has been the case for me.

Eternal Laws at Work

The God I know is one of order. Many laws of nature or of the Universe play out all around us, and mostly we remain unaware of them. Researchers have identified some of these laws, and we are beginning to understand aspects of them. You likely have heard of the two big ones associated with abundance—the law of attraction and the law of vibration. The movie, *The Secret*, that came out in 2006 made the "law of attraction" more widely known.

There are primary and secondary laws. The law of attraction is actually a secondary law, meaning it is subject to a greater law—in this case, the "law of vibration." *Everything* in this world emits a vibration or frequency. Even you and I give off an overall frequency. According to the work of some writers and spiritual teachers, the majority of humans vibrate at a low frequency or resonance, a very contracted and restrictive place. People in this state give off or live mostly in negative energies. This might look like anger, impatience, frustration, deception, selfishness, blame, shame, and guilt.

The energy we send out enacts the power of the law of attraction, meaning we attract back to us what we are emitting. When we are taking a healing journey and raising our self-love, self-awareness, forgiveness, and hopefulness we bring our vibration up into a space of positive attraction. We will begin to experience freedom from trauma, belief that our lives can improve, and an increase in our faith in God. It's like lifting a heavy, dark, suppressing blanket off of ourselves, so we can see the light and visualize a better future.

Energy healing is a massively effective tool for helping one shift off the weight of negativity and embrace higher vibrational feelings. At this time, any human who can genuinely emit a high vibration are the folks doing amazing things in the world, who are loving, compassionate, open-minded, hopeful, forgiving, and trusting. They have learned to let go of trauma, wounds, or anger. When we reach these heights, we attract back to ourselves more experiences of joy, love, abundance, and peace. (For more insight into this topic, Google "images on studies of the frequencies of emotions.")

Those at a higher vibration still experience heartache or stress, but they have learned how to feel negative energies and then release. They can and do choose to return more readily to a place of peace and trust in God.

Religion & Community

I have spoken of a lot of spiritual ideas and tools thus far in this chapter. Would it have made sense to put religion into one of the first two categories? Possibly. Likely. However, I wanted it as a stand-alone because I believe spirituality and religiosity are not the same thing.

Someone can be very spiritual and not religious. Vice versa, someone can be very religious and not at all spiritual.

I define spirituality as having a great desire to actively seek connection with God, Spirit, and all things metaphysical. It increases our awareness of the grandeur of God and helps us develop humility. We are happier, expanded, loving.

Religion is more about structure with creeds, beliefs, doctrine, policy, rituals, and culture. It is totally possible to practice a religion faithfully and yet have little relationship with God. This reality, which can feel like hypocrisy, harms many youth and turns them away from religion—because they know imperfect, toxic, or abusive people who claim to know God because they practice religion. Christ speaks of this type of person in scripture saying, "They draw near unto me with their lips, but their hearts are far from me."

For me, I need religion *and* a focus on spirituality. I like my religion for offering me a path, giving me a sound moral compass, and allowing me close ties with other people who have similar beliefs. A religion can provide community and belonging. Gallup reports "rigorous" research supporting a connection between regular church attendees and increased wellness and life satisfaction over those who do not attend or rarely attend church.

We all need a healthy community where we belong. Having other people you can turn to—to share your thoughts, feelings, hopes, or concerns on your journey toward God—is critical. I caution against social media as *the* source of your community. This is a counterfeit community. Can it provide some comfort and good? Yes, of course there are healthy ways to incorporate online community into your life. But if you do not have living, breathing, next to you, near you, actual people that you can rely on, you will still wind up feeling alone in the world.

Kitty leading us to seek community.

Books, Personal Development, & Education

The practice of continual self-improvement via education and self-study is crucial for becoming a changed individual. Bringing in new thoughts, ideas, practices, and processes can enrich our ability to overcome all old patterns of living and thinking. It can provide daily or weekly encouragement and motivation to keep going. I have read *many* books in whole or in part over the last eight years of my life that have given me knowledge, power, hope, and played a role in helping me grow and change. Some books covered subjects I find interesting (like cats). Many books helped me grow spiritually or to heal from old wounds. Some were memoirs of others to learn from their personal journeys. Books on physical wellness and healing have increased my capabilities as an energy healer.

Here are a few of my top picks for non-theological books I have found useful for growing & changing:

- *The Emotion Code* by Dr. Bradley Nelson
- *The Body Code* by Dr. Bradley Nelson
- *The Gifts of Imperfection* by Brené Brown
- *Remembering Wholeness* by Carol Tuttle
- *Judgement Detox* by Gabrielle Bernstein
- *The Universe Has Your Back* by Gabrielle Bernstein
- *Signs* by Laura Lynn Jackson
- *Life Colors* by Pamala Oslie
- *Love from Heaven* by Lorna Byrne
- *Medical Medium* by Anthony William
- *Why Woo Woo Works* by Dr. David R. Hamilton
- *Messages in the Numbers* by Alana Fairchild
- *Power vs. Force* by Dr. David R. Hawkins
- *Breaking the Habit of Being Yourself* by Dr. Joe Dispenza
- *The Science of Getting Rich* by Wallace D. Wattles
- *You Can Heal Your Life* by Louise Hay
- *Making the Shift* by Dr. Wayne Dyer

Energy Work & Healing

If you only glean a few things from this book, let this be one of them—energy healing is one of the best ways to heal yourself emotionally, mentally, spiritually, and even physically. It works for your cat, too. Pick from the *many* modalities available. I have personally tried Reiki, Rapid Eye Technology, Emotion/Body/ Belief Code, Foot Zoning, T3 (Three-Dimensional) Therapy, and Emotional Freedom Technique (tapping), among others.

Heart Walls

Heart wall elimination is the energetic removal of the hardness of one's heart. The hardening happens over a lifetime of painful, traumatic, sorrowful, shaming experiences. Not everyone has a heart wall, but most do. Young children often have not formed heart walls, but the more traumatic events encountered at a young age, the greater their chance of carrying around a hardened heart. The "hardening" is symbolic, but the energy wall created around the heart to protect someone is real. Our subconscious mind often builds this wall as a way to reduce the amount of pain and hurt we feel the next time something terrible happens to us. However, this protection ultimately hinders someone seeking to connect with God, to feel real love in their life, and to be open and vulnerable in healthy ways. I haven't used other modalities of energy work to address this specific concern, but know the Emotion Code and Body Code tools will help someone release their heart wall. How much better will our cat-human bonds become without hiding behind walls of protection?

Shielding

Energetic shielding is a powerful protection tool and, like energy work, a great one to incorporate into your life and especially into the care of your cat. This practice involves intention and visualization.

I use energy shields in this way:

- **To protect my entire body** by visualizing the shield around myself and asking or praying for the the following: that the shield will protect me from harm, evil, and accident; that it will be strong and powerful; and that it will only allow for positive energy exchanges except for a circumstance needed for my highest good or the highest good of someone else.

- **To protect my heart** by keeping my subconscious from rebuilding a heart wall should I feel stressed, fearful, or hurt. I visualize a specific small shield around my heart. I ask or pray for something along these lines: that my heart will be protected; that I will keep a soft heart, one connected to God and the Heavens; and that I will remain open and vulnerable in healthy ways.

- **To protect my cats** by shielding them before they leave the house to go outside or to go to the clinic for a procedure. I visualize their individual shields around their bodies and will often say something like: "Please stay up and strong around this kitty. Protect him from harm, evil, accident. Allow him to move safely while he is on his own".

- **To protect my car** while I am driving. I visualize the shield around the entire vehicle and ask or pray along these lines: that we will be protected from any accident, that we will not harm any other living creature as we drive, and that no other driver will harm us.

- **To shield my home** by picturing a powerful energetic protection around my entire house. I might ask for something like this: to be safe from harm, accident, and evil; that my home will have a sure foundation and even in the event of an earthquake that it would stay strong and secure; and that everyone in the home will be safe that night.

❧ **To protect any person or object in my care or purview.** An example of this is when I first moved to my condo. The main road leading there was large but the area still somewhat rural. Drivers frequently hit and killed deer and other creatures. My heart sank every time I passed a body on the road home. I started fervently shielding the road in my mind's eye every night before bed. I asked and prayed that the shield would protect the animals crossing, that it would prevent them from crossing at a dangerous time. And you know what? While I did this, I witnessed a dramatic decrease in the deaths on that road. Eventually, construction on the road put up massive walls on either side making it nearly impossible for deer to be at risk.

When you visualize a shield, you think about the color, shape, and possibly texture of the shield. Usually when you first create it, you get inspirations of color and shape, movement and texture of the shield. Don't over think it. It should pop into your mind and feel right. Over time, the shield may need to adjust in shape, color, movement, and texture as we change or the person or pet we are shielding has changed.

Shielding is an intentional behavior. Therefore, setting a shield once and never coming back to it in your thoughts or actions is not very effective. It is a daily request of power and protection.

Note, you can shield your children and pets. However, you cannot or rather should not shield someone who could choose to shield themselves, a.k.a. other adults. They have their agency. You can try to teach them and encourage them but unless they are compromised in some way (like mental incapacitation) you should let them dictate their own lives.

When you want to help others but don't want to overstep, ask for Angels to attend them, to protect them, to try to get through to them. I do this sometimes: I see a person on the street, and I sense their sorrow or pain and pray quickly that Angels will help and protect them, to lift them and allow them to feel God's love for them. Or if I am standing in a line at the store, I look around me and ask for a blessing to descend on all of those people that they might be supported, protected, have their wants and needs met, and feel God's love for them. Carol Tuttle first introduced me to this practice in her book *Remembering Wholeness*.

Meditation & Visualizations

This practice is one I wish could do more of. I struggle to carve out time in the day that is sans cats. Trying to meditate with a bunch of cats wanting my attention and crawling on me is moot! I have to shoo them all out of the room and close the door, but then some of them just sit outside and yowl or jump up to try to knock the handle and open the door.

When first beginning, follow someone's guided meditations. Select a person you trust to listen to. The practice of meditating involves quieting your space and mind, then focusing on the now, your breathing, and relaxing into potential different brain wave states of alpha, theta, or delta. I tend to be drawn to the theta state as I prefer visualizing in meditation. All of these brain wave states will lend to helping someone become more spiritually in tune, relaxed in life, successful at achieving their goals, and potentially more enlightened and peaceful.

Affirmations

I love affirmations! If any of you readers are as old as I am, you might remember the character Stuart Smalley from *Saturday Night Live*. He looked at himself in the mirror and repeated phrases like "I'm good enough, I'm smart enough, and doggonit people like me." While humorous, at that time I was a teenager and that sketch influenced me to think that people who did affirmations were silly and foolish.

On the contrary, affirmations can be quite powerful in helping us shift our mindsets. Creating affirmations is a skill; you have to understand how the words impact you. For instance, someone might decide on an affirmation of "I am going to get thinner," not realizing the "going to get" aspect constantly pushes what they want into a future time. A more powerful statement looks like, "I am living a healthy, active, holistic life, which gives me joy and vitality." 'I am' is always the strongest form of affirmation selection over words like 'I hope', 'I want', 'I will.'

Say your affirmations daily, several times a day. Create a short mantra around the thing you wish to shift most quickly and say it one hundred times a day in your mind and out loud.

Crystals

I am a fan of crystals because I love pretty, iridescent, and sparkly things. I find great joy in the fact that God gives us an abundance of natural tools to help with our wellness. I have relished selecting stones I have felt drawn to over the years and amassing a collection. As I buy a new type of crystal, I learn about its metaphysical properties. I have several crystal books to reference along with Google.

I can't say that crystals *alone* bring substantial healing. However, I do find them to be great supportive care to go along with other methods and strategies for healing and changing. The key I have found is akin to shielding—we have to have clear intention when using crystals. Our intention, prayers, and hopes increase their effectiveness.

My throat chakra is often a weak spot for me. I find that when I wear a supportive stone around my neck like Owyhee blue opal or aquamarine and ask for it to help me speak effectively, powerfully, and vulnerably, it truly makes a difference. Or on days when I feel insecure, I wear a fire agate pendant and ask for it to help my confidence, and it does.

❁ *A part of my crystal collection.*

Crystals are more than placebo. I don't have room to go over it here, but scientific studies prove crystals carry unique vibrational frequencies and when you pair those with specific needs it offers true support. You can check out the book *Why Woo Woo Works* by Dr. David R. Hamilton for this specific topic and others in the alternative healing realm.

Healing Frequencies

My understanding of this topic is rudimentary, but I do know that having a variety of different frequencies that we absorb into our bodies via sound, vibration, or gentle electric stimulation can support healing and wellness.

The cat's purr vibrates between 25 and 150 Hz, a frequency proven to support a myriad of health benefits. Their purr not only releases endorphins in their own brains, but in the human brain, too! These endorphins help reduce pain and stress. This frequency range, especially on the lower end, is known to help muscles, bones, and tendons heal faster. I love that some cats, well bonded with their humans, will seek out their companion when she is sick and just sit with her and purr. Kitty is actually trying to help her feel better—not just emotionally but physically. And when we become better humans through all these healing modalities, we can return the favor.

Frequency devices are available to purchase for in-home use. They can range into thousands of dollars, so before purchasing do your research to ensure the product is genuinely effective so you can be confident it will help you, your loved ones, and your cats. I have such a device and like crystals, it supports but isn't meant to be the lone healing source. Some holistic doctors will have the correct equipment to do frequency therapies for you in their offices.

You could join a drum circle class or use singing bowls to help you. YouTube has a huge selection of healing frequency music that tout different levels of hertz and will last ad-free for hours. Turn it on low in the background while you work to help keep your mood more peaceful and open.

These healing frequencies address physical, emotional, mental, and spiritual health. All can be impacted. Charts exist online that will give you the ranges of hertz that support a specific body part, relaxation from anxiety, spiritual awakening, and more. My frequency device comes with a myriad of programs already attuned to a variety of health and wellness needs.

Animal Communication

This is an interesting way to get to know your cats. I suggest you do some research on who you hire to be sure you feel comfortable with them and that they have good reviews. I enjoyed the experience myself. The communicator really did know things about the dynamics of my cats that she could not have known without being in tune with their energies. She knew things about me, too—like that I was procrastinating writing this book! I found the session most healing for me but my cats did do pretty well with our move (the reason I sought her help). The adjustment was huge because of restricted space in which to roam at the new place and ongoing construction for a month after we moved, but they did much better than I imagined. I made sure to provide the things the communicator told me they wanted most in the new environment, and all went pretty smoothly. It wasn't stress-free for the cats by any means, but I expected dramatic increases in fights between them and in potential litterbox concerns because that happened the previous time I moved, but it didn't happen at all.

❀ Beaux appears to be a bit forlorn as I pack for my vacation.

You can communicate directly to your cats yourself. Really be focused and intentional. The cats benefit when we explain things to them. Ask for Angels to help translate your words to kitties, so they better understand you. This is mostly about an energy exchange; we can't expect kitty to stop a behavior just because we talked to them. I used this technique in the weeks prior to a nine-day vacation I took, telling my cats over and over that I was leaving but that I would come back. That they would be fine, and I arranged for two people to take care of meeting all their needs. The cats seemed to be fine as reported by my father and my cat sitter with no additional squabbles and no signs of stress.

Physical Wellness

I'm adding this additional level of healing concepts because our physical bodies are important to our overall vibration. It supports our actions day-to-day, and if we feel ill, tired, in pain, we'll find it harder to focus on the things that truly matter. Certainly, many of the healing tools above will contribute to better physical wellness.

I am not the arbiter of physical perfection. My body is aging less gracefully at times than I'd like. I struggle with weight, and one of my vices is comfort food. I have desire to permanently change my lifestyle to one more ideal for optimal health, and though I have made strides, as of yet, I haven't fully shifted. Know there is zero judgment from me on how you currently feed your physical body.

Like anything, the physical body is merely part of our strength and wholeness. The mental body, emotional body, and spiritual body all need nourishment and support too. If we fixate on the physical alone, and the American culture puts the most emphasis here, we are not achieving wellness. If we only focus on the others and completely ignore the needs of the physical body, we are not arriving at our full potential. We must strike a balance in order to have increased capacity to help others, like our feline friends.

Healthy Eating

The American diet contains numerous toxicities. We have become so busy that our food choices tend to be last minute and with the priority on convenience. I am prone to these weaknesses myself. As a single woman, grabbing restaurant food is easier and faster than planning and preparing a meal for one. However, in general, takeout foods do not nourish us properly. We need to choose foods for how much life, energy, and vitality they emit. Fresh, alive foods have the highest vibrations. Foods that are dead, or fermenting, or processed, or heavily cooked have lost significant vitality and resonate at lower vibrations. We actually *are* what we eat. Hence, if we choose more alive foods—organic, fresh, crisp, and beautiful—their vibrational energy will lift our own.

Water

Humans consist of up to 70% water, and we cannot live without it. All life contains water. I love that Christ identified himself as "living water." We have to have water. Not just liquids that contain water, but pure, clean water. We should drink about 50% of our body weight in ounces every day. If you weigh 150 pounds, you should drink 75 ounces of water daily. If you want to drink other things like coffee, milk, soda these do not count toward your 75 ounces. If you drink alcohol, you will need even more water daily to flush out the toxicities.

Water can vary greatly in its quality. Tap water in many places is not the best thing to drink. Do some research on the water that comes into your home. If you can afford to, have a good filtration system installed to purify your water. (Remember that our skin is a huge organ, and it absorbs toxicity from the things we put on it, like water from the shower.) Using spring water to drink is often more healthful. Purified drinking water can vary. Get water testing kits and test your own favorite brands. If your water comes in plastic jugs, do what you can to offset the use of plastic to help out our environment.

Essential Oils

I have used essential oils for more than a decade now. I use them every day for myself. I use orange oil in the morning to lift my energy. I use lavender oil at night to help me relax. I use lemon, peppermint, clove, ginger, and others on a weekly basis to help with digestion, to clean, to use on wounds, to flavor food, and more. I make many of my own toiletries like deodorant and toothpaste, and essential oils are important ingredients. I diffuse oils in the air to lift my mood or freshen the home. Replacing some toxic everyday items in your home by using pure essential oils is a great idea for helping to increase your wellness.

Since many essential oils on the market are contaminated and not healthy, invest in Certified Pure Therapeutic Grade essential oils (CPTG). For instance, you may find an organic essential peppermint oil at the grocery store, and yet the label says, "not for consumption." Why is organic peppermint not edible? Because for profit, companies dilute with hidden ingredients that are toxic if ingested. You can utilize therapeutic-grade oils safely for more than merely aromas in the air.

Essential oils *can* be used with cats. You have to get your instructions from a highly reliable source. You *cannot* use an essential oil remedy intended for dogs on your cat. Dogs metabolize differently than cats, who lack certain enzymes to help process remedies via their liver. This practice of using oils on cats is not something I have done a lot myself to date because early on in my use of oils I used them inappropriately with my cat at a time when she was already gravely sick. I was clueless on her scent sensitivity levels. Since discovering my mistake and feeling terrible about it, I have generally avoided essential oils with cats. Some oils are toxic to cats and their high intensity is too concentrated to use on cats without significant dilution. If you want to use oils with kitty, do so *only* when powered by reputable holistic vet research and remedies, but for you, they can serve as a powerful healing tool.

Supplements & Vitamins

Like essential oils, the vitamin industry has a large gap in supplement quality and absorption value. Because this industry has less regulation, some supplements contain toxic ingredients. Buying a popular item that is more scam than healthful induces such risks.

I stick to a few brands I trust, having researched them, and I trust recommendations from qualified holistic medical professionals. I like organic whole-food supplements. Supplements offer vital support in increasing healing and energy levels as our conventional foods are no longer as nutritious or safe as they should be. When we feel good, we have more patience and energy to care for our cats.

Homeopathy

I am just beginning my journey into homeopathy and cannot give you enough significant information other than, if it works, it might be a safer choice for you and for kitty over intense chemical compounds like pharmaceuticals. Homeopathic doctors and veterinarians are out there, but they are hard to come by. My state has a single homeopathic vet, and it often takes two to three months to get in to see her.

Chiropractic, Acupuncture, & Massage

I love the story of chiropractic medicine's journey because it gives me hope for energy healing and other holistic methods that many still view as "woo woo" or "snake oil" in our society. I remember in the 1980s, a vibe existed

❀ *Kitty massage*

around chiropractic care on the level of witch-doctor hooey, and that people who went to a chiropractor were being duped. Today almost everyone accepts chiropractic work as a valid form of health care.

Along with these muscle and bone adjustments, massage has a lot of health benefits. It can promote relaxation, release endorphins, stimulate the discharge of free radicals from the body, and potentially free negative energies as well.

I've done acupuncture a few times. In my mid-thirties I had Lyme disease, which caused a lot of joint pain. Acupuncture sessions were helpful. I recall lying on the table, tears seeping out of my eyes. It was not from pain. I didn't know at the time that crying is common when negative energies are leaving the body.

Lights & Lasers

Medicinal light therapy can be very relaxing and bring a feeling of peace. Like my experience with acupuncture, I would frequently shed a few tears when resting under light pads. I found the infrared and blue spectrum lights helpful—there are many brands to look into—in easing physical pain and lifting my depression. However, like crystals and frequency devices, lights are a supportive tool most useful when paired with other health and wellness care.

There are more and more veterinary practices offering laser treatments to help with joint pain and other ailments in our pets. I had a kitten who had a leg amputated and used light therapy on her a few times a day to speed her recovery and help with depression.

Wrapping up this part of the chapter, I want to reiterate that I qualify as a professional and expert only in the modalities of Emotion Code, Body Code, and Belief Code. However, I have personal experience with each of the methods mentioned here. Even though I am not a qualified expert to speak on them at length, please know I am bearing testimony that these tools were and still are a part of my healing journey of over a decade. Some I look forward to exploring further. To even consider trying

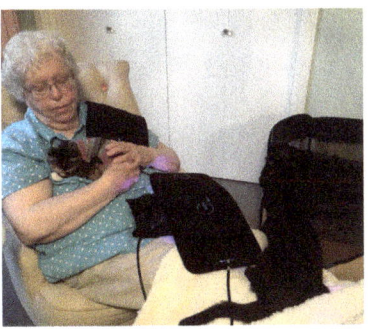

❀ *My mother and kittens receiving light treatments (LumiCeuticals).*

all of these techniques at once would overwhelm anyone, so I suggest you select three or four to explore and try out for yourself.

With sharing these holistic modalities, I am not negating other traditional physical or mental treatments out there. If you are utilizing western medicine practices to help you heal, power to you on the journey! I mix both all the time, but personally prefer to lean heavily on the alternative, holistic, and spiritual.

HOW TO RECOGNIZE MIRACLES, MERCIES, & HELP FROM THE "OTHER SIDE"

The key to seeing the mercies and miracles is gratitude. Sound simple? Yes and no. When we have struggled for a long time, gratitude might elude us. Is it cliché to recommend an "attitude of gratitude"? Don't smack me yet! Early on in my personal growth journey, I threw a book across the room in frustration and anger because what they were teaching really pushed my buttons.

It may be difficult to start with, but ultimately it feels really good to develop the ability to spot little blessings in our lives every day. When we stop to acknowledge them, and more importantly to thank God for them, we open ourselves up to the potential increase of good things.

As we do the work of healing physically and mentally, growing emotionally and spiritually, we increase our overall vibration, which means according to universal laws, we should start attracting more positive encounters and opportunities. Life won't consist of rainbows and good luck all the time, but pause to take note of every good thing. A great healing practice is to keep a gratitude or happiness journal. At the end of every day, reflect back thinking of five things that made you thankful, smile, or feel good and write them down.

When you are struggling with your kitty relationship, look for and add to the journal anything positive or good that kitty did that day, e.g., "Kitty didn't miss the litterbox today!" or "I was feeling sick, and kitty sat next to me and purred," or "The cat was comical today; I am grateful to have laughed." We raise the vibration of the relationship when we take time to express gratitude for the other individual.

The higher our vibration, the closer we come to God. The closer we come to God, the more support we receive because we are asking for it, hoping for it, and even expecting it. You will see and experience miracles. You will recognize them as such because you have become more humble, more grateful, and more at peace.

PURRRITO WRAP UP

I hope you can take the time needed to digest and deeply ponder all of the options and tools listed in this chapter. I have found them helpful in my personal growth and healing. If you have not yet taken your spiritual development or emotional healing seriously, a great place to start is by reading or listening to books on these topics. I provided a list of potential starting points, but there is a vast array of good books you can seek out and learn from. Once you have found and read a few books, say on energy work or on seeing signs, put them into practice. Ask in prayer for God to magnify the efforts you are making, so that you will receive a clear message of their validity. If you schedule an appointment with an energy healer, pray to recognize clearly and quickly if this is a good path to your healing. If for any reason you do not get a confirmation of efficacy after a few tries, move on to a different healing tool. Recall that you will always get better results if you practice several methods to achieve wholeness and wellness.

Okay, we've talked a lot about ourselves in the last few chapters. Let's focus now on some of the biggest behavioral concerns cat owners deal with. We'll ask a lot of good questions and see things from the cat's perspective.

PART 2

Cat Behavioral Concerns

❀ My "Spring Flower" foster kittens seeing an adult cat for the first time.

CHAPTER 5

Cat Behavioral Concerns: House Soiling

In this segment of the book, we will discuss common cat behavioral concerns. I intentionally chose to focus on the word "concern" more than "problem" or "issue." When kitty behaves in a way we don't like or approve of, she, in essence, is trying to communicate with us. We should show concern for kitty and resolve what is upsetting her. She is saying "help me" or possibly mirroring back to you that she feels stress because *you* feel stress.

Cats are sensitive creatures. Studies demonstrate that cats, among a few other mammals, have a broad range of emotions. Other studies show that cats have empathetic qualities with their humans and cat mates. I have certainly observed a wide range of feelings among my own cats and fosters. Some cats are highly expressive of their feelings, usually displaying through eyes, ears, and tails. My cat Trixie has the best looks—they are heart-on-sleeve readable and make me chuckle. My favorite happens when I tell her "no" to getting in my lap and hold out my palm in a "stop" sign. She flattens her ears and slits her eyes like, "Please woman, you know it's going to happen, so stop delaying the inevitable!" Moreover, she manifests obvious jealousy if she has been trying to get in my lap and another cat swoops in first. I've seen her nip tails, bite bums, or give off an expressive meow as if saying, "Hey, I was here first!"

🐾 *Trixie trying to get onto my shoulder after I'd said "no" a few times.*

Side Note: Positive Reinforcement

If you respond *at all* to bad behavior or to unwanted actions, whether with kindness or frustration, you reinforce the activities of the cat. Any form of attention becomes "positive reinforcement" even if you scold. To stop undesirable manners, ignore kitty while she is doing them or walk away. When she does things you like, praise, pet, and offer treats to reinforce those behaviors. We will get into more details on training later, but I wanted to point out that I am aware my own actions with Trixie, as mentioned only a moment ago, constitutes a form of positive reinforcement.

Guardians should realize that their furry friends, as emotional creatures, may not feel comfortable or happy with the current arrangements in the home. Cats have opinions. They are not, however, intentionally devious; they cannot lie, and they don't plan out revenge despite common myths or trending memes. They feel fear, anxiety, stress, restlessness, love, jealousy, excitement, anticipation, hurt, heartbreak, abandonment, loneliness, overwhelm, disgust, interest, boredom, pleasure, satisfaction, betrayal, hopelessness, rejection, resentment, humiliation, shock, panic, confusion, amusement, contentment, confidence, low self-esteem, depression, and more. Your cat, if acting out in negative ways, is trying to tell you she is not doing well and needs your help to fix it.

In my experience discussing cat behavioral concerns with numerous clients, much of the time (approximately 75%), *the people* are making mistakes in the care of their cat, thus causing the negative acting out. About 25% of the time, the animal has a medical concern. Less than 1% of the time, the animal has an unfixable inherent behavioral condition, though in some cases, options like anti-anxiety medicine, training, or energy work may help.

However, in my experience with owner surrenders and clients with cat behavioral upsets, they assume 80-90% of the time something is inherently wrong and unfixable about the cat; therefore, it is a "bad cat." 10-20% of the time, they may

❀ *A variety of kitty feelings.*

consider a medical problem, but it really is the last place most people look to lay blame for the behavior. Usually, they place blame squarely on those tiny kitty shoulders.

I am here to lovingly say, most likely you, not the cat, are the problem. You simply need to up your awareness of cat well-being, and you are doing that by reading a book like this. Kudos to you for making an effort. I appreciate that, and your kitty does too. I assume by your presence here you are open to the idea that you may need to make some changes.

A lot of cat owners I've worked with won't change. They think the pet needs to bend to their will and not the other way around. I have worked with many who disregard sound counsel, and usually they end up relinquishing the animal. We live in a culture that for decades has emphasized that everything should be easy—otherwise, it just isn't worth it. Love should be uncomplicated. Marriage should be unproblematic. Jobs should be fun. Food should be fast and effortless. Packages should arrive in under two days. Everything should be gamified. Entertainment must be at the touch of a button. Communication should happen instantaneously. Well, many tend to lump pets into the "should be easy and fun" category and not in the "I will take full responsibility for the commitment I made to this animal when I adopted it" category.

Story Example: Unwilling to Change for Kitty

I want to share an example of someone unwilling to change. A person I know and really like came to me for help with his now senior cat who refused to pee in the litterbox. He wanted me to see if energy work would fix the concern in the cat. Digging deeper during that session I discovered several things:

One, this man did not really like cats but he rescued this kitty when a family moved out of his condo complex and abandoned it. He took compassion on the cat and tried but failed to find a home for kitty. Even though he preferred not to, he kept the cat. Because of his kind heart, he would not allow the cat to remain isolated and hungry.

Two, when this man traveled (he traveled for extended periods of time for work) he either boarded the kitty or placed it at a friend's home.

Three, the kitty never had any litterbox concerns when she stayed at the boarding facility or at anyone else's house. She only had litterbox difficulties at home.

Four, this man owned an automated litterbox. The cat would poop in it but not pee in it.

Five, this man had a serious aversion to poop—scooping feces was too much for him. I discovered via energy work that this went back to his childhood where he always had the weekly chore of picking up the family dog's poop in the backyard.

I counseled him to perform an experiment. Get a regular litterbox and see if the misses stopped. Automated boxes often make cats uncomfortable. This cat was willing to risk it for poop, because likely she was a cat that needed to bury the poop, but she could pee anywhere else and feel safer. I advised this man that if his scooping aversion truly threw up a roadblock, he should hire a neighborhood kid to come every day to scoop. Pay them $10/week for that daily 5-minute chore.

I checked in twice with this person after the session, but he had done nothing to fix the situation. Not wanting to change the arrangements in the home, he fell back to rehoming the cat. He hoped for a quick fix via energy work. Unfortunately, energy work won't change the nature of a cat wanting a safe place to urinate.

LITTERBOX BEHAVIOR CONCERNS

With that story as our intro, let's first look at this most common reason for cats losing their homes. Around 40% of cats surrendered result from house-soiling concerns. Usually, it is an ongoing difficulty before the worst happens, but it had a beginning. The first time you discover the cat has peed or pooped somewhere other than the litterbox, stop to make some assessments on kitty. If you don't know which cat in a multi-cat home did the deed, set up some inexpensive home security cameras in areas most soiled to discover which kitty is struggling. Once you know which cat to help, you will need to do some additional investigating.

1. Is this a bladder release or is it urine spraying/marking?

You can usually recognize a full release (inappropriate elimination) because the urine consists of a fairly large spot or puddle on a horizontal surface like a towel on the floor, in the laundry basket, on a blanket, the bathroom mat, or next to the litterbox. You will likely smell it as your first warning that something is awry. Urine spraying, however, *usually* appears on a vertical plane. It is typically a few drops of urine that run down the surface. Kitty intended to mark the territory more strongly with her scent

2. If it is inappropriate elimination, why might she do that?

If this is a first time, ask yourself a few questions: Did kitty somehow lose access to her litterbox? If no, is the litterbox clean? If no, how full is it and how smelly? Did I recently change litter types? Did I just put out a new style of litterbox? Is there a new stressor that may cause upset for my kitty, like a new member of the household or lots of commotion and packing for a move? Did I declaw my kitty at any point? Is my cat acting sick? Is she getting too old or overweight for the style of litterbox? Is the litterbox too far away or hard for kitty to access?

Access to Potty

Healthy adult cats typically need to pee on average two to five times a day. Some may pee once a day, and some may pee eight times. In my experience, if a cat only urinates once a day, it usually dislikes the litterbox setup and wants to avoid it as long as possible. An adult cat can hold her urine for about 12-24 hours. Holding urine on a regular basis can lead to urinary tract health complications. If kitty loses access to her litterbox, she will seek out the next best option in her mind to relieve herself.

Story Example: Needing a Potty

One time I went on a week-long vacation, and my brother and his kids cat-sat Stella. Her litterbox stood in the unused shower of my guest bathroom. The day before I returned home, they came per usual, scooped, put out food, visited with Stella, and left. However, one of the kids had gone number two in the guest bathroom while there, and according to their family's house rules, she turned on the fan and closed the bathroom door behind her when she left. I didn't arrive home until the evening of the next day. I saw the closed bathroom door and knew Stella hadn't had access to a bathroom for well over 24 hours. I discovered that she found the next best solution to pee, in my dirty laundry basket. This was in no way her fault. She had to go and tried her best to make it right.

A similar situation happened more recently to my parents' cat Minnie. The same family came to visit, and their youngest son, about four years old at the time, closed the closet door that housed the cat's litterbox. Neither of my parents noticed. The next morning Minnie was pacing and yowling, and my parents did not understand the problem until she hopped up on the bathroom counter and peed in the sink.

Side Note: Multiple Boxes

If we had known, understood, and practiced the recommendation of having two litterboxes for one cat, placed in separate locations, we could have avoided both of these situations.

Clean & Comfortable Pottys

Cats prefer and need clean litterboxes. The best, no-fail recommendation: scoop once a day. Some cats need you to scoop two or three times a day. However, if you have one cat and an extra-large litterbox or two litterboxes for her, scooping every other day should suffice (as long as kitty isn't upset by that schedule). If you use clay-clumping litter, add a layer of fresh litter to the box about once or twice a week. When using a quality odor-control clumping litter, and you have a cat that demands strict cleanliness, you should dump and refresh the litter completely every one to two weeks. If using a non-clumping litter, change out the litter completely every other day if your cat needs a very fresh box. Clean the box itself every week or two. When you wash the box, clean with hot water and unscented soap. Dry before putting in fresh litter. You can use a stronger cleaner like white vinegar or bleach, but some cats are particular about scents and may not like the box if it smells differently. I personally use a small amount of bleach because of my multi-cat home and fostering situations, and I want to sanitize the boxes more effectively. My cats are okay with this.

Story Example: Stress Marking

A few years back, during a period of illness and depression, I didn't scoop litterboxes downstairs for weeks. The lone box I scooped regularly was the one upstairs. I was shaken out of my lazy haze when I noted that a cat had marked with urine the hallway walls, the guest bathroom walls, and even the exterior of the clean upstairs litterbox. The marks stated to the other cats, "I claim this one because it's fresh!" I immediately washed all the urine markings and scrubbed the boxes downstairs. The spraying stopped.

Illnesses

Typically, you can quickly identify or rule out a lack of litterbox access or cleanliness stress as the cause of urinating outside the box. The next step in figuring out why your cat is urinating out of the box is to go to the vet to check for any infections or illnesses. Many litterbox complications arise at the start from urinary tract discomfort. Veterinary clinics will often take urine samples and perform bloodwork to diagnose urinary tract ailments.

Sometimes cats will pee right in front of you and even look at you while doing so. This isn't spite! It's communication. If you aren't around, she may go right outside of the box as a way to help you pay attention to her needs. She may be telling you that something is wrong, that she feels sick. Since she cannot talk and say, "it burns when I pee," kitty has to show us.

Story Example: Communicating Pain

My Beaux kitty tried to get my attention this way a few years ago. He had never interrupted me when scooping the litterbox or intentionally peed in front of me before, but on back-to-back days he hopped in to show me he had something wrong. He had to "tell" me three times before I pieced together that he was experiencing a partial blockage or pain when peeing. One sign is taking a long time for the

❀ *Beaux with his summer haircut.*

cat to release a small amount of urine. Since Beaux couldn't tell me, "See Mom, it hurts, and I don't know why," he communicated by showing me.

I took him to the vet, who discovered that crystals had formed in his urine which lead to blockages. Using sound research on his illness, I put him on a new diet of predominately quality wet food. I also give him a regular supplement for urinary support, and he has healthy urine now.

Urine crystals most commonly appear in male cats, but occasionally in females too. Around 25% of male cats will experience this in their lifetime. One of the main causes is commercial cat food, especially cheaper dry foods full of fillers not part of a cat's natural diet, like grains, vegetables, and even ash. Cats need quality proteins in their diets to keep a healthy pH level in their system. Too alkaline and a cat's body creates crystals in the urine from excess magnesium, phosphate, and ammonium. These crystals can become tiny stones that may partially or fully block the urethra.

If you notice kitty has stopped peeing for any length of time over 24 hours, this is not good. This is another reason why scooping every day is valuable: you can see changes in bowels or fluids. If the cat will allow you, check her tummy below the ribs. Do you feel a tight, orange- or grapefruit-sized ball? If you do, this could be the bladder at max capacity from a blockage. Blockages require surgery to remove. Some veterinarians have learned to alter the male genitalia to mimic female genitalia by enlarging the urethral opening in male cats prone to blockages. To avoid these costly surgical procedures, whether male or female, preemptively feed your cats a healthy diet. If your cat shows signs of crystals, start a quality urinary tract support supplement. I personally use Amber Naturalz UTR formula. Your holistic vet can recommend other brands as well.

Cats with environmental stress commonly have inflammation in the urinary tract. It is possible, too, for both female and male cats to get bacterial-caused urinary tract infections (UTIs) that require antibiotics. When it hurts to pee, cats often choose softer locations to expel their bladders; perhaps they think it will ease the discomfort.

Kidney disease or failure is also a possibility to rule out with a vet. This problem often plagues senior cats due to a natural decline of health from aging, but young cats can experience this, especially if they have encountered something toxic. A cat suffering from kidney complications will likely have other symptoms like lethargy, lack of appetite, vomiting, fever, weight loss, dehydration, drinking a lot of water, or standing over a water bowl with head hung low but not drinking. Does she object if you touch her on the belly or sides? If so, it could indicate pain. Organ failure is serious, and you need immediate veterinary support if you see any of these signs. Remember, cats hide illness and pain well; therefore, you must become a pet guardian who notices changes in behavior, appetite, water consumption, waste, and more.

Side Note: Pain in Litterbox

If kitty has experienced pain in the litterbox, she may now see the box as more threat than safe place, and even after clearing a urinary infection, cats may avoid the litterbox. Cats can form habits quickly, and what began as an illness may turn into a behavioral concern. If kitty receives the medical care needed but still goes outside the box, look at other litterbox triggers and at retraining with positive rewards. You will need to reassociate the litterbox into a positive location to urinate.

Style of Litter or Box

There is no full-proof litterbox style or substrate that works for *every single* cat. However, commonalities between *many* cats for litterbox preferences do exist. When reviewing this content, understand two things about cats:

🐱 Some cats may have *tolerated* a litterbox or substrate style previously, but that doesn't mean they liked it. When stressors reach a max, they may avoid what they used to use because it's "the last straw" in their ability to cope.

🐱 Cats will often stick to their learned preference in kittenhood as long as it doesn't become painful (like pellet litter on arthritic paws); however, if all else fails, resort to the substrate of the cat's ancestor—sand.

If kitty is urinating outside the box and you recently changed litter types, go back to the old litter. This may immediately correct the concern. If you really want to change litter brands, you must do it slowly by adding in the new type with the old type in a several week transition, putting the new litter on the bottom and old substrate on top. Know you may never succeed at getting your cat to prefer what *you* like. You could try several new types of litter at once to see which one the cat picks. Dr. Elsey's Kitten Attract or Cat Attract litter is a great tool for bringing cats back to using the box, but it is not the final say in figuring out how to resolve the concern. Since it's the cat's litterbox and not yours, purchase litter based on her needs and preferences and not your own. In general, cats do not like large pellet litters and favor small granule clay or sandy textures. Do not buy scented litters, and don't fill the room where the litterbox is located with scented plugins, air freshening sprays, essential oils, incense, or scented candles. The cat's sense of smell is very keen compared to our own, and they do not like floral, citrusy, perfumy aromas.

If kitty is urinating inappropriately and you recently changed litterbox styles, revert to the old style. Some cats will not use lidded boxes, especially top entry boxes. Some may not like the box moved to a new location that feels suspect, like next to the furnace or washing machine that randomly comes on and makes noises or in the garage where the loud automated door may suddenly open.

Many cats do not like auto scooping boxes. If you have confident kittens and they get used to it from a young age, an auto box may work. Otherwise, shy cats, high-strung cats, or cautious cats will not appreciate the moving parts or machine sounds coming from the place they are expected to visit for private business. Besides, automated boxes tend to have small areas in which to eliminate waste. Generally, the box should be one and a half times the length of the cat on the longest side.

A good practice with any litterbox change is to do it gradually, whether switching litter products, the type of box, or the location of the box. If you haven't found the right setup, please reach out to a cat behavioral professional like me to help you figure it out. We often have additional tricks up our sleeves that may just win out in the end with your kitty.

Side Note: Figuring Your Cat's Potty Setup Preferences

You could perform a litterbox and litter type test. You do this by offering three or four different style boxes and three or four different types of litter at the same time. This helps you discover the cat's preferences. Set up the boxes, then after a week note which box kitty used the most. Next, switch the litter contained in each box to a new type that it didn't hold the first week. This should help you discover what is more important to the cat: the box shape or the litter type. To perform a good test, try two open style boxes, one with lower sides and one with high sides, and two lidded boxes, one with an easier front entry and one with a top entry. With substrate, try clay clumping, crystal litter, a natural substance like wheat, corn, or grass seed, and pellet litter like pine or newspaper. (Make sure all types are unscented and dye free as cats are sensitive to potentially toxic odors and chemicals.) Do the test in the same location. Pick a location your cat prefers for going potty. Don't set up the test in the garage when the cat fears the garage door. If the cat prefers your bedroom, then grit through it for a few weeks by having four boxes set up in that spot. If you set up the boxes in separate locations around the house, then you must also factor in location preferences and the test will take longer (by additionally switching styles of boxes/litter in the various locations).

Stressors

Many stressors can trigger kitty to have litterbox concerns, such as bringing home a new baby, having an out-of-town guest, a romantic partner moving in or spending more time in your home, getting a new pet, moving the furniture around, packing boxes and getting ready to relocate, the death of a resident pet, taking kitty to the vet, and more. Again, consider the feelings of the cat. See it from her eyes for a moment and how you might help her adjust to bring more peace and security into her life.

Some ideas for helping a stressed kitty might be to use a more soothing voice around her. Steer clear of loud, violent, aggressive TV shows. Quietly play classical or healing frequency music and avoid noisy, beat-heavy music. You could use calming pheromone room sprays or diffusers, like Comfort Zone or Feliway (not all cats are helped by these synthetic feline facial pheromones—FFPs). Set up more resources in the home like food stations, water stations, and litterboxes. Offer new cat trees, cubbies, or higher perches. Try energy work on your cat. The Body Code is a great tool for helping animals feel better when stressed. Place healing and de-stressing crystals like amber or amethyst near kitty while she sleeps.

If a new person is causing the stress, help build a relationship between that person and kitty. Have the individual start to give meals and treats to the kitty. Let the newcomer be the one to play with or offer catnip to the cat. Teach this person to let the cat dictate touch and petting.

Something else to consider is that if the litterbox is really old or was used for a previous cat, the residual odor in the plastic (plastics absorb odors over time) could be upsetting the cat. Might be time to throw an old box out and purchase a fresh one. Or if you have new pets around, your resident cat may feel threatened, frustrated, or insecure. She might react by protecting the litterbox with her scent. She may start to pee high instead of squatting low in the box. This new way of peeing will be a full urine release mixed with the instinct of vertical spraying. This places their urine on the side walls of the litterbox. If you have a low, unlidded box (which is ideal if you have no complications), the liquid will start to spill over the edges and around the box.

Story Example: Peeing High

When I started fostering kittens, my cat Prim felt unhappy about it and shifted from squatting to pee, to allowing her urine to hit the walls of the box and slide down into the litter. I don't like it, but I understand why she does it. Luckily, I had tall litterboxes. The rare occasion when I have a low box with no lid out, her urine puddles around and under the box. When I had construction going on down in the basement, Prim refused to go down to the storage room (even though no construction was going on in that room) to use the litterbox. She started peeing on doormats and bathmats upstairs. I had to rethink my litterbox plan in my new home and bring one upstairs for her. She immediately stopped going to the bathroom inappropriately and used the box upstairs, which felt safer to her. (I now have several litterboxes upstairs and down.)

Side Note: Box Liners

Avoid using litterbox liners. Some cats dislike that their claws get snagged in the plastic and may develop an aversion to the box. Plus, the digging and scratching punctures the bags, and they prove less helpful than you'd like when changing liners.

Declawed Cats

Another cause of possible litterbox concerns is if you have previously or recently declawed your cat. This procedure is traumatic to kitty and incredibly painful even long after the procedure. Short-term effects of declawing surgery may include depression and discomfort, which could lead to litterbox difficulties. One of the long-term side effects is that many declawed cats, at some point in the aging process, find litter painful on their feet, most especially when combined with arthritis. Imagine if you were missing the tips of all your toes, had bad arthritis in your feet, and yet were expected to stand in a shower with bumpy rocks on the floor in order to bathe. Painful. You might stop showering all together, right? With this in mind, try not to get angry when the declawed cat chooses not to use the torturebox, er, litterbox.

Sometimes, changing out the litter for these cats to a softer, finer grain can help bring them back to the litterbox. You might use real sand or a product like Pretty Litter or Sustainably Yours which has really small granules. Make sure kitty has easy access into the box where she can gently step in without jumping and landing on her paws. As a different soft option, you could try using a layer of shredded paper in the litterbox, which will need changing one or two times daily. You could switch to using puppy pee pads in the litterbox and changing them out once or twice a day. I wouldn't recommend the pee pad practice for any cats other than those in pain because they often like to dig to bury their business. Or use no substrate at all in the box.

It is always a tragedy when declawed cats, maimed by their own people, are punished for stopping litterbox usage. Almost always these cats face surrender, abandonment, or euthanasia when they start having too much pain to use the litterbox. My own sweet Pepé, my childhood cat, lost his life in this way.

Story Example: Declawing Leads to Euthanasia

Pepé died when I was about twenty years old and away at college. Unfortunately, my parents had Pepé declawed as a little kitten in order to protect the furniture, not knowing back in the 1980s the cruelty or long-term ramifications of doing this to a cat. At around ten years old, Pepé started peeing outside the litterbox. My parents had recently paid for new carpet, and my dad chose the carpet over the cat and had him put down. I was angry and hurt when my mom told me after the fact what he'd done. And even angrier at my father when I learned he left Pepé's body at the vet for mass cremation. Back then my parents blamed the cat and were frustrated with him—but now we all recognize that his litterbox concerns resulted from declawing.

Ongoing Urination or Defecation Concerns

If the cat habitually chooses inappropriate spots in the house in which to pee or poop, the best course of action is to clean them up as thoroughly as possible, removing all odor traces. If it makes sense, placing a litterbox near the problem area with a litter like Cat Attract can help in the retraining process. This can be frustrating if the target is, say, on your bed or favorite chair. In these instances you can protect the surfaces with a thick plastic drop cloth or similar material until you are able to reassociate these areas for other activities. *Sometimes* getting kitty eating or playing in that area helps. You could also block off the area, like a certain spot on the floor, by moving a piece of furniture over that place. This tactic may help, *or* kitty just finds a new undesirable location to go. Over time, you can slowly shift the litterbox from the problematic area toward a more practical location nearby.

It can be important to note that if they are choosing to urinate in a human scent heavy spot, like the bed, favorite chair, couch, or on your clothing, this isn't a spiteful act! The opposite is often true; the cat is likely trying to claim, blend with, or relate more with that human.

Story Example: Trying to Belong

One woman I consulted had a cat that urinated on her husband's side of the bed and on his clothing. Luckily, she always caught the urine mess quickly, and her husband remained unaware (or at least never said anything). The husband was not a pet person and remained uninterested and unaffectionate toward all the cats in the house. This particular cat was attempting to connect with him through scent-mingling conduct. However, this man would *not* have found this endearing or be compassionate about the behavior. He declined to work on the relationship by bonding with the cat via feeding, play, or affection. I suggested, and she followed through with, setting up more litterboxes in the house and creating a safe space for kitties with her. Her youngest child moved out, and she claimed that bedroom as her new cat room. She set up cat shelves, scratchers, and a litterbox so her cats could bond more with her during the night without upsetting her husband and emphasizing the emotional distance between himself and the cats. This cat has done much better about using the right place for potty as he feels a little safer in the home.

Now, if medical reasons and not simply emotional reasons cause this urinating behavior, the tips I've given thus far will not solve the concern. If the elimination behavior stems from a health concern, the cat will likely ignore the uniquely placed boxes and find a new spot that feels more comfortable to go potty in or on. When medical reasons create the inappropriate elimination, the cat associates pain, stress, or discomfort with the litterbox itself. The *dis*-ease needs to be addressed to allow the cat to feel at ease again with using the box.

POOPING OUTSIDE THE BOX

If the cat is defecating outside of the litterbox, you want to address this quickly.

1. Why is the cat pooping outside the box?

Ask yourself questions like: Is the litterbox too full of waste? Did the kitty get really scared? Is the litterbox big enough? Does the cat show other symptoms of being sick like lower appetite, fever, lethargy? Has kitty shown any signs of being in pain? Is kitty constipated? Did we recently change the litterbox style or litter type? Did kitty get into something toxic? Is kitty declawed? Is the cat getting older, and could she have cognitive or incontinence struggles now?

First off, if you are a new cat guardian, make sure that what you see on the floor is actually poop and not a hairball barf. They often have similar shapes and colors. Secondly, decide if the cat actually pooped outside the box. Or did she start in the box, but poop clung to her bum or fur? When this happens, you'll usually find a single lump, and not the entire bowel movement. The clump can randomly drop off, or the cat may try to wipe it off via scooting on the floor. Often if a cat swallows long human hair, thread, or even long blades of grass, poop can get stuck or looped together on that stringy substance. This situation is messy and gross, but not intentional, so your cat doesn't have a litterbox problem (unless it happens all the time, in which case I suggest a vet or behavioral visit).

Sometimes the pooping out of the box is completely accidental. I have seen cats get so petrified that they poop where they stand. It just comes right out of them. We really can't be upset at this. We need to focus on compassion for our cat who was so scared in that moment she couldn't control her bowels. Understand what triggered that kind of fear and avoid future instances by not recreating or allowing for that situation to happen. For instance, if she poops in the car on the way to the vet, figure out a way to make the next trip less scary. Offer treats, speak kindly and comfortingly, put her favorite blanket in the carrier, cover the carrier in a towel, try a homeopathic stress relief remedy, and play soft classical music on the car ride there.

Side Note: Cat Carriers

You can make the effort to desensitize the kitty to the cat carrier or car ride. Do this by leaving the carrier out and open in the house. Put treats inside the carrier. Every now and then, close the door to the carrier when kitty goes inside to eat treats. Use calming tones while she is in the carrier. Praise her for being brave. Open the carrier door a minute or so later. Slowly extend the time closed inside the carrier. Pick it up and carry it around the house and put it down and let kitty out. Next time, take the carrier to the car and put it in, but don't go anywhere. Simply sit in the car with kitty. Get back out and take her inside and let her out of the carrier. Give her a treat. Eventually, go for short drives and back home. Give treats in the car or when you arrive back home. If at any point the cat gets too upset, backtrack a step to where she felt more comfortable and repeat that for a while longer before progressing forward again.

Sometimes when you find poop directly outside of the litterbox, the cat simply had an accident. This can happen when bums hang over the edge of the box, and kitty unintentionally misses. A simple fix for this is getting a larger or taller box.

Story Example: Box is Too Small

A young teen who adopted a few kittens from the rescue I was working with had what she called litterbox and behavior issues with one of the kittens. I was asked to consult with her. This teen had a know-it-all attitude, quick to disregard my questions and combat every tip I gave her. During our conversation I had to grow firm and ask her to stop being contrary, answer my questions, and listen to my advice. I told her, "It sounds like you just don't like the kitten." (Everything she told me seemed normal and I felt she had over dramatized his "problems".) "Are you really telling me you want to bring him back or do you actually want to address any of these concerns?" She fumbled a moment and said she wanted to keep him. One of the things angering her was that he pooped on the floor. Well, this *is* a concern, but when I dug deeper with questions, I discovered she only offered one of those tiny kitten litterboxes, but he was now about five months old and 6 pounds. He got in the box and dug a hole but then accidentally dropped his poop over the side of the box almost every time. I told her the kitten did not have a behavior concern. He was doing everything right, but she wasn't providing what he needed. The fix was simple; get a larger litterbox with taller sides. Unfortunately, this girl ignored my advice and several months after our consult returned both kittens at about nine months old. Usually, adopting out older kittens is harder, but luckily these two boys found a new home the same day they were surrendered.

Changing litterbox style or litter products can cause defecation out of the box, even if cats still urinate in the box. Not all cats dig to pee. It isn't necessary, but they usually dig to poop (some cats are vice versa). If the litter feels uncomfortable or painful on her paws (especially for declawed or arthritic kitties), she may decide it is not worth it to use the box for pooping. In a lidded box, the odor of her poop in that small space may overwhelm her. A cat's sense of smell is up to fourteen times more powerful than our own. Likewise, if you are not scooping the litterbox, the cat will eventually stop using it all together because of the filth. Imagine if you were expected to use a bathroom covered in urine and feces. You would seek alternatives too.

Story Example: No Clean Potty

I once helped with a hoarding case not a cat hoarding case per say, but the home was crazy covered in stuff and extremely dirty, an unhealthy environment for everyone living there. We found a litterbox, but I couldn't say when the last time someone scooped it because it was so packed with cat waste. As a result, the cats went anywhere and everywhere in the home.

Medical reasons can cause a cat to stop pooping in a litterbox. Take your cat to the vet for an exam. They may have suffered an injury. Pelvic, spinal, or tail breaks or other injuries can create difficulties with house soiling. Some breeds of cats are more likely than others to have medical complications around defecation, like any type of bobtailed or tailless cat. Cats bred to keep a deformity, like no tails or stubbed tails, have an increased risk of health issues that come along with that deformity. Tailless cats may have spinal damage which can lead to neurological problems, incontinence, or constipation. An aging cat may start to have litterbox struggles due to arthritis. Some breeds of cats, like Scottish Folds or Munchkins, commonly suffer from early onset osteoarthritis. Other causes like declawing, cognitive impairments like dementia, incontinence issues where the anal or urinary muscles are degenerating may be at play. A very sick cat, a cat who ate something toxic, or a cat with a bowel obstruction may have difficulty using the potty. If your cat poops and pees inappropriately, do not get angry. Get compassionate. Consider that kitty may need medical help immediately.

URINE MARKING

1. If this is urine spraying or marking, what do you do now?

Earlier in the chapter, I asked you to decide if the urination was full a release or urine spraying. Marking usually consists of a few droplets of urine sprayed on a vertical surface, though not always. Sometimes a cat will spray horizontally or use small puddles of urine to mark her territory. If you are unsure if your cat is marking, but occasionally you catch a whiff of urine, buy a blacklight flashlight. Use this tool at night. Turn lights out and walk slowly around the house, focus on areas where you caught a whiff of urine. Look closely at the first twelve inches of all walls and surfaces. Point the light at furniture or carpets, looking for spots that fluoresce. Obviously, with a black light, anything white or light-colored will take on a glow. What I am talking about is organic material illuminating under the black light. Blood, urine, barf will all pop out a bit under the blacklight. On some fabrics or surfaces it is harder to tell as they absorb the light and don't reflect back very well. Keep sticky note tabs in hand as you do this and place a marker of your own in any spots you find that need cleaning. In the daylight, you can go back around with cleaners to remove the biological material from the surfaces.

Cats marking territory with urine frustrates their humans, but in the life and language of cats, expressing territorial stress or dominance is normal behavior. It is also a normal mating practice if cats, especially male cats, remain sexually intact.

Sexual Behavior

If your cat is not fixed, getting him or her altered may help end the spraying. I can empathize with anyone who has a concern that spaying or neutering takes away the animal's right to live a more complete and full life. I have worried about that myself. However, in our current culture we have domesticated certain species, and if we allowed them to procreate indiscriminately, it would put hundreds of thousands, if not millions, of their lives in imminent danger of either living a harsh life in the wild as fully or partially human-dependent animals or getting rounded up and slaughtered to prevent neighborhoods from becoming overwhelmed. We have seen this as a society already; it is not an exaggeration. While numbers are going down, shelters euthanize hundreds of thousands of cats every year. Until we live in a more perfected and peaceful world, fixing domesticated animals is a kindness to them and to ourselves.

To avoid urine marking, get cats fixed *before* they reach sexual maturity. Males can reach sexual maturity around six months but as late as twelve months. In females this can occur as young as four months but generally transpires around six to eight months. Along with the negative outcome of unwanted litters, both genders may spray their territory to try to lure cats for mating. Males perform this ritual more often than females as a sign that they are available, but females can be culpable. If your cat goes into heat or starts mating rituals that include urine marking, the behavior will likely stop, but not always, after alteration. Ninety-five percent of females will not urine mark once spayed. Males are about twice as likely as females to continue spraying. This is of course regarding urine marking as a mating practice turned habit. Cats may still urine mark over territorial and resource concerns, especially in multi-cat homes, both males and females.

Territorial or Resources Concerns

Urine marking is a higher concern in multi-cat homes. The more cats you have, the greater the risk of this behavior manifesting. I started experiencing urine spraying in my home when I kept my fifth cat, Honey. I dislike the behavior as much as the next person, yet I am savvy enough to recognize that when this happens, I failed to meet a furry someone's needs. If you have cats with resource concerns (food, water, litterbox access, sleeping spots, human attention) or territorial frustrations (being bullied, trying to renegotiate their social standing), they may manifest this stress via spraying urine.

With resource or attention concerns, territorial arguments occur, and lines are draw with spray. One cat is communicating to another that they claim that location, at least at certain times of the day. The message contains data for other cats that we may not even fathom. The urine can tell another cat the time the spraying cat was last there and when they may be back. For insecure cats, their own urine smell comforts them.

Typically, the spot being marked has some meaning or significance. The story I mentioned earlier about marking the hallway, bathroom, and exterior of litterbox, was a clear message that I had failed to keep all the litterboxes clean enough. Other times cats may mark exterior doors or walls around windows, which might indicate that she worries about an animal outside that regularly prowls the yard. A cat may mark favorite spots in the house to try to claim it from other cats. A cat may mark her "safe space" as a comforting behavior when she is being bullied.

2. It is important to try to decode the message when a cat marks with urine.

Set up inexpensive security cameras around the house, especially in places frequently urine marked to discover which cat is spraying. Ponder the concerns and frustrations this cat may be experiencing. Think about the locations of the urine spray and see if you can discover the reason based on that. Ask yourself: Is another cat chasing her non-stop? Is she bullying another cat? Is she upset with a dirty litterbox or claiming a preferred litterbox? Have I noticed a new neighborhood cat wandering in the yard? Can she not access enough food because of other cats in the home? Did she recently reach social maturity (two to four years old) and now wants to "climb the ladder"? Did I recently add or remove a cat or other animal from the home?

If You Think It's About Potty Access

Make sure you have enough clean and comfortable litterboxes in the home. The general recommendation suggests one box per cat plus one more for safety. Locate the boxes in different places throughout the house and on all levels if you have multiple floors. Don't position boxes in corners if bullying is going on. It's not a good situation to have a cat pinned down by a bully cat while trying to go to the bathroom. If this happens, you need several exit points around the box. Try to improve the bathroom setups for the cats if you see urine marking around litterboxes or have witnessed bullying at the litterbox. You may have to situate an open box in the middle of the room for a time to help resolve the disputes. Remember to keep it clean inside and around the litterboxes. Don't make bathroom time more stressful with perfume smells and room sprays. Try using feline pheromone room diffusers plugged in near litterboxes to help ease tensions.

If You Think it is About Food or Water Access

If a cat is too shy or afraid to eat with all the other cats or if one cat pushes others away from food, set up more food stations. In my home, with six cats, I have five food stations, some with two to three food bowls. I had to do this because certain cats refused to eat near other cats. They just didn't feel safe enough. I have four water stations. It's best to have some water stations set up away from the food bowls. Cats will likely drink more this way.

❀ *Skippy at one of the water stations.*

If You Think it is About Favorite Sleeping Spots or Perches

If cats bicker about that one spot in the sun or on the top of the solitary cat tree, offer more spots in the sun and additional cat trees. Buying another tree, adding more cat shelves, or inserting cat furniture to a space is a simple fix. Kitties generally prefer sleeping in the same places you like to spend your time, in other words—where your scent is strongest, like couches, beds, and favorite chairs. Ensure bullied cats get time in those prime spaces each day. The spot most desired and squabbled over in my home is my bed, where I have a heating pad that stays on low all the time. It may seem silly, but rotating cats' access to certain parts of the home may help if one spot is *the* hotspot. Again, try calming pheromone room sprays or diffusers in this location. Place calming crystals in that zone like blue lace agate, selenite, or aquamarine. Additionally, set up a similar space in another room. I added a second always-on heating pad on a chair with a cat bed over it. Though not as popular, the cats use that spot now, too.

If You Think it is About a Lack of Personal Attention

Cats can get jealous of one another. I see it in my home all the time. One wants to be held, but I say no and put them down, so they sit nearby. Another cat hops into my lap, and I may give them some attention before removing them. Meanwhile, the first cat looks jealously on, jumps up again to push the other cat away, or makes a vocal complaint. Trixie will nip the bums of cats if she feels thwarted by them. If you find yourself favoring one cat over others, they will notice. I admit that Skippyjon gets away with sitting in my lap almost every time he leaps up because he snuggles in my arms like a human baby, so I have to ensure every cat gets at least one snuggle session in my lap each day. If I can't hold a cat and must reject them, I try to do so with love and kindness. See things from the cats' perspectives and adjust your schedule to give each some of your love and one-on-one attention daily.

If You Think it is About Outside Cats or Animals

This one might prove trickier to fix, but you could start by blocking the view of the ground through the windows. You can do this cheaply with cardboard and tape or choose solid rollup blinds. Textured clear vinyl sheets can block views but still allow light. If the cat's favorite tree perch is at the window, make some adjustments and move the perch to another interesting spot, like in front of a fish tank or next to your favorite chair. Try to figure out who owns the roaming

cat and see if they can help you out by not letting their cat out or by limiting how often it goes outside. Look for non-lethal deterrents to put in the yard like motion sensor sprinklers, coyote urine spray, or ultrasonic sensors.

Side Note: Feces Marking

This behavior, called "middening," is fairly uncommon with cats. A cat may strategically place poop around the edges of a territory, marking her ownership of said territory. If you think this is happening in your home, please reach out to a professional cat behavior consultant for guidance.

CLEANING UP URINE & FECES

Clean up waste messes and urine marking completely and thoroughly as soon as you discover it. The longer it stays, the more the odor works its way into your floors, baseboards, and fabrics. If left uncleaned or partially cleaned, cats often return to the places they previously urinated or marked to do it again. Other cats in the house may smell it and decide to add their own urine scent to it. Cats' sense of smell far outstrips our own, so removing odors completely for them can be challenging. You must clean with an enzyme cleaner specific to breaking down urine chemicals.

If you need help finding all the urine spots, use a black light in the dark to see what fluoresces. Don't be alarmed at everything that will fluoresce on the walls. Sneezes, hard water droplets, food, and more fluoresce. For urine elimination, look for puddles on horizontal surfaces. For urine spraying, look for two to three splashes, starting 8-12 inches up the wall, that drip down. If you have white baseboards, you might see a few yellowish drops there.

I recommend that you disinfect in several steps. If a urine-soaked item cannot be tossed into the washing machine, first dab up as much as you can with a dry rag towel, pressing lightly. Then saturate the spot with cold water and a rag. Gently press again to remove moisture with a dry towel. Next, use a professional enzymatic cleaner for urine with *urease* in it, either spraying or pouring onto the surface. I personally use Nature's Miracle, Bac-Out, and Bissell's Pet Pro Oxy solution. I usually let the enzyme cleanser sit on the spot for twenty minutes or more before taking a dry towel or wet vac (depending on hard or soft surface)

and drying the spot by soaking back up as much of the moisture as possible. Avoid pressing too firmly on soft surfaces, which is why a wet vac is helpful.

When cleaning up vertical urine sprays, the steps are similar, but you don't need to saturate and soak in the same ways. Thoroughly wash all the crevices and cracks on the vertical surface with vinegar water. Try not to leave behind any urine. Then use the enzyme cleaner by spraying and letting it dry. Come back later and spray again. Wipe down the wall or surface with a water-dampened rag and then a dry cloth to remove any residue from the enzyme cleaner.

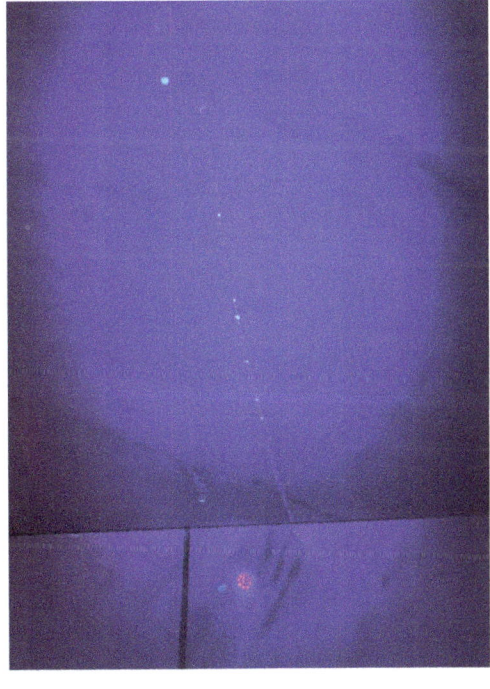

❦ *Example of urine spray under black light.*

If you can put the items in the washer or dishwasher, do so. You can add some bleach, baking soda, enzyme cleaner, vinegar, or OxiClean odor remover to the wash. (Not all of them at once—pick one.) Look at the stain and smell it before putting in the dryer. For urine-soaked items, try washing on cold several times before drying to eliminate all traces of urine. If you dry before the stain is removed, stains set in the heat.

When cleaning up feces, except watery diarrhea (in which case I hope you head to the vet's office asap), first pick up and flush chunks of poop. Observe the shape and how hard it is in case you need to see the vet about it or relate to a consultant what the poop is like. Then follow the same steps as above for saturated urine spots. If diarrhea, carefully clean up with paper towels, removing as much as possible from the spot before dabbing with water and soaking with enzyme cleaner.

I do not recommend using bleach or ammonia-based cleaners on your floors, walls, or upholstery. The odors left behind by these cleaners may compound the issue of a cat coming back to that spot to mark or eliminate again because something in the chemical makeup of these cleaners reflects the smell of urine to some cats. I also would avoid steam cleaners as *the* clean-up solution. They really serve to spread the urine and do not (alone) kill the odor. If you want to steam clean, do it after you apply the steps above and the odor is removed first. I find that the Bissel and their formulated Pet Pro Oxy solution do a good job on fabric or carpet. (It's especially helpful with barf staining.)

SPIRITUALLY SPEAKING: HOW TO HELP HOUSE SOILING CONCERNS

When it comes to urine and feces messes with kitties, as humans we tend to feel frustrated and disgusted. It is *far* from okay in our own human culture to leave our bodily waste around the house. However, cats commonly use urine and feces to communicate in their own culture. Try to keep this in mind to help maintain your patience as you work to resolve concerns.

Remember to use your spiritual and alternative tools to help yourself & kitty. I suggest:

- **Offer prayer.** Ask God to help increase your patience. Ask for help identifying kitty's triggers. Ask to be led to the right person to help you resolve concerns. Ask for miracles of healing if kitty is sick.

- **Employ crystals**. Obtain a crystal pack or collar necklace to help with either stress, confidence, reducing dominance, or urinary tract wellness. Use them daily with intention to help kitty cope or heal.

- **Utilize vibrational frequency** devices or music to help with your cat's stress, pain, or healing. Use it on yourself to reduce your stress and increase positivity.

- **Ask for Angelic support**. Ask for them to help you to intuitively understand kitty's needs in this situation. Ask for help catching the "culprit" if something outdoors is causing kitty stress. Ask for guidance to solutions your cat or household needs.

- **Use energy work**. Tapping, Body Code/Belief Code, or Reiki could help both you and kitty. Specifically look at addressing energies that contribute to kitty acting out in this way.

PURRRITO WRAP UP

Do not let urinary or defecation concerns go unchecked for long. Cats create new patterns and habits very quickly. Even if it began as a medical complication, it could become a behavioral concern over time if left unaddressed. Go to the vet to rule out health issues. If health complications are found, do what you can to immediately address them with appropriate procedures, medications, increased water intake, or diet changes. Identify the stressors for kitty and try to eliminate them. Absolutely avoid punishments when trying to address the litterbox concerns. Do not yell, hit, set up traps, shock, or water spritz. Please discover what has led your cat to make the decision to use the bathroom outside of the litterbox and address it appropriately. The best way to change behavior is to do so with love, patience, rewards, and good sense.

Hopefully, the information in this chapter addresses any house soiling concerns you may have. I certainly desire that positive changes will help reestablish a healthy relationship with your furry friend and strengthen your loving bond. If for any reason your litterbox concern persists, I recommend that you reach out to a qualified cat behavior professional and have them review the details of your situation, what you have tried, and how long it has been going on. They will help you discover what is happening in your cat's mind or world and will come up with a customized plan to correct the concerns. Please choose to spend a few hundred dollars on this service before giving up on your cat. Some folks find success with litter retraining by confining a cat. The confinement may take many weeks or months. I am not personally a fan of this, most especially if confinement involves a cage. It can make the cat more stressed or feel abandoned or depressed by isolation, *but* if a professional advises this approach, then follow their counsel as it may be necessary for positive long-term outcomes.

CHAPTER 6

Cat Behavioral Concerns: Aggression

Aggression is another major reason people surrender cats or seek professional help for cats, so this chapter discusses common aggression concerns that can occur when living with a cat. Kitty does have real weapons—his claws and teeth. Living with an animal is hard if you are scared of him or constantly getting wounded. Conversely, if living in a state of continual stress and fear, no wonder kitty acts out violently when approached. Alternatively, if in physical pain, he will do what is needed to protect himself.

Unfortunately, about 30% of surrendered cats lose their homes because of aggression. In most cases, the human family actually causes this aggression by how they physically handle the cat, offering inadequate resources, failing to do slow introductions when bringing a new animal into the home, or neglecting medical treatment when the animal is in pain. A very small percentage of cats *do* have diagnosable aggression not caused by a lack of care or a history of abuse, but these cats are not common. Most aggression difficulties improve or resolve for a cat by identifying his stressors, fears, pain, or illness and eliminating them. Furthermore, training kitty into positive behaviors may be required.

Let's try to define what aggression is and *is not* in a cat or kitten. Everyone comes at this from their own perspectives, and if someone has little experience with a cat, they may perceive something as aggressive that is, in fact, not. And an overly patient, huge cat lover may allow themselves to be hurt more than they should.

Body language often identifies aggression in a cat as he warns with his animate tools (ears, tail, eyes, sounds) *before* scratching or biting.

Normal cat behavior includes:

- Climbing your legs to get closer to you while standing, seeking attention and affection (often only in young kittens). If accompanied with negative signs like growling or hissing, this is not normal.

- Using claws to climb onto furnishings because they are too small to jump.

- Having claws out when jumping or landing on something to help grip and balance. This could include when they jump onto your back or shoulder.

- Stretching, sharpening claws, shedding outer claw sheaths, leaving scent, marking territory—often this winds up labeled as "inappropriate scratching" of furniture when not trained to use appropriate surfaces.

- Using claws and mouth/teeth to play, e.g., snatching toys out of the air, bunny kicking with back legs, or play wrestling with other cats or animals.

- Showing a strange or larger animal, like a dog, that they are tough by piloerection (fluffing out fur), swatting with paws (claws out sometimes), hissing, growling, spitting (when really scared)—these show the dog or strange animal the weapons the cat possesses to defend himself.

- Using teeth to play; young kittens especially are very mouthy, exploring the world through biting and chewing.

- Pouncing on our feet, especially when under blankets and wiggling.

- Kneading or "making biscuits" while purring is a loving sign. Sometimes claws are felt, especially when untrimmed.

- When startled or scared, using claws to launch from a surface, like your lap, to escape faster.

- Capturing and killing prey using claws and teeth.

- Giving love bites or grooming others using mouth (and by default teeth).

Actual aggression looks like:

- Swatting at a person with claws out—scratching skin, bunny kicking, and potentially drawing blood—when accompanied with any hissing, growling, or irritated body language like ears back and tail swishing.

- Launching themselves at animals or humans with hissing, growling, swatting, climbing, teeth baring (only incredibly fearful cats will do this except for a few cats showing territorial dominance).

- Cat-on-cat aggression can sometimes be hard to tell from cat-on-cat wrestle mania games. When it's too aggressive, look for excessive vocalizing from one or both cats, like yowling or growling, tufts of fur flying, or rolling around as one angry ball of fur.

- Warning bites when petting or touching tells you it is unwanted and to stop. These bites don't usually break skin but will often leave red indentions.

- Incredibly fearful cats may skip a warning bite and go right to a deep puncture bite, drawing blood and causing serious pain.

Cats give off oodles of cues with their bodies, but many people don't know how to read those signs. Let's review positive and negative body language in this chart.

Body Part	Positive Signs	Negative Signs
Eyes	Normal pupil size for amount of light, soft blinking of eyelids, closing eyes when around you, narrow pupils can reflect pleasure (analyze other body signs to be sure)	Wide pupils can indicate fear or anxiety, narrowing of eyelids in annoyance, staring intently, widened eyes can mean aggression (or excitement, so analyze other signs)
Ears	Perky ears, rotating ears to pick up sounds	Ears that are flattened to the side or all the way down on the head
Paws	Claws tucked in while playing with you, claws out while playing with toys/hunting, "making biscuits" or kneading (with claws somewhat out), placing a paw gently on you in an affectionate way	Swatting paws offensively or defensively with claws out, sometimes cats will place a paw on you to stop you doing something that is annoying them
Tail	Tail straight up, tip of tail bent slightly, quivering of tail can mean they are excited to see you, presenting their bum to you, small contented swish of tip of tail (unless showing other negative signs)	Swishing entire tail side to side angrily, piloerection (fur standing up), dragging low to the ground, quivering of tail while backed up to a surface to spray urine
Fur	Well groomed, clean, shiny	Piloerection, dull fur, unkempt or matted fur, overgrooming creating bald patches or sores
Posture	Relaxed, belly showing, sleeping, loafing, curled up in a ball, wiggle butts, pouncing playfully, laid out in a long stretch	Arched back, cowering, slinking low to the ground while not "hunting," tight ball to protect self
Mouth	Rubbing mouth/lips/gums on you, offering soft (usually) love bites, vomeronasal reactions (the funny open-mouthed sniffing that makes them look like they smelled something awful), tongue out can mean relaxed, yawning	Licking lips is nervousness (or a sign of negative energy releasing), barring teeth, snapping, warning bites and hard bites, tongue out frequently can also be a sign of health concerns
Sounds	Chirping, meowing, purring, trilling	Growling, hissing, spitting, yowling, purring is also a self-soothing tool for a cat who is terrified, injured, or sick

Side Note: Intensely Aggressive Cats

Circumstances where a person or family may legitimately need to surrender or consider euthanizing a cat because of serious aggression and safety concerns do occur. One of two things likely happened in these scenarios: 1) The family took on a feral or semi-feral cat and then unintentionally created a very stressful environment for the cat or, 2) The kitten arrived socialized to humans, but the environment did not provide a healthy life for the kitty; hence, it adopted intense defense mechanisms to survive. It is *extremely rare* when the environment is perfect—the cat was well-socialized during the critical period as a kitten, no identifiable triggers arise from stress (like health complications)—but the cat is still intensely aggressive. Cats get a bad rep in media for being "tiny psychopaths." The reality is, humans likely turned the cat into that fiery-fur-ball-with-teeth-and-claws by making a series of bad choices in the care of and interactions with kitty.

If a cat in the home poses a real danger (deep bites and blood drawing frequently) to you or your children, consider removing kitty. Neither your family nor the cat should live in constant fear. Consult with professionals about the layers of the situation to help you make the right choice. Earnestly understand what your home environment and human interactions may have done to create an aggressive animal and learn how to become a good cat guardian before you adopt another cat. This book provides great tools to set you on the correct path for your next cat relationship if you must surrender this kitty now. Don't rehome to someone unless you know them, and they are fully aware of *all* concerns. If you surrender to an organization, disclose all the facts and leave out any over-dramatization. When surrendering a cat to a community shelter with an "aggressive" label, they are highly unlikely to get adopted from the shelter setting and will likely wind up euthanized. You might try your luck at finding a good rescue group who will knowingly look to rehabilitate kitty in a qualified foster home.

Sometimes, just leaving the environment and moving into a safer one helps kitty to calm and change. You could seek for a permanent placement in a no-kill cat sanctuary, however, they are hard to come by. Euthanasia is an option for cats when rehabilitation or training has not worked or when it is ultimately the kindest things to do for the cat.

Story Example: Cat Bites!

Severe cat bites require immediate medical treatment. My sister Ellie had one of her cats bite her deeply and repeatedly. He'd escaped outside and had been missing for almost a month. Ellie had been searching for him, handing out fliers to all the neighbors, walking around the neighborhood calling for him, and setting up cat traps, but she only caught the neighbor's cat and a giant raccoon. One night she saw him outside in her cul-de-sac, and when she called to him, he came over and wound himself around her legs, so she decided she could pick him up. She felt the Spirit tell her, "If you don't hang on to him and bring him home tonight, you will never get him back." The cat was terrified out of his wits when she snatched him up. He bit her hands around thirty times as she hurried to the house, but she would not let him go until she had him safely inside and the door shut. I told her she was a cat rescue *warrior* for doing that. Most of us would drop a cat after bite one. Her husband, livid at the cat for mutilating Ellie, wanted him gone or put down, but Ellie refused to give up on her pet kitty. She washed her hands to rinse away all the blood and applied Neosporin and essential oils, but she didn't realize cat bites are considered a dirty wound and didn't go to the hospital until her hands turned red and swollen, about 24 hours later. When she arrived at the emergency room the following evening and reported that she'd been bitten by a cat about 30 times the previous day, they rushed her in, and the doctors' and nurses' concerned reactions surprised her. She didn't realize how much danger she was in. Certainly, a hundred years ago these wounds would have meant her death, and today they are still serious. The attending physician admitted her to the hospital immediately and began an IV antibiotic drip. At first the doctors gave her the worst-case scenario possibilities of a week-long hospitalization,

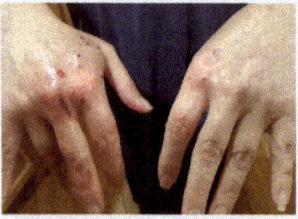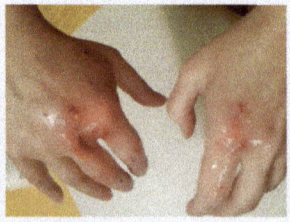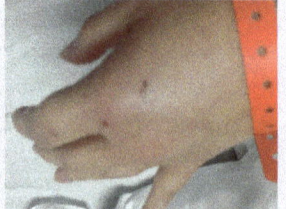

❀ *Ellie's bite wounds and swollen hand.*

possible surgeries, sepsis, or even the loss of a hand. Despite the strong antibiotic IV drip, her hands became swollen to the point her skin split. It was the week of Christmas, and her son's wedding was scheduled for a few days after, so of course her family and extended family sent up a lot of prayers for her healing. Miraculously, she stayed in the hospital for only three days and was healed enough to go home. Her hands bothered her for a long time afterward, but she now has full function in both.

The moral of the story: **if you receive a cat bite that is more than a surface wound, seek medical care immediately**. Rinse deep puncture wounds with water, or disinfect with iodine before heading into urgent care or the ER. Don't place other remedies on them if you have access to western medical care and get that started first. Afterward, you can apply your natural remedies as a support to healing. Bites that merely indent the skin with red marks, scrape the skin to form a scratch, or barely break the skin with tiny amounts of blood are treatable at home and would all constitute a "warning" bite given from the cat.

Some people, and sadly even a few veterinarians, declaw cats as a solution for aggression. This maiming operation is *never* the solution. If the cat is afraid, in pain, or stressed, removing the claws will not improve the cat's behavior! It only adds more stress, pain, and frustration to his life. A cat who no longer has claws, but still feels the need to protect himself, often starts using his teeth as his first defense. Bad cat bites are much worse than scratches. This chapter contains solutions to end aggressive scratching. Please don't choose declawing.

1. What or who is triggering the aggressive behavior?

When searching to understand why kitty is aggressive, start with asking yourself some questions: Is this aggression new or ongoing for some time? Is it simply associated with playtime? Only petting time? Or playtime *and* petting time? Is it related to jealousy of my time regarding other cats or family members? Is it about pain—is kitty limping or protecting a certain area of his body? Did I declaw the cat? Is there a certain person in the house who the aggression is geared toward? Is the kitty just mean to strangers? Did a family member or family pet recently die? Did the cat recently experience a trauma?

In this book we will discuss the most common forms of aggression, but not all types. For a deeper dive into all forms of aggression read *The Cat Whisperer* by Mieshelle Nagelschneider. Don't let aggressive behaviors persist or worsen. Make changes and seek guidance early on.

AGGRESSION AT PLAYTIME & PETTING TIME

Playtime

If aggression happens at playtime, reflect on how you taught your kitten to play. Or if you adopted an adult cat, realize the previous owners may have created complications around playtime. We should *never* use our hands to play or roughhouse with our kitten or cat. When we do this, our hand becomes the target, the prey, the threat. The frequent result—any time we attempt to touch the cat for *any* purpose, he attacks. We (or a previous owner) taught him to do this, *or* he was never fully socialized. It will take very real effort and a fair amount of time to retrain your cat to not see your hand as something that triggers attack mode.

For cats, playtime equals hunting time. As kittens they practice hunting by running, jumping, pouncing, and wrestling with siblings and toys. The play fights and hunting games would later turn into real fighting skills for territory and mating and actual hunting for food and survival. With cats as indoor pets, playtime mimics the hunt for kitties. It's about engaging their brains and their bodies to help use up energy. Using your hands, letting them scratch and bite you, may not seem bad as tiny kittens, but when they grow up, the aggression turns more substantial and painful. Cats learn patterns and habits very quickly, so you can't hand wrestle them when little and expect them to stop on their own when they grow up.

❀ *Playing tug of war with foster kitten Sugar.*

We should always use toys as an extension of our bodies when playing with cats. Again, our hands are *never* toys. The right body extensions for playtime include wand toys with feathers, fleece string toys, wire toys with tiny mice attached, large stuffed kicker toys, laser lights, and balls or lids to play fetch with.

We want cats to view our hands as positive things, an ally—not as threats or prey. Hands feed. Hands give love. Hands groom. Hands give treats. Hands give medicine. Hands pick up kitty gently. Hands hold toys.

Petting Time

If kitty only lashes out during petting time, try to get better at understanding how the cat prefers affection. The cat should have given signs early on in your relationship or is still giving signs that he doesn't like something about what you are doing. He will pull back or flatten his ears, emit a low growl, stop purring, flinch or ripple his fur and skin, thrash his tail impatiently, or his pupils will dilate. These warnings tell you to stop what you are doing. You may have some trial and error but try to discover more consciously which areas kitty likes petting and which he does not. Most cats appreciate petting around the head and chin. An exception might be if the cat has any painful teeth, so that area becomes off limits. If you have a kitty who starts pulling away from head petting, have the vet examine his mouth. Most cats also like a good scratch around the base of their tails, but not all cats. Many kitties appreciate gentle strokes all along their spine. Some do not.

❀ *Gigi, exposing her belly while she sleeps because she feels safe and cozy.*

Some areas of a cat's body are not ideal for touching. For instance, if you pet the head and get purrs but then pet the belly and get smacked, you should learn never to pet the belly. Cats generally restrict that area as a "no-no" zone. They may show you their tummy by rolling around on the floor in front of you, but that doesn't equal an invitation to touch them like it does in dog language. In cat language, showing the belly says, "I'm comfortable and feel safe." More rarely, some cats, who feel very trusting, will actually let you pet their stomach or brush their fur there. I have six, and all regularly show me their tummies. However, only Beaux lets me pet his tummy a few times with gentle strokes. Too much and I get a warning bite.

Another area cats may not like having touched are the paws, especially if declawed. If you adopt a kitten, I recommend you work daily at desensitizing paw handling by lovingly touching the little toe pads, gently squeezing to push out the claw, stroking the top of the foot nicely, or softly holding the paw in your hand. This interaction helps, over time, to make claw trimming easier. If you have an adult cat who doesn't like their paws touched, do your best to respect that. My cat Honey, who I had as a tiny bottle baby, dislikes having her paws touched. She gets upset at my pushing her paw pads to reveal her claws for trimming. I performed the same desensitizing technique with her all through growing up, but she is my most sensitive-to-the-touch kitty. Honey's skin flinches and ripples at anything nearby, even air movement around her fur.

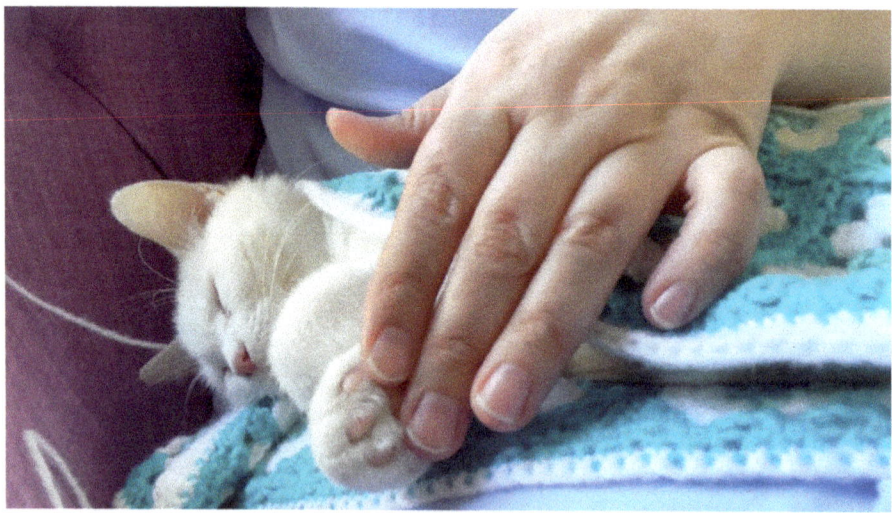

❀ *My foster kitten Hero, working on desensitizing his paws.*

❀ *Beaux and Skippy demonstrating the soft, one-finger offering.*

HOW TO REINTRODUCE HANDS

If you have made the mistake of using your hands to play and roughhouse, stop immediately. If the cat attacks your hands during petting time as well, then stop petting the cat completely until the reintroduction to your hands is successful. Everyone in the house *needs* to abide by the following instructions. This will not work if one person in the home insists on still using hands to harass or play with the cat. It will also not work well if merely one person reintroduces their hands and no one else does this process. Everyone must participate, but ideally the most nurturing and calm adult should retrain and reintroduce first, setting the pattern. While this happens, everyone else remains totally hands-off with the cat.

To reintroduce your hands slowly and purposefully, start using toys at playtime and give treats to kitty for playing with toys. If he still tries to go for your hand, get up and walk away. Wait a few minutes before coming back and trying again with the toy extension. If he keeps insisting on attacking your hand, end the play session by walking away. Try later in the day or the next day. Eventually, the cat will understand that playtime ends if he goes for your hands.

Once kitty has mastered that playtime is about toys (and little treats) and does not involve direct contact with hands, you can slowly reintroduce hands. When the cat is in a mellow mood, get down on his level and calmly, slowly hold out your hand in a non-threatening way, i.e., have only one finger extended gently while keeping the others tucked into your palm (think Michelangelo's *Creation of Adam*). Do not touch kitty. Allow kitty to come on his own to your finger to sniff, lick, or rub his head on your hand if he chooses to. If he does this, give him a treat. Have it hidden in your palm and release the treat for him after he behaves nicely toward your hand. Give verbal praise as well. *Do not* push this exchange by immediately lifting your hand over him to pet. It may come across as a threat. If you've had success with finger sniffing or rubbing, praise and treat. If the cat lashes out instead, slowly remove your hands and say "no" calmly. If the cat is not too upset, stay there, and speak gently and kindly to the kitty. Blink your eyes slowly at him to show you are not a threat. Do this for a few moments before ending the session. Try again later. With soft blinks and sweet words, gently show your hand again with the single finger out and others tucked back. Try not to feel stressed or scared during this process. Cats pick up on that nervous energy, and this will set them on edge. Keep yourself calm, confident, kind, and steady.

You will need to repeat this pattern and process over and over every day for several weeks. If kitty is doing well with you and your hands, gradually allow other family members to reintroduce their hands, too, by following the same instructions. Only when the cat feels calm and trusting of this touch may you gently attempt to pet the chin/cheek area. Do not lift your hand over kitty's head to pet his back until confident kitty won't fear it.

AGGRESSION TOWARD A SINGLE PERSON

If kitty singles out one person in the house for aggression, there is likely distrust between the cat and human. It is very important to figure out this brokenness and to address it appropriately. Once trust disappears, it takes intentional effort and patience to regain. Sometimes the person targeted with aggression genuinely has no idea what they did to cause the problem. Other times the person regularly harms the cat in secret, then claims innocence to the cat owner. Or the human openly abuses or antagonizes the cat. I think the hardest to deal with is the person who acts innocent but is not, because they will be least likely to change. As the cat's advocate, you must figure out what is going on. You could set up a nanny cam if needed or bring in a professional cat behavior consultant to figure it out. It often takes an outside party to recognize obstacles we've become blind to because we live with them day in and day out.

Side Note: Innocent Target?

Sometimes the human target *is* innocent. We then need to consider "redirected aggression." Something else is amiss in the cat's environment, and the cat just happens to lash out at that poor individual over and over again. Generally, a cat takes out his redirected aggression on anyone or anything close by when the cat is triggered, but it is possible for the cat to be triggered  and then seek out that same person to lay into. If you cannot pinpoint the cause of the trigger with redirected aggression, seek professional feline behavioral advice.

A cat may distrust a specific person for a myriad of reasons, but let's go over some ideas:

- Maybe the person yells at the cat with a threatening voice. Yelling is unhealthy in general for everyone because it makes a home unpleasant. Adults have no need to yell in an angry voice at animals (or children).

- Possibly the person accidentally hurt the cat by tripping over him, and if a preestablished bond of trust hadn't formed, the cat could think it intentional.

- Maybe this person really dislikes the cat, and the cat has picked up on this negative vibe and dislikes this person in return. Cats, like most animals, are pretty intuitive creatures and readily pick up on the energies and feelings of humans.

- This person in your life may be purposely abusing the cat physically, psychologically, or even sexually. When abused, cats have very similar responses as humans. Some retaliate to protect themselves and some cower because of overwhelming fear. Some get depressed; some get angry. Some may lash out at others they are less afraid of in an effort to feel some control in their life (redirected aggression). Ponder all considerations when figuring out the cause of the discord—the person receiving the aggression may not be the cause but actually someone else in the house, only the cat is too afraid of the instigator and so retaliates on others.

Story Example: Stressed Queen

Years ago, a woman called looking for help with her cat. This family had several young children and lived in a small space. The queen delivered a litter of kittens. Prior to giving birth, the cat seemed to handle all of those little kids fairly well. However, in a natural and instinctive effort to protect her young, kitty started acting aggressively toward the children—biting and scratching when they came near the kittens. Unfortunately, it took too long for the woman to figure out she should intervene. Even as the kittens aged, mama cat got worse. This woman really wanted to do what was right for the cat and kittens *and* for her family. She responded positively to rehoming mama and kittens with a foster temporarily, adopt out the kittens, get the mama cat fixed, and then bring her back to their family. So, I arranged this scenario with her through the rescue I volunteered with. After deciding on this arrangement, the woman told me the mama cat bit her hard, creating a puncture wound. This was worrisome. As a rescue, taking on animals with a history of bad bites is a challenge. We still had her take the kittens and mama to the foster home to officially surrender them to the organization. Once there, this woman opened up further about the difficulties with the cat to the foster home mom. Apparently, a week before she called me, her husband violently kicked the mama cat across the room when she scratched one of the kids. After this traumatic event, the cat became exponentially more aggressive toward everyone, including the woman who loved her. When learning this, the rescue leaders decided not to return the mama cat to that household. We had a hard conversation with the woman about the abuse the cat experienced and that rehoming the mama after the kittens matured was best for everyone. The woman tearfully agreed. The family could have avoided losing a cat they loved had the parents been mindful, proactive, and compassionate from the beginning to the queen with tiny kittens. A mama cat needs a safe space to care for her young. She cannot have the stress of three or four busy young children clutching at her or the kittens. The parents should have put firm boundaries in place with their children to help mama cat out. Also, parents should not own cats if their first instinct is to physically harm an animal who protects themselves against small, grabby hands. In the foster home, a quiet house with parents and one teenager who all respected and understood kitties, mama cat never showed *any* aggression. She showed love toward the humans there, sharing head bonks, purrs, and kisses. The mama cat was relieved to no longer endure the daily stress and unsafe feelings of her former life.

Broken bonds between a human and a cat can be mended, *if* the person is willing to learn how to change. Obviously, a toddler will not have the capability to do all items I list below if they are the human the cat targets. However, as the child ages, they should do as many of these suggestions as possible. Teaching the child to respect kitty's wishes will help heal the relationship. The person with the rocky relationship with kitty should work on the following list to reestablish safer interactions. Of course, this method will prove ineffective if the person does not stop all threatening or abusive behaviors toward the cat.

What you can do to reestablish trust:

- **Feeding the cat.** Be the person to put down the food every day. Let him associate you with this vital need.

- **Playing with the cat.** Establish a better friendship and trust through play. Tormenting the cat for your own amusement during playtime will not reestablish trust. Keep playtime respectful and genuine. Use toys and never your hands to engage in play.

- **Scooping the litterbox for the cat.** Cats like a clean potty and will notice who helps them have a more comfortable place to eliminate.

- **Speaking kindly to the cat.** Your tone of voice is a big deal. Use kind sounds. Be real and not sarcastic. The tone alone does not suffice. The words themselves need to be positive. If you kindly and sweetly call the cat "little jerk," "butt head," or other worse insults, you aren't fooling him.

- **Softening your eyes when looking at the cat.** In cat language, staring is not merely rude, but threatening. When looking at the cat, soften your eyes by doing long, slow blinks. It works even better if you get on the same level of the cat instead of towering over him. Lay down on the ground several feet away from kitty and slow blink at him. Close your eyes for long periods, showing the cat that you feel safe with him, then he in turn can feel safer with you.

- **Reintroducing hands and feet to cat.** If you used your hands or feet to hurt kitty in the past, you must reestablish with the cat that your body isn't going to hurt him anymore, that those appendages won't lash out at him ever again. Only use your body to show affection, compassion, and support toward the cat. Follow previously given instructions on reintroducing hands. Apply the practice to your feet if you have pushed kitty with feet, kicked, or allowed your feet to be "prey" too frequently.

- **Respecting boundaries with the cat.** Understand that the cat has a right to safety, space, and freedom. If he doesn't like something, stop doing it immediately. Don't force him to do things or try things. All kitties have unique personalities and spirits and will have different needs, weaknesses, experiences, and wants. Learn to read his body language effectively and show respect.

Cats are smart and intuitive. None of the actions listed will make a difference if the cat senses the person still dislikes him—the person has to have a shift in attitude with a sincere desire to care for and love the animal. Performing the listed acts of service for the cat will help create that love. Serving someone unbegrudgingly always increases our compassion toward them. As well as, the person struggling with the cat might consider doing some inner work of healing and growing. Identifying triggers and those old inner child wounds that need addressing are huge steps. Find outside help and support to release anger and pain in more productive ways, so it's not taken out on kitty. If this person is a young child, consider that we as the parent may need to make some changes in our parenting style. We may act in a controlling, overprotective, or even abusive way. Our actions may lead to a frustrated, angry, and hurt child who lashes out on the creature in the house they can have some power over—the cat.

AGGRESSION TOWARD EVERYONE

My first question for this section is whether or not your cat was truly domesticated when you adopted it. **Feral cats distrust humans** and will typically hiss, growl, and slap with claws out. If truly feeling threatened they will bite with full force, skipping the oft-used warning bite that domesticated cats use on humans. **Semi-ferals** or under socialized kittens know *how* to live indoors, but often distrust humans. Semi-ferals develop when a person finds and takes in a young cat or when rescue groups take in older kittens (over six weeks old) from a feral colony. If the foster who has taken on these kinds of kittens doesn't truly know the taming process, those kittens may not fully socialize. Yet, they still wind up at adoption events.

Feral or semi-feral cats may act aggressively toward everyone in your home because that wild side of them was never truly tamed. Yet, putting out a cat—because you've given up hope of domesticating it—that you've taken care of for months or years is dangerous for the cat. After living indoors and having food provided, they may not be able to survive outside on their own, especially if you brought them in as kittens. If you already have a feral or semi-feral cat in your home, I hope you make the effort to tame again, this time with appropriate tools. If you really need to remove a feral or semi-feral from your care, do your best to enlist a skilled TNR group (Trap Neuter Return) to rehome kitty to a colony that is being fed or to get him into a working barn cat program.

Taming Ferals

Domestication of these less social, more wild kitties is possible. However, the process takes a lot of time and consistent daily effort, using correct methods. The success rate increases with kittens less than eight weeks. With adult ferals, they may or may not tame and will take longer in the attempt. If you want to help ferals in your community, usually the kindest thing to do is to *not* take them into your home. Instead, work with a TNR group to get as many fixed as possible and offer to help feed the colony. Your local shelter or rescue groups should have contact information for people working in TNR.

The Kitten Lady website (www.kittenlady.org) has information and videos on domesticating feral kittens. You could also watch videos on YouTube by Kitten School or Flatbush Cats on taming ferals. In general, you have to work slowly and consistently to gain the cat's trust. Often you want to start out with the cat or kitten in a small, contained space like a bathroom or bedroom. Many situations may even require using a large kennel or crate to start with. If they have full access to the house, the cat will likely hide in places you can't imagine, and it's hard to tame them when you can't find them.

You want to use food rewards as the way to tame. Use super tasty foods and allow the animal to get hungry (but not starved). Do not leave food in his environment. Food appears when you are around, tastes really good, and comes directly from your hands. For safety, you can start with spoons as an extension of your hand, but eventually you want the cat to eat directly from your fingers. Baby food in turkey or chicken flavors is a good food tool. A really yummy kitten wet food works great, too. As you progress in taming, get the kitty to play with you using toys as an extension of your body. Use treat rewards for the kitty when he relaxes and engages in positive ways. Throughout your efforts work on petting and picking up the kitty. He needs to be relaxed and unafraid when you touch him because the ability to pick up the cat is important in order to give meds, rescue him from bad spots, or put him in the carrier. Dive deeper into the process by finding quality resources like those I suggested.

If your cat's aggressiveness toward everyone seems abnormal or comes out of the blue, the cat may be **injured or sick** and physically in pain. The hostility likely stems from that. Cats hide illness and injury amazingly well, until it gets unbearable. His aggression may seem like "zero to sixty" to you, but the cat may have been in pain for days, weeks, or months without you realizing it. Now, kitty is simply trying to protect himself. If this is the case, get kitty carefully into the carrier and off to the vet as soon as possible.

NO PAIN   SOME PAIN   INTENSE PAIN

Another reason for cat aggression toward everyone emanates from **stress in the environment**. If he must always remain in hyper-vigilance mode, he will more likely lash out with teeth or claws. Often small children unintentionally create unsafe environments with cats; children commonly grow so excited about a cat that they squeal, yell, grab, and chase kitties. Parents have to proactively teach children to respect the cat and enforce boundaries to protect the cat. If an entire household is currently struggling—going through a divorce, major illness, mental illness, abuse, trauma—a cat may react aggressively to the stress of his humans. Typically, in these taxing situations that indirectly impact him, a cat will become more aloof or clingy and not aggressive, but aggression is a possible reaction.

As I wrote previously in the story sample, another reason aggression may start is **if a mama cat has kittens**. Her protective mode skyrockets as her instincts to care for her young kick in. If you provide safety, privacy, and calm, mama should not react aggressively toward humans, but she may still react aggressively to other pets in the home because other cats or animals could pose a threat to her offspring. She can react in an offensive mode. Offering her a private room is ideal.

As you analyze the situation, decide if the aggression arises from the environment. Make a plan to change the situation to help the cat feel safer and then implement that strategy. If you have a hard time identifying all the stressors, hire a cat behavior professional to help you pinpoint triggers you may have missed or may not recognize as an issue.

AGGRESSION TOWARD STRANGERS

If your cat just turns on outsiders who come to your home, you may have an "attack cat." Like attack dogs, they protect their family and territory. This is not a common phenomenon. Mostly, cats hide when strangers come into the home or yard and may take minutes, hours, or days to come out from hiding while the newcomers stay around. I have one cat who doesn't hide upon the doorbell ringing. I have three that come out within minutes and two that come out within hours. Now, if it's a big crowd, most will stay hidden the whole time.

Gratefully, none of my cats act aggressively toward strangers. However, I have several that will hiss at young children as a warning to keep their hands to themselves. That seems fair to me. I always instruct children to let the cat choose to come to them by offering a single finger to sniff. If the cat doesn't come, they must leave it alone.

Humorously, cats often are drawn to guests with allergies to or disinterest in cats. This makes

❀ *Beaux and Trixie welcoming my sister when she visits.*

it a bit awkward for that person. When that happens, I typically remove my cats to another area of the home and close the door. Instruct guests who like cats or want to interact with them to let the cat come to them by offering a single finger to sniff and accept before attempting to pet the cat. Some people who come into your home may not consider the cat's feelings and approach quickly and confidently, thus putting the cat on defense mode. Many people like animals but have little experience with them, and they don't know the appropriate etiquette. You are your cat's advocate. Make sure guests in your home treat your kitties respectfully. You can accomplish this without alienating the person. Simply giving them friendly tips or warnings should suffice before they interact with your kitties. When I go to other people's homes and they have cats or other pets, I never just reach out to touch them. I wait until the cat or dog shows interest in me and then I allow sniffing, and if they desire it, I will pet them.

Things you can do to avoid your cat acting aggressively to your visitors:

- A simple solution is to put the cat in a quiet, safe room that contains all the things he needs—food, water, toys, litterbox, window perch, cozy bedding, hiding spot.

- If guests are staying more than a day or two, consult with your vet. They may offer a mild relaxant for the cat during the visit.

- Purchase over-the-counter items to increase relaxation of the cat like Comfort Zone room diffusers or an herbal or floral remedy for inducing calm like Bach's Rescue Remedy for cats.

- Warn guests to steer clear of the cat and not to approach.

- Be sure the cat has out of reach upper-level shelves or cat trees throughout the house. He can watch the new person and not feel as threatened.

If this person is a new significant other and the cat really dislikes them, analyze what may cause that. Ask yourself: Does this person fear cats or really dislike them? Are they taking up all of my time, causing the cat to become jealous that I don't have as much time for him? Is the cat upset that the person's scent is replacing his own on the bed or couch? Did I move the cat's belongings to make space for my partner? Am I having sex in front of the cat and does this upset him?

If the romantic friend plans to be a part of your life for some time, this person should build a relationship with the cat by feeding him, scooping his box, playing toys, or offering treats. The cat needs to see the person as another source of good things and not as the person taking up the attention and time of his beloved human. If kitty is stressed when he sees you touching the partner, make some shifts. Not all animals get upset by this, but some do. I counseled a woman whose cat got mildly aggressive toward the man in her life every time they got near each other. I recommended that they stop having sex in front of the cat and the situation improved—the cat no longer targeted the man aggressively.

If the cat is prone to lunging at, scratching, and biting the newcomer, and the behavior is completely (or seemingly) unprovoked, please call a cat behavioral consultant to help you analyze the cat's resources in the home and try to uncover why the cat is intensely protective of his territory. Visit the vet and discuss if the cat would benefit from anxiety medication. Behavior training still needs to be happening while on meds, so hopefully the cat can come off them at some point. Having a connection to Spirit and prayer can help you here as well, to know the right course to take for the cat and your family.

Side Note: Lotion Protection

Wear a citrus- or floral-scented lotion as a quick temporary fix to keep attacking cats at bay. Generally, cats loathe them and will steer clear of you for a short while. Avoid using lotions with mint or menthol as this can stimulate some kitties. My Stella, who was not aggressive at all, would bite my face in excitement when I used a minty face cream.

Additionally, you could concoct a water spray bottle with pure lemon essential oil in it. Ten drops in 3-4 cups of water should do. Shake well and then spritz it all over yourself as a body spray. Never use this spray directly on kitty. Citrus can be toxic to cats, and while the amount of lemon will not harm, it's unkind to make kitty uncomfortable in that way.

❀ *Honey and Skippy demonstrate some play fighting. They are pretty good buddies and will play wrestle-mania every day. Sometimes it gets too rough, but it isn't real aggression, merely play. It helps burn energy.*

AGGRESSION TOWARD OTHER CATS

Because they are very territorial by nature, it is common to deal with some **cat-to-cat aggression** in multi-cat homes. Ordinary spats will occur. This may surface as fussing over a prime sleeping spot. Sometimes one cat feels bored and tries to engage another cat who doesn't want to play. You don't need to sweat these sibling squabbles. To diffuse them, use a calm voice, never an angry or yelling voice. I typically say something like "Everything is okay. Let's be nice kitties." If needed, I walk over to the cats to calmly steer them away from each other. This is typically enough to end spats.

Bigger problems arise if cats legitimately push each other's buttons and move in the direction of an actual fight. If you are new to cat ownership or to multi-cat households, you may be unsure of what comprises playing and what constitutes fighting. Cats often play-fight as a way to blow off steam. This should be permitted as long as both cats consider it a game. If mutual, they will chase each other, take turns pouncing, and refrain from a lot of vocalizing. Ears may be back, and they may occasionally growl or hiss, but they really are having fun. If one starts to have enough, the game ends without concern.

In actual conflict, hunks of fur start flying. But before that happens, the cat being bullied will give a lot of warnings—ears back, hissing and growling, fur raised, or often they take a more submissive stance or try to escape around the bully cat. If the bully cat chases the one attempting to escape, the fight tends to escalate. You may hear loud vocalizing that sounds hurt or fearful. If the cats draw blood through scratches or bites, it damages the relationship. The more fighting that happens, the harder it is to repair the connection. Curb these types of skirmishes as quickly as possible to prevent truly aggressive fighting.

Existing Cat-to-Cat Conflict

Daily or frequent intense disputes that involve growling, hissing, licking lips, swatting, stalking, chasing, piloerection, and fur wads flying isn't pleasant for anyone. Discourage and curtail it quickly. Do not escalate the quarrels yourself by yelling or punishing the animals. Your role is to *de-escalate* by gently separating, using calming words, and showing love. If the cats are in an all-out fight, rolling around as one body, with fur flying, biting and blood, this approach is too late. Do your best to divide the cats without putting bare hands in the mix as you may accidentally get wounded. Grab a blanket to throw over them and scoop it around one cat to pull them apart. Use a large solid object like a cookie sheet or big pillow to try to block the cats' view of each other. A broom could force them apart. Once separated, place each cat in a different room and close the door. Cats in this high arousal state may use redirected aggression, so avoid picking up the cat if you think it might hurt you. Make those rooms dark. These actions serve as time-outs, not punishments, giving kitties space to decompress. Speak in soothing tones to both cats. Turn on low classical harp or new age music. Once kitties have calmed down enough, inspect them for wounds.

If you find injuries, you will need to treat them. Depending on the severity, you may do this from home or go to the vet. First, rinse out and clean any wounds. Use warm water or saline solution for this. If it's just a scratch, you could apply a regular antibiotic ointment or food-grade coconut oil after cleaning. However, cats will lick or groom off the medicine pretty quickly. If injury involves a bite, they are considered dirty wounds and have the potential to become infected. Cleaning with water or applying an iodine solution may prevent an abscess or may not. Do not put gels or goopy ointments on a deep puncture because it can trap infection and compound it. Nor use hydrogen peroxide or rubbing alcohol to disinfect as these are toxic to cats. Keep a close eye on the wound over the next several days. Should a swollen, inflamed area appear on the injury, possibly with visible pus, go to the vet immediately to get the absces drained and cleaned and to get kitty on antibiotics. If left untreated, the infection could spread to the blood stream, the cat might become septic and, not to be an alarmist, if untreated kitty could die.

After a big fight like this, you should do a methodical and intentional reintroduction for these cats that may take weeks or months to accomplish. My number one recommendation is not to mess around with figuring out how on your own or with books, but to hire a professional cat behavior consultant to review the concerns and come up with the plan. If you simply do not have the money, Jackson Galaxy's book *Total Cat Mojo* gives good instructions for reintroducing cats who have fought like this. A few episodes of *My Cat From Hell* show parts of this process in action. *Cat vs Cat* by Pam Johnson-Bennett provides another book resource. I will give a brief overview of the concepts in the next few paragraphs.

It is important to give the cats *complete* separation from each other for several days or weeks after the bad fight and before starting reintroductions. I suggest during this time you seek out energy work for both cats to release negative emotions they associate with each other. The first step to reintroduction is smell swap with *no* visual sightings of each other. Over time, as each cat accepts the other's scent, you may allow distance viewing with a partially blocked see-through door (glass or screen). If they attack the door, backtrack to no visuals and simply smells. Give treat rewards and praise rewards for any calm behavior when exposed to the other cat either by scent or by sight. Helping them each associate the other cat with positive things like treats and play builds rapport. It is important that neither cat feels rejected or that they have less access to valuable resources like litterbox, food, water, prime sleeping spots, or human time. Jealousy will *not* improve things. Swapping their spaces every other day may keep frustration and jealousy at bay. This will allow for each cat to maintain their scent throughout the environment.

Use the same cat brush on heads, cheeks, and shoulders (no rear-end brushing) on both cats every day. This really helps to create a polite "group scent" and develops acceptance of each other. Do not force a cat to wear the other cat's scent; allow them each to sniff the brush and accept it. Give treat or praise rewards when they accept being brushed. If you have more than two cats, include all in this daily brushing ritual. If brushes in general are not liked by one or more cats, use a cloth instead.

Eventually, if the process proceeds smoothly without any aggressive body language or vocalizing upon seeing each other, try to get them to eat closer and closer together (with the clear door or gate still between them). This will help you understand if reintroduction is working. Cats on high alert or that feel threatened cannot relax enough to eat. If this feeding time succeeds, gradually let them eat close together through the door. If this works, next allow them to share the same space for short periods of time with supervision. Place them apart from each other in the same room. Use calming tones and soothing music to support a good vibe in that space. Have large crystals supporting love and relationships like rose quartz, clear quartz, and chrysoprase in the room. Give treats, praise, and pets for all calm behavior. If all goes well, eventually encourage them to play about ten to fifteen feet from each other (but *not* together). Never let the toys cross each other as an accidental run in with the other cat may set things back. If you live alone, take turns playing with them. Mature cats typically understand whose turn it is with the toy. Let them watch each other have fun. All throughout this process, again use treat rewards, affection, and praise rewards for the behavior you want to see in both cats.

There are excellent clicker training approaches to support healthy reintroduction processes. Please hire a cat behavior and training professional to teach you first-hand how to train with these techniques.

During this reintroduction process, if you have other cats in the home not involved in the conflicts, do your best to keep the existing relationships alive and well. If you have cats that get along well with one or both of the fighters, let them stay in the room with one stressed cat, then swap the peaceful cat into the other space with the other stressed cat. Make sure redirected aggression is not aimed at the calming cat and that the slow reintroduction process doesn't cause a new problem with non-conflict cats in the home who were getting along fine with everyone.

Story Example: My Cats' Conflicts

I did not do a traditional slow introduction with the resident cats when I chose to keep Honey because I'd fostered her since she was a tiny kitten. My cats had seen and smelled her for months before I decided to keep her. While not one of my felines was happy to have Honey staying put, no fights ensued during that first year. However, when Honey matured, she showed herself to be a more aggressive cat. She decided to bully Trixie. Prior to this, my multi-cat household only had play fights or normal sibling squabbles. Though small, Trixie has proven herself very scrappy when necessary. Honey would push and push until Trixie would let her have it back. I would break up disputes when I saw them, but I still had to sleep and go to work, so the fights escalated.

One night while I was sleeping, a brawl between Trixie and Honey got really bad. I flew out of bed to separate them. Fur floated everywhere, and Honey's ear was torn and bleeding. Blood speckled the wall. I didn't discover until it abscessed that Honey also received a bad bite on her tail. The vet had to drain and clean the wound and give her an antibiotic shot.

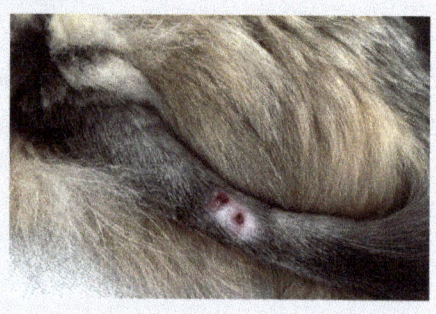

❀ *Honey's bite wound after our vet visit.*

This bad conflict happened in early 2020. I separated them at night and while at work to keep both safe, but the fighting didn't stop. I started praying for help; what do I do? The pandemic hit, and it actually became a small blessing to our problem with my transition to working from home. I quickly curbed all squabbles using gentle tones, splitting the cats up, and showing both affection.

I did not do the official reintroduction process as recommended by many experts. I felt hope still as there had merely been one or two bad fights. I am not suggesting that you should mimic me. Judge how extreme your situation is and make choices based on your unique circumstances and hopefully with professional counsel. Some cats reach social maturity and decide to promote themselves amongst their cat peers with aggression, so I am not sure that a slow introduction in the beginning, when Honey was small, would have avoided the later fights.

After more than three years of working from home and stepping in immediately, disagreements rarely occur, even though Honey still feels the need to push Trixie. However, both girls now understand when I say kindly to them, "Let's be good girls. Be nice. Be nice girls." Once I say that, they both tend to back away. Something else that helped ease tensions for these cats, who needed more territory and space from each other, was allowing them time outside. We followed the guidelines of outdoor safety I'll lay out later on. For now, their tension predominately takes place at the front door over who gets to go outside. I have placed a Comfort Zone diffuser there, and I use sweet words and gentle pets for both when I let one of them out or back in. Letting cats outside may or may not be wise for you in your own circumstances. There might be other, safer ways for you to expand territory in the house. (More on indoor-outdoor cats on page 269.)

While Honey and Trixie had the worst fight of any of my cats, unfortunately the relational conflicts haven't stopped there. Gigi and Prim became "police officers" in the early days of Honey and Trixie's fights. Gigi always targeted Trixie and Prim would take Honey. They chased the girls away from each other and scolded them. Unfortunately, Prim started taking her role too far, preemptively chasing and punishing Honey. Then I had to additionally keep things chill between Honey and Prim (this is mostly over now). Whenever any squabble happens with Trixie nearby, Gigi targets her immediately even if she was totally an innocent bystander. I have to coax Gigi down and comfort Trixie. Gigi is a good girl and will walk away, but still, managing all of the relationships requires a fair amount of effort.

Adding to all of this, recently, when Skippy turned about two years old, he decided to bully Prim. Primrose makes such a fuss about it; he can't resist doing it. If she stood her ground with Skippy, he would let her be, but he can't refrain from chasing her when she flees. He is learning the meaning of my words when I say, "Skippy, leave her alone, walk away." The night before I first wrote this paragraph, Skippy did walk away for the first time without my physically guiding him. It was a great break through! I praised him for being such a good boy. He has since learned my expectations and follows through (with some reluctance) when I say, "Walk away, Skip."

Side Note: Cats are Not Pack Animals

Cats are not pack animals; thus, no real alpha emerges in a clowder (group of cats). Their dynamics are diverse. When you have a large multi-cat home like mine, "rankings" definitely depend on who is interacting with who. For instance, Gigi seems to mostly rule the roost as all the other cats accept her punishments or priorities. Honey tries to push back on occasion but always loses to Gigi. Beaux is a chill alpha-type with the other cats but regularly succumbs to Honey because she always slaps him in the face when he has done nothing to deserve it. Honey tries to dominate, but, really, she can be controlled by Gigi and Prim. Prim concedes to Skippy in such a sad way but prevails over Trixie. It is all about personal, individual dynamics between kitties. Cats do not have a leader; still, I call Gigi "the matriarch." Cats in general often seek power in a territory to feel secure.

When you have a multi-cat household, you too will become a good "cat herder." The Internet abounds with jokes implying it is impossible to herd them, to get them to do what you want, but that is not true. Cats can be taught. Repetition and rewards bring good results. Clicker training can speed up the learning. Pick up Karen Pryor's book called *Clicker Training for Cats.* Rewards include food, toys, catnip, affection, or praise. (Be aware catnip can increase aggressive behavior in some cats. Like alcohol does to humans, catnip makes some cats mellow and some cats mean.) Another tool I used earlier on when experiencing higher conflicts was putting jingle bell collars on Prim, Honey, Trixie, and Skippy. These sounds acted as a forewarning system to the other cats to reduce any cat's capacity to sneak attack the other.

Learn from me. Having more cats leads to more inter-cat-relationship tribulation. When I had four cats, they never had any major upsets, just little normal cat-spats. The more cats you add to your home, the more territorial complications will arise. If you do not want to spend time every day herding your cats, curbing squabbles, and managing interactions, simply have two or three cats in your multi-cat home. Granted, it only takes two to have a bad relationship, but I'm conveying that the pressure for the cats increases the more felines you ask them to live with.

Multi-cat aggression disputes might be addressed and resolved by looking at triggers in similar ways as those from unwanted urine spraying on page 113. Set up cameras around the house to help you decode what sparks the warring cats. A quick recap on that:

🐱 Sexual behaviors may be the impetus. If one or both of the cats are not fixed, altering them may be the most important answer. This is especially true of two unaltered male cats living together.

- Resources: do you have enough? Food stations and bowls, water stations, cat furniture, prime sleeping spots, toys, litterboxes, and more. If one cat feels that they have to protect resources from another cat, simply adding additional resources may ease the tensions.

- Jealousy could be the reason. Do you give one animal more love, affection, or time? If so, equalizing your attentions may help resolve conflicts.

- Is one cat overly stressed about a cat outside that it can't get to? He may want to defend his territory, and the frustration may become displaced, targeting his cat roommate instead. Try non-lethal options like motion-sensitive sprinklers to deter the outside cat from coming around.

As recommended before, do not hesitate to find a professional to help you analyze your specific cats and circumstances. A cat behavior pro can create a tailored plan and check in with you to see if it's effective and make adjustments where needed.

Side Note: Look Away!

With cats, fighting almost always starts with the aggressor encroaching the other's space and staring at them. A great training tactic with aggressive cats is to get them to learn to look at and then away from their target to prevent them from staring. They learn that *not* staring gets them a reward. The technical training term is "Look at That" or LAT. However, I have made some tiny adjustments in how I use this tool. As many times as you can, use the words "look away" *or* "look at me" *or* make an obnoxious kissing sound with your mouth. When the aggressor who is staring at the target cat then does look away or looks at you, praise them, give a treat.

If a fight is about to ensue, quickly block sightlines by placing an object in front of the aggressor—a large book, cardboard, or throw pillow. If you don't fear for yourself, and kitty doesn't ever attack you, you could place your hand in front of kitty's eyes (with love and calm, not aggressive energy). You can give treat rewards for kitty when they look away or at you to reinforce not staring at the other cat and heeding your vocal cue. Use "walk away" or "go to place" and reward them for coming to you, leaving the room, or sitting in a designated spot. Remember, your role is always to diffuse with calm.

Preventing Cat-to-Cat Aggression from the Start

When you plan to add another cat to the mix, kitten or adult, do it thoughtfully. Select a cat with which you think the other animals already in residence will get along. Know that you cannot drop the new kitty into the home and simply expect all the animals to "work it out amongst themselves."

Instructions on steps to take:

- **Set up a segregated space** for the new one. Include all his supplies like food, water, toys, bedding, litterbox. A small space with no hard-to-reach hiding spots is best, such as a bathroom for a kitten or a bedroom for an adult cat. Keep the cat in isolation for as long as it takes to accomplish the introduction process. Block under the door with a draft snake.

- **Do scent swaps**. Take bedding or towels rubbed on kitty heads to the other animals, so they can sniff out details about each other. Let them smell each other on your clothing or hands. Use a shared brush between all the cats, brushing the head, cheeks, and shoulders at least once a day. Do not force acceptance of brushing; let each cat sniff the brush before you begin; if they pull away, keep working on other ways to establish scents.

- **Swap spaces**. Allow the resident cat to go into the bedroom or bathroom of the new cat, and allow the new cat some additional space in the home to explore. Do this without the cats seeing each other. I suggest for the new cat, select a portion of the larger home, something closed off like a bedroom because a scared cat or kitten out about in the entire home for the first time may hide, and you may not find them again for hours or days. Swap for an hour and then put them back into their respective spaces. Do this more and more to allow the new cat to acclimate to the rest of the home without the resident cat stalking them or hissing at them.

- **Allow kitties to sniff each other** after several days or weeks of scent and space swapping. Do this under a door or screen/glass door with sight lines partially blocked with a towel or carboard. Either or both parties may hiss or growl; it's normal. Give treats to both (preferably not while hissing)—a highly desirable food reward to associate the other cat with yummy, good stuff. Offer praise and petting rewards to both if they act nicely and curiously.

- **Allow the cats to see each other up close**. Do so safely. Use an interior glass or screen door to try the visual introduction with one cat on either side of the door. You might put the new kitten in an enclosed play pen with a cave bed inside for hiding. The two can see one another with that barrier (I'd not recommend crating or placing one in a tight space as the fear of no escape may increase dislike of the other cat). One cat could be leashed, if trained. Again, reward with praise for good behavior. Use calming words if either hisses or growls. Keep these first few visuals short; no need to push tolerances. It's best to end before any negative signs.

- **Try supervised mingling** when the cats have managed steps one through five. Keep the situation calm with soothing words. Play some soothing classical or harp music in the room. Sniffing bums is normal. Some hisses to keep distances is normal. A big cat smacking a little kitten is normal. However, don't encourage the negative. Try to keep the meet-and-greet positive with treats, praise, and fun. (Careful not to associate "treats" with behavior like swatting.)

- **Play with a favorite toy**. Don't push them to interact with the toy together. Play with one cat and then walk a few feet away and play with the other. Something about watching each other play helps to build a more peaceful relationship. However, kittens don't always understand about taking turns and may launch after the toy and land unexpectedly in front of the resident cat and cause conflict. If both show interest in playing together without hissing or growling, that is a great sign and will help them get to know each other. Offer praise and treats if this is the case! Keep it short.

- **Never leave them alone together until you are confident** that both cats will tolerate one another and not create any conflict. Aim for tolerance, not necessarily "best buds." If they do become friends, great! Recognize that once the kitten reaches about two to four years old (social maturity), they may start conflicts with other cats.

🐾 **Take the pace cues from both cats**. If both cats warm up quickly and introductions go smoothly, then trust the process and move forward. If one cat resists or becomes upset, go more slowly.

AGGRESSION TOWARD DOGS

These two species can be friends, but when it comes to larger dogs, remember that kitty sees a real threat to their life upon meeting. Do very slow introductions to avoid fights or tragedies. If you have conflict in your home already between a cat and dog, you should reintroduce them following a slow and careful plan. I am certified in cat behavior, not dogs. Consequently, this information is meant as a high-level download. If you need extra help with this subject, read *ComPETability: Solving Behavior Problems in Your Cat-Dog Household* by Amy Shojai or another competent resource. Hire a certified dog and cat behavioral consultant or one of each to help out.

When a cat meets a dog for the first time, kitty will likely stand his ground to show how fierce he is so that the dog understands kitty can and will protect himself. This will look like hissing, swatting the dog's face (sometimes with claws out), piloerection, possibly some growling, slinking, or an arched back. If you have a gentle, well-trained dog, she will likely handle this first attack with grace, but an untrained dog's reaction could be lethal. Exercise caution when bringing a cat into a home with a dog who is larger and whose temperament toward cats is unknown. **I cannot stress enough the need for slow introductions to ensure safety and tolerance between the different species.**

The slow intros above when introducing two cats have similar parameters for new cat-to-dog relationships. If the cat is already in residence and you are introducing a new dog to the home, make sure the resident cat has his full territory and the dog goes into a safe room. Getting a puppy may work out best for helping an adult cat accept a dog, but not always. Puppies are very playful, and a big puppy could be hard on an older cat. You will have to keep an eye on their interactions and the cat's tolerance level. The following suggestions assume the dog already resides in the home and kitty is the newcomer.

- Before you ever bring home a kitten or cat, **make sure your dog is trained**; that she sees you as the alpha and will obey several basic commands like "sit," "lay down," "drop it," and is leash and kennel trained. Trained dogs are far easier to introduce to a cat than an untrained dog.

- **Keep kitty in a safe room** with all his needed belongings. I described this setup previously.

- **Block sightlines**. Block any crack over a quarter inch under the door to the safe room. You could block with a rolled-up towel, but either a cat or a dog could easily shift this item when you are not looking. I recommend duct taping cardboard that goes all the way to the floor on one side of the door or using a weighted draft guard.

- **Begin the process of scent swapping**. When the animal shows interest and curiosity with scent swapping, not animosity, offer treat rewards to help associate the scent of the other animal with positive outcomes. Avoid offering treats for negative responses to the smells. Do offer kind and comforting words.

🐱 **Space swap** after scent swapping for a time. Remember, the new cat or kitten will likely be timid in the larger territory. For that reason, instead of whole house access all at once, allow them to explore a single room that contains the dog's smell. You can widen the kitty's access over several days if he remains calm and curious. These swaps should last for 30-60 minutes. Make sure the animals do not visually see each other during swaps. Give treat rewards for calm or friendly attitudes during the space exchange. If there are two adults in the home, do swaps simultaneously; if not, place the dog in a closed off area of the home and spend time with kitty as he explores. Then put kitty in a different closed-off location for 20-30 minutes and allow the dog to explore the cat's safe room. Never reward hissing, growling, ears back, or any other negative response. Do not reprimand either. Just speak calming words to the animal.

🐱 **Do visual introductions** if space swapping goes well. This can happen through a door, or with dogs, easily done while the dog remains either kenneled or leashed. A two-person team, one for each animal, always makes these types of interactions easier. Encourage each animal to stay calm and reward them with treats in the presence of the other. If either will not eat a treat or food, then there is stress to at least a minimal degree for that animal. If stressed, increase the distance between them or end the session. If you are introducing kitty to multiple dogs, do steps 1-5 at the same time, but for visual intros, do one dog at a time. Select your most congenial dog to go first. Do several days in a row of controlled, distance viewing. If all goes well, make the next step.

🐱 **Allow kitty to approach dog at his pace**. Have doggie on a leash or kenneled. Give her praise and ask her to stay calm. As mentioned before, most cats, especially if they have never spent time around other dogs, will show physical signs of fear when up close to a dog for the first time. Expect fur raising, hissing, growling, swatting, crouching, arching, and dilated eyes. If kitty exhibits none of these body language signs and he remains calm, you are on a good track. If you see fear signs, speak soothingly and encouragingly to kitty. Ask doggie to stay calm and seated (lay down if a large dog). Offer treats. If a kitten or young cat, try getting him to play in front of doggie with a toy. If he starts to play, this is good. If too fearful to play, don't push it. Keep session short if the cat is afraid. Do this meet-and-greet again and again until kitty is neutral to or interested in the dog. Praise and reward dog for staying calm and patient.

- **Interactions with dog**. If all these steps go well, allow dog to slowly approach kitty. I'd recommend keeping the dog on a leash, so you can step on it if needed. Do not ever allow the dog to chase kitty when kitty is still anxious or unsure. This will certainly damage the relationship, even if the dog is playing. For kitty, dogs, larger ones in particular, are a threat to their lives and a chase when there isn't a bond of trust or friendship will harm a positive connection. Once the kitten trusts the dog, he will want to play, but a big dog should always be well-mannered with the smaller cat.

- **Be extra safe**. Until 100% confident that they are pals, never leave the home without securing one of the animals. In fact, I might suggest that if you have a kitten and an excitable dog, do not leave them alone together at all, even if they love each other, until the cat reaches maturity. Always provide escape routes for kitty, like high perches and shelves that doggie can't reach.

- **Take the intros at the pace needed for both or for the most resistant animal**. Remain patient in this process and do not rush or force it. It will not help either animal. If they adapt quickly, wonderful. If not, please take the needed time to improve the situation. When you have made the correct efforts with the intros and the animals still don't accept each other, it's time to call a dog trainer and a cat trainer to see what additional steps to take before giving up on one of the animals.

What to Do When a Relationship Turns Ugly between Cats & Dogs Who Used to Get Along

Try to find or recognize what triggered the relationship going sour. Set up in-home security cameras to identify what triggers the upset. Is it mealtime? Is it territorial disputes? Is it because the dog can't leave kitty alone? Is it because one animal is in pain? Did one reach social maturity? Are they both fixed? (Hormones may be causing the problem.) If fixed, is the dog or cat harassing the other via mounting attempts? A large variety of causes could disrupt their relationship.

If you can identify the main trigger or the biggest disputes, then you can work to resolve the conflict concerns. For actions that kitty might take to harass the dog, involve a cat behavioral professional. For actions the dog takes to upset the cat, involve a dog behavioral professional. You can find experts trained in the care of both species, and they will be your best option in these situations.

Story Example: Kitty Stressed by Dog

A man I worked with had cat behavioral concerns, some of which stemmed from one of the large dogs in the home harassing the kitty. Because of this nuisance, she was forced to remain upstairs while the family and dogs spent a fair amount of wakeful time downstairs. Many of the conflicts started immediately when the kitty came down the stairs—the dog would corner her on the steps. A few things were happening:

- The dog had recently gone off medicine that helped calm his anxiety.

- The cat, as a small kitten, was very possibly mauled by a large dog, as evidenced by the story the shelter gave that the kittens all had wounds and were found next to a dead mother cat with injuries that likely came from a dog.

- The dogs were trained but not entirely obedient because they were high-energy dogs and not getting enough activity in their lives.

- The cat really didn't have any escape routes out of the dog's reach when downstairs. A large cat tree stood in a corner far away from the stairs and kitty would get cornered under pieces of furniture on the way there where the dog would growl at her, and she would cower and hiss.

We made a lot of changes in the home for the cat. Gratefully, the cat guardian genuinely wanted to help kitty feel happier and safer and followed through quickly on suggestions for changes in the environment. One of the changes created a path with wall shelving from mid-way down the stairs into the living room. The guardian also moved the cat tree to the corner closer to the stairs, so kitty could safely come downstairs. We blocked access to underneath furniture where kitty was getting trapped. We added feline facial pheromone plug-ins around the home to help calm kitty as well. A week after our meeting the guardian sent a photo of the cat and the dog in question sleeping near each other on the couch a few feet from the diffuser, something he had never seen before from the animals. While things did not become 100% perfect in the dog-cat relationship, it vastly improved, and kitty is much happier in a space where she feels safer.

Having a well-trained dog will go a long way in creating a healthy relationship. Dogs, often but not always, are more excitable and higher activity animals than cats. Cats, who generally prefer calm and relaxing environments, can find this energy annoying. When planning ahead, research which dog breeds do best with cats. Research which cat breeds might be most compatible with certain types of dogs. You can of course make things work beautifully with mixed-breed dogs and regular domestic cats, but having knowledge ahead of time helps because in the US a high percentage of dogs come from breeders. For instance, imagine pairing a very high energy, active dog breed like an Australian Shepherd with the docile, lounging Persian cat (the smush faces often create sinus and breathing difficulties, so imagine how hard it would be for a cat like that to live with a dog constantly trying to herd it).

Please use care when mixing cats and dogs together. Sometimes it flows with no issues. Other times, well you know, cats and dogs can be like oil and water, never emulsifying together without sincere effort. Do not allow dogs to chase cats and vice versa when it is not playful for *both* parties. Do what you can to immediately correct conflicts between the species, and don't let struggles inflate or linger for months on end. Call on a professional for a personal review of the circumstances and for the creation of a plan of action using training and behavior methodologies to bring the two creatures into at least more peaceful cohabitation. While we love it when cats and dogs become friends, sometimes the most we can achieve is safe tolerance in a home.

SMALL PETS WITH CATS

You may want your cat to live with smaller, common pets, such as bunnies, birds, lizards, hamsters, mice, rats, smaller snakes, and fish. Almost all of these are at risk as potential prey when bringing home a new cat. We've all seen the cute memes and videos of "unlikely friends" with cats and their natural prey buddies. It's super cute and heartwarming. However, if you assume *all* cats will behave kindly toward their natural prey pet buddies—please think it over carefully.

Getting a kitten seems the most obvious choice when you have other small pets. Young kittens will more likely accept new types of friends, and if raised in a home from birth, they haven't specifically learned to hunt live prey. *However,* that prey drive doesn't go away, and instincts remain strong. Once grown, your cat, even though it thinks it is being gentle during playtime, may wound, seriously maim, or accidentally kill the smaller pet.

Some ideas to keep smaller pets safe around kitty:

- Never leave the pets unsecured but kept safely in their enclosures.
- Do scent swapping before introductions.
- Only let the pets mix when you are supervising closely.
- Give treat rewards to both cat and other pet to help them associate the other with pleasantries.
- Curb any roughness on the kitten or cat's part by immediately taking the small pet away and back to safety. Conversely, reward the cat promptly with treats for showing gentleness.

With your small pets, encourage cats to leave them alone and walk away through clicker training. Helping kitty to know the expectations when you give commands like "drop it," "walk away," "leave it alone," "be nice," "sit," can go a long way in teaching them not to hunt or kill the pet rat or the pullets (teenage hens) in the backyard. Clicker training is the fastest way to engrain the knowledge into kitty, but you can also train kitty with just words and a lot of repetition. My cat Trixie doesn't get clicker training at all. She is so treat-focused that she completely ignores the clicker. However, I can get through to her with simple word training, like "sit." I haven't associated this word with any food treats for her, simply praise rewards, but she is learning. Buy a cat training book—Karen Pryor is a great expert on cat and dog training—and make sure you have good tools. More training tips on page 195.

SPIRITUALLY SPEAKING: HOW TO HELP AGGRESSION CONCERNS

Your approach to getting guidance or making spiritual adjustments might differ when dealing with cat aggression toward people versus aggression toward other animals. I will mention alternative healing solutions along with the spiritual.

- **Use prayer**. When praying, ask for guidance to understand what triggers kitty's violent reactions. Ask to be led to the right resources for help. Ask for patience while you figure out what to do. If kitty is truly scaring and wounding people in your home, pray to know the best decision in regard to keeping kitty or surrendering. In some intense violent circumstances, you may need to ask God for help in knowing if euthanasia is the right solution.

- **Ask for Angelic help**. I do this all the time with my cats who have squabbles on the regular. If you are trying to sleep, in the bathroom, or have full hands, you can't always get to the cats to separate them or shepherd them away from each other. I ask Angels to intervene, to help calm the cats, to get them to walk away. I find this helps a great deal in diffusing potential fights. I do the same thing when I travel from home for long periods, asking Angels to watch over the cats and help them get along and avoid conflicts.

- **Do energy work**. I highly encourage energy work for aggression concerns. Everyone involved in the conflicts will benefit from energy healing modalities. For humans, it can help remove fear, jumpiness, anxiety, and more from experiencing wounds or attacks from a cat. For cats, both the aggressor and the bullied cat need to clear away past negative energies associated with fights. Energy work combined with other environmental changes and training protocols will go a long way in amending relationship challenges.

- **Try supplemental support**. There are many options to try in regard to reducing aggression, stress, and anxiety in kitties before heading to long-term pharmaceutical options. I find that supplements help, though not typically the complete answer. I have good experiences with Bach's Rescue Remedy for cats. This product promotes itself for situations like going to the vet but can be used daily. Other companies offer flower essence blends as well to help calm. CBD oils, a true quality oil designed for pets with no THC in it, can help kitties in a variety of ways. The right dosing may calm a cat, although too much can create a sleepy or agitated cat. FFPs (pheromones) can help. I recommend diffusers around the home and personally buy Comfort Zone for multi-cat households. Not all cats respond to FFPs, but some do. It's worth a shot. L-Theanine can potentially reduce aggression or stress. Some homeopathic remedies like Thuja reduce fear and anxiety. Premade homeopathy pills can be made into tinctures by dissolving into fresh water and dropped directly in a cat's mouth or put on wet food. For any of these options, use wisdom, consult with a vet, or find a homeopathic vet online.

- **Apply crystals**. I value crystals for their subtle support and protection. Use these tools in conjunction with other efforts. Keep larger stones that promote feelings of love and calm around the house like rose quartz, clear quartz, selenite, blue lace agate, celestite, amethyst, chrysoprase, and more. Place smaller stones near where kitty likes to lounge and sleep (pick them up after use, otherwise kitties will bat them around and lose them under furniture). I make and use crystal necklaces for cats and find they help as well in diffusing conflicts. Kitty can wear a necklace for several hours a day with calming, loving crystal beads helping to reduce conflicts. Remember, always have clear intentions with crystals and keep them clean and charged.

- **Play calming frequencies or music**. If you have a frequency device with programs to reduce stress, anxiety, or fear, utilize it. Place the device near kitty once or twice a day while he snoozes. Kitty may enjoy it, or he may get up and walk away. Please let him dictate his exposure to the device whether for two minutes or forty. If you do not have a device to use, YouTube has a selection of frequency music pieces that promote peace, calm, and healing. You can usually find these compositions listed under their hertz numbers. I suggest 528Hz or 174Hz or both together. You can find curated playlists already for cats, dogs, or humans. The music lasts for hours and hours. Play it softly throughout the home or in the areas cats spend most of their time.

PURRRITO WRAP UP

A cat may display many forms of aggression, and I covered most of them in this chapter. If your cat expresses a different type of aggression than those discussed here, seek the help of a professional cat behavior expert. The biggest tips for avoiding aggression are to adopt a well-socialized kitten, raise the kitten safely with no roughhousing, have children respect cat's boundaries, keep kitty happy in the home with great resources and enrichment, learn to read the cat's body language and cues and back off to keep the peace, and when bringing in new animals always do slow and structured introductions.

Retraining an aggressive cat takes effort, consistency, and patience. You can usually find solutions to reduce conflicts and engender peace; however, not all cats are safe to be around. Surrendering or behavioral euthanasia are options you should discuss with professionals like your veterinarian *and* a cat behavioral professional. No one should live in daily fear in their own home, including the cat. Before adopting another kitty, make sure you and your family have learned how to create a safe home for cats.

CHAPTER 7

Cat Behavioral Concerns: Destruction, Shyness, & Other Behavioral Concerns

In this chapter we will talk about other behaviors in cats that might cause stress or frustration. While not as common for surrendering as house soiling or aggression, these other concerns can still cause some humans to call it quits in their cat relationship. Of these destructive or odd quirks, people most frequently surrender cats for clawing up the furniture or flooring, but a few cats also struggle with chewing objects and destroying them in that way. Many cats push items on tables or counters onto the floor, and sometimes those things break or make big messes. Some cats continue a sucking or nursing habit into adulthood that can be irksome, particularly if they want to suck on you.

Furthermore, we will look at behaviors like shyness, seeing what we can do to help kitties come out of their shells. I want to help you with cats that insist on dashing out the exterior doors every time you open one. And we are going to discuss overweight cats, sharing tips on getting kitty back to a healthy weight.

SCRATCHING FURNITURE

Cat's claws tend to present a big problem for many people. In reality cats have eighteen little, tiny blades that can hurt and destroy. We need to understand when we bring a cat into our lives that these are not solely weapons of survival that they won't need in our homes. **Claws are intrinsic to being a cat.** Claws support who they are at the core. As cat owners, if we take away the claws, we damage the cat in very real and lasting ways emotionally, mentally, physically, and even spiritually.

Cats know through their DNA that they are small animals in danger at any moment from a threatening predator. Taking away claws damages or removes the cat's safety, confidence, agility, escape options, and more. Cats use their claws not only to protect themselves, but as a balancer when they jump, climb, and land. They use claws to help them stretch deeply to keep muscles agile and strong. They use claws to mark territory; territory safety is huge for cats.

Understanding Declawing

Please, never take away the cat's claws. Many negative ramifications result from it. Any "positive" outcomes absolutely benefit humans and are not "real" or lasting in many cases. Does every declawed cat develop behavioral or pain issues after surgery? No, but far too many do, so it is a high risk, no reward procedure.

❦ *Taking away claws because you have small children you don't want scratched?* Declawing takes away the gentler of the two weapons a cat has to defend herself, meaning the teeth are what remain. A bad cat bite is far worse and far more threatening than a bad cat scratch. Respect that the cat has the right to defend herself against the stress, fear, or pain small children may cause with their untrained or unsupervised handling of the animal.

❦ *Removing claws to protect your furniture or carpet?* I cannot tell you how many owners I have come across with declawed cats that have litterbox aversion concerns. Many people come to me and demand help, threatening to put kitty down or surrender to a shelter because she stopped using the litterbox. I try to keep my cool amidst the demands and threats when I inform them that a common side effect to declawing is litterbox avoidance, because the box is too *painful* to use now. I help them recognize that *they caused the behavior* with their choice to amputate the cat's claws. They disfigured the cat to protect the furniture and carpet but now get angry at the cat because it pees on furniture or carpet. Taking the time to train kitty to scratch appropriate locations would have better served the cat (and them) than declawing and its outcomes.

As a result for many cat owners, when I have the conversation with them about what declawing actually involves and what it really did to their cat, they begin to doubt veterinarians. Now understanding the negative outcomes (like cats biting to protect themselves, having chronic pain, and not using the litterbox) and that 42 countries deemed the surgery an animal cruelty act and made it illegal, they stand there in shock and clear regret. Then they almost always say in frustration, "Why didn't my veterinarian tell me this?" And that is a truly good question.

Gratefully, this surgical practice is becoming more outdated, and more vets are becoming savvy to the way it makes them look to still offer this surgery on a cosmetic level. However, in the US about 75% of veterinarians will still perform declaws. I do not know individually why a vet would offer this cruel practice when the premise of their career would suggest a love of animals and they vow to "do no harm." But broadly I can say that this surgical procedure is highly lucrative to vet clinics who offer declaw; typically, they charge $250-$600 (or higher) for a 10-15-minute procedure, giving them a high profit margin and thus a good way to help sustain their businesses. Some vets think they save the cat's life by performing the surgery as clients will tell them they will give up the cat if they aren't declawed. Interestingly though, some data from way back in the 1990s said that merely 4% of owners would have surrendered the cat if the vet didn't perform the surgery, whereas the veterinarians responded that 50% of the owners would have surrendered had they not performed the surgery; clearly a big miscommunication or a justification. I wonder in these situations if the vets throughout the decades accurately described to the client what the procedure entailed. Did they forewarn them about possible behavioral and medical complications after the procedure? The Paw Project cites that a scant 11% of veterinarians think that bringing up and discussing behavioral concerns with their clients falls under their purview. Many people have a huge misconception that declawings simply remove the claw, and they liken that to a permanent claw clipping. In their view—like no more than taking off fingernails. But our fingernails regrow. The only way to stop a fingernail from growing back would be to chop off the tips of every finger. *That* is declawing. It is a ten- or eighteen-digit amputation surgery.

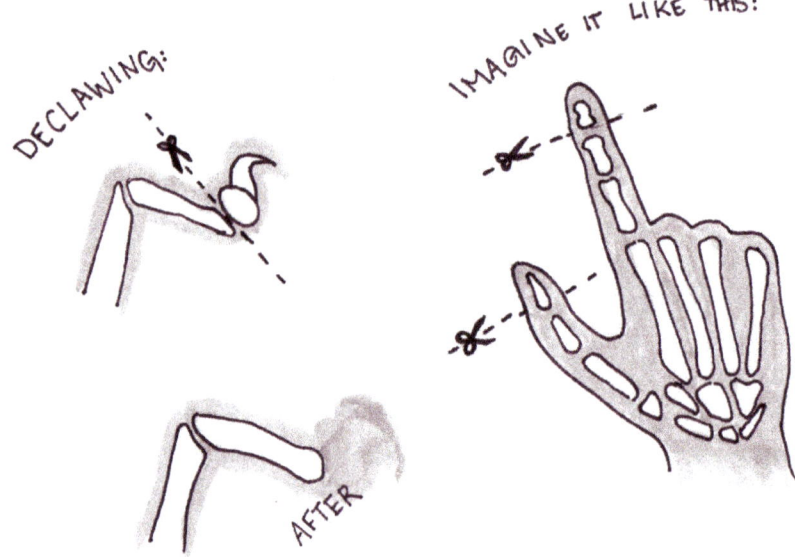

No wonder most cats experience great pain for the rest of their lives. Some folks who have declawed will balk at that statement and say, "My cat never showed any pain!" Cats are brilliant at masking pain, so that they don't appear weak. In the wild, larger prey target the weak animal as an easy kill; cats learned to hide it well (a response written in their DNA). Nevertheless, the pain will lead to litterbox difficulties. It hurts the cat too much to jump into the box and land on grainy or lumpy substrates, it is painful to stand on the substance, and to dig around in it is even harder. Not surprisingly, they begin to seek more comfortable ways to eliminate. Sometimes these litterbox difficulties don't manifest until years later when the development of arthritis in the paws, as they age, compounds kitty's long-term pain.

Here is a quick snapshot of data found at The Paw Project's website. For more information on the facts about declawing, please visit www.pawproject.org.

- Up to a 55% greater chance of litterbox problems for declawed cats over those not declawed.

- Nearly 74% of declawed cats have related medical complications post-surgery.

- Nearly 50% of cats, post-surgery, returned to vet to help cope with pain, and the study cited that up to two thirds of owners witnessed visible pain from their cats post-op.

- 33% of cats in one study developed behavioral concerns post declaw surgery (as cited by owners who can be less reliable on making connections between surgery and behavior).

- Nearly a 20% increase over non-declawed cats in instances of biting.

Understanding Why Cats Scratch

They have to scratch. It is part of who they are—a natural behavior that we need to provide the right outlets for. What makes it important, you say? Let's go over some of the big points.

- Scratching helps kitty perform personal pedicures, removing old claw sheaths, sharpening claws, and preventing claws from getting too long.

- Scratching is part of kitty yoga, allowing for long deep stretching, muscle use, and strengthening.

- Scratching keeps kitty feeling safe in her territory because it allows her to both mark with her scent (paw pads have scent glands) and visually say, "I live here."

- Scratching other creatures is a first-line defense when kitty feels in danger. It helps show the threatening party that if pushed to it, she will fight back to survive.

We must accept that kitties need claws. So then, how do we live with it? I have a large multi-cat household, and I have had items destroyed. It's frustrating at times, but as you become a true friend to felines, you become more accepting and patient. Combined with your new traits of patience, you can absolutely work on training your kitty to scratch in the places you designate and not indiscriminately scratch anywhere and everywhere.

 Outdoor kitty yoga.

How to Keep Claws & Protect the Home

First, we take care of the claws and offer appropriate scratching options. Then we work on training kitty to seek out the right places to scratch. Moreover, we can make choices that will reduce stress and worry about cat destruction when we furnish or build our homes.

Here is a checklist for helping kitty with her claw needs:

- Trim claws regularly. It's best to start desensitizing kitten's paws early on with this regular practice. You trim only the tips and avoid clipping into the quick as it causes pain and bleeding. If you make too many mistakes of cutting the quick, kitty will begin to loathe the event, so take it slow and steady when doing this task. Waiting until kitty is drowsy helps, as does consistently trimming every two to three weeks. You can pay a groomer or vet for this service, but it should be totally doable at home with some desensitization, training, and rewards.

- Provide a variety of appropriate scratching surfaces and scatter them around the home and most especially have them in the rooms where you spend your time, because you want kitty to feel welcome there.

- Provide both vertical and horizontal scratching options, and ensure scratching objects weigh more than the cat by about one and a half times. This way the surface or post won't slide or tip when she uses it.

- Experiment with different types of scratching surfaces. Commercially, the easiest to find are cardboard, carpet, and sisal rope. Also try different styles of carpets, fabrics, wood, or bark.

- Buy scratchers that actually meld with your couch or chair—some drape over arms, some wrap around sides and corners.

- If you must and can afford the regular expense, try nail caps for claws. I don't love these as an option, but if you feel desperate for a fast solution, these may help. However, for a kitty already struggling with stress and fear, don't take this route as it will most likely compound negative behaviors from the cat. I suggest that you not try to put the caps on yourself but see a groomer to apply them. Like human fake nails, they will need to be reapplied every few weeks.

To train kitty to use scratching posts & to avoid harming your furniture, follow these tips:

- Draw positive attention to the cat posts by sprinkling catnip on them every few days.

- Use clicker and target training to teach and reward kitty for using the scratching surface. This is the most impactful way to train to scratch appropriately.

- Use a lot of verbal praise for scratching in the right spot. If you catch kitty scratching in the wrong spot, don't reinforce the behavior by drawing attention to it, but try to disrupt the behavior quickly—make a loud noise that ideally seems disconnected from you. Pop on the stereo, or shake a jar of coins.

🐱 Wrap the exterior of the furniture with a thick plastic or vinyl wrap. Though not super aesthetic, it can help with retraining. Try using thicker plastic sheets; simply pin or adhere into place.

🐱 Use non-harmful deterrents on surfaces you want avoided.

🐱 You can use double-sided sticky tape, which works for some cats. However, others think this is meant as a game and pull it down quickly. Note that tape strips when swallowed form a choking hazard or potential bowel obstruction.

🐱 You can use motion-activated compressed air that hisses and sprays when kitty gets near her scratching spot on the couch. Personally, I don't like this one because it may train kitty not to come sit with you on the couch.

🐱 You can spray pheromone sprays every few weeks all around the couch sides and back to prevent scratching. It mimics the scent of cat marking and if it already smells, kitty has no need to scratch. This works for many, though not all, cats.

🐱 There are other deterrent sprays or essential oils with scents intended to revolt kitty, so they don't want to touch the surface, but I honestly haven't found a truly effective one, and again it might keep kitty from sitting near you on the couch if successful. Another downfall is how frequently you need to reapply.

🐱 Offer scratching posts right next to the surface being scratched in a similar substance. For instance, if the cat is scratching your leather sofa, offer a leather wrapped post instead. If kitty likes the soft padded upholstery, wrap quilting batting and fabric around a scratcher post.

When buying new furnishings or renovating your home, consider these ideas as a cat guardian:

🐱 Buy inexpensive upholstered furniture just in case kitty damages it. It might be easier to swallow damage on the $2000 couch versus the $6000 couch.

- When buying upholstered items, remember that the looser the weave in the fabric the easier claws damage it. Tight weaves like a velvet or microfiber are harder for claws to shred.

- With carpeting, cats tend to like looped better and can create damage faster, versus cut carpet.

- Plan to buy couch and chair covers to protect from cat fur, barf, and scratching. Choose items easily washed at home on a regular basis.

- Consider going all hardwood, luxury vinyl, or tile in your home, so kitty does not have an option to scratch carpet. If you change from one type of flooring to another, cats might freak out a bit without help during the transition. To smooth out the switch for kitty, place rugs around the home and work with her to desensitize to the feel of the new surface on her paws.

- When buying rugs, contemplate the newer washable type, or purchase inexpensive ones. Acrylic rugs with printed patterns offer a low-cost option versus real wool rugs with woven patterns.

- In a renovation, talk with a carpenter about building in a climbing wall, ceiling walkways, or built-in scratching posts to really catify the home.

SUCKING & CHEWING

These two behaviors can be odd ones for a kitty to assume. Though not super common, they happen enough that I need to address them here. Let's first broach the sucking aspect.

What Is Sucking?

Sucking consists of a nursing action that the kitten persists in well after weaning. Often the cat selects objects like a blanket or stuffed animal to "nurse" on. Some call this "wool sucking." Sometimes kitty chooses clothing to latch on to. Sometimes she will try to nurse on another pet in the home, which may annoy that animal. The most concerning aspect of this behavior is if kitty chooses to suck on your skin, earlobes, fingers, or hands. Most people don't need kitty hickeys in their life, so curbing this behavior is useful.

Most commonly this habit starts right after weaning age. When you adopt, you could ask the foster home or breeder up front if your kitten still sucks on items in a persistent manner. (It is uncommon.)

Story Example: *Marmalade*

I have raised *one* kitten that had this behavior. This orange tabby boy endured some rough situations during his upbringing. First, he came to me as a singleton between one to two weeks of age. During a family's move, they found him under some exterior stairs. A few weeks later he got really ill along with three others in the group (I had added other singletons to the mix after quarantines). Marmalade, the name I gave this kitten, was the biggest and strongest of the group and healed up well. However, only a day or so after he got better, one of the kittens (who had been unknowingly exposed at another foster's home) came down with different illness, this time panleukopenia. I vaccinated Marmalade and his sister with their first vaccine the same day as the diagnosis on the other kitten. They were six weeks old and healthy at that moment. I wanted to offer as much preventative support as I could to them. Skippyjon was in this group.

❀ *The kittens in this story.*

❀ *Sweet boy Marmalade getting one-on-one time after all the illness was over.*

I moved the kittens into a sanitized room and started preventative support for all of them. About a week later, Skippy came down ill with panleuk and then the sister. Marmalade, gratefully, never showed any major signs of panleuk. He didn't develop the fever, continued to eat, and didn't become dehydrated. However, he did get a bit neglected as I had to focus heavily on tending the other two to keep them alive. For more than two stressful weeks, my attention was pulled from Marmalade. I have wondered if the stress and emotional neglect he experienced in kittenhood contributed to his need to self-soothe by nursing.

🐾 *Marmalade in his new home.*

He liked to nurse my skin, in particular my earlobe. I had a home lined up for him and his sister. They were twelve weeks when going together to their new home. The family was aware of Marmalade's sucking habit ahead of time and that I had been working to redirect his focus away from my skin and onto something else with some success.

In his new home, he selected the mother there to suck on. She didn't love this behavior, but together we successfully retrained him to choose blankets and stuffed animals to suck on. In a recent update, I was told he still nurses fuzzy blankets.

Some adult cats will pull up a corner of a blanket, straddle it, and knead their paws and purr. This is most common in males. This action is comforting and soothing and in some ways mimics mating. I don't discourage this action in my cat Beaux, who enjoys this behavior every now and then.

When redirecting the sucking action away from you and onto a more appropriate object, do so with kindness. Yelling, fussing, pushing do nothing but stress the bond and potentially intensify the cat's need to self-soothe via sucking. It also reinforces the behavior through the discouraging *attention* she receives from you. If kitty starts to nurse you, simply get up and move without any more action than that. She will eventually learn that you leave if she sucks on you. When she is on her own and feeling sleepy, you can present kitty a blanket or stuffed animal that she can choose to "nurse" if she likes. Make sure to offer quality fibers that don't easily pull out and non-toxic fibers as kitty will swallow some of these. The least amount she swallows the better. Like hairballs, these fibers can build up inside kitty. You can offer a good oil each day to help fibers through the digestion tract. (See page 201 for ideas.) To end the habit entirely, do the above while working on environmental enrichment and emotional bonding. If kitty feels safer and loved, the behavior may eventually lose its appeal.

If kitty is "nursing" another pet in the home and that pet does not discourage it or cannot get away for some reason, redirect kitty's attention *before* she begins to nurse on them. You may have to separate the pets entirely for a time. If you find yourself in this circumstance, I recommend working with a professional cat behavior expert to help create the right plan of action.

If you have a sweet kitten who nurses on you, try to curb this behavior early on. It might seem cute right now, but when she is full grown, you will inevitably wish she would stop. It is easier to break a habit when it has had less time to become engrained.

What Is Chewing?

Have you discovered the edges of your books with fang holes? Do the corners of kitchen cabinets appear to have teeth marks? Does cardboard get chewed up with kitty biting and tugging out chunks? Do any wooden furniture legs show signs of being gnawed?

There is chewing and then there is pica. You may need a veterinary behaviorist or cat behavioral expert to help you distinguish which one you are dealing with. Considered a diagnosable disorder, pica can be difficult to put a stop to. Chewing, on the other hand, is fairly common among young kittens exploring their worlds orally. However, for adult cats, chewing may indicate boredom or oral pain. The professional you enlist can create a plan that is specific for your situation and cat's needs.

In general, make sure to put away items that kitty could consume that are dangerous to her. Offer more environmental enrichment. Have items acceptable for chewing, like cat-specific chew toys (watch her while she uses them so as not to ingest large pieces) or provide catnip and grasses. Recent research points to nutritional deficiency as the cause behind the chewing or full-blown pica, and you could try giving kitty probiotics, psyllium powder, digestive enzymes, iron, B12, and other vitamins. Please consult your holistic veterinarian on what to try for your kitty.

Ingesting foreign, non-food items is truly dangerous to your kitty. Bowel blockages are very costly to surgically fix, and if not addressed, deadly. Fortunately, cats chew up foreign items less often than man's best friend, the dog, but it is still a possibility. Signs of an obstruction in the digestive tract could include loss of appetite, weight loss, lethargy, vomiting, straining to poop, no poop for several days, tiny bits of diarrhea that are all that can be expelled, pooping outside of the litterbox, reacting in pain, and possibly aggression when you touch kitty in the area of the intestines. Please take your cat into the vet as quickly as possible to receive the right imaging diagnostics to check for an obstruction.

Oriental breeds of cats have a reputation for higher occurrences of wool sucking and pica. By oriental, I mean the *breeds*, not coloring. If you have a domestic shorthair (DSH) or domestic longhair (DLH) cat with distant Siamese-mix ancestry and coloring, the risk isn't higher.

SUPER SHY, SCAREDY CATS

If you have a shy cat who hides a lot, spooks easily, or runs away from you when you walk around the house, it usually means they missed getting enough human interactions during the critical period of socialization as a kitten. The best bet for helping kitty to come out of her shell is to try as early on in her life as possible to build confidence. If you adopted an extremely shy twelve-week-old kitten, work on this concern *now* instead of waiting until she is five years old to address it.

❀ *Timid foster kitten, with ice blue eyes, showing fear signs in a new situation.*

The term "wallflower" is sometimes used for describing very shy cats. Some experts explain that these cats are not happy because they cannot fulfill their natural cat instincts when in a constant state of fear. Experts instruct that cats like this must not be shy in order to fulfill their full cat potential. I understand these beliefs and do agree; however, I think that if kitty missed any of the critical period of socialization from age two to nine weeks, a guardian can only do so much to help kitty develop more confidence in the human world. We should not expect that a shy cat will become a super bold cat. Though we *should* set expectations that a shy cat can confidently be out and about in the house with those she trusts and loves. She may still dash away if you walk toward her, and she will certainly dive under the bed when the doorbell rings. For me, this is completely acceptable behavior and doesn't have to be trained out of the cat.

We need to recall that cats are *small* predators which means they are also prey to larger creatures. We should not try to train self-preservation out of them, especially when they were under-socialized with humans. Instead, accept it as a part of their nature now.

Story Example: Two Terrified Cats

One of the rescues I worked with had two adult cats surrendered that were originally adopted out through the organization seven years earlier. The older couple cited new allergies as the reason for surrender, but it felt like an untruth or at least a partial truth to me. Because they originated from the rescue, we knew a little about their kittenhood. Scooped up as older kittens around ten to twelve weeks of age from a feral colony by a TNR group, they came into the rescue and merely lived with a foster for a few weeks before being brought to adoptions. This was a failing of the rescue in my opinion, adopting out feral or semi-feral kittens. The two cats were both very beautiful, which gave them a big leg up at adoptions. One was a lilac point color, and the other a lynx point color. They both had long hair; one had blue eyes and the other more rare "ice" blue eyes.

In their quiet home with the older couple, they did all right. While still very skittish, they each bonded with one of the adults. Sadly, this couple ignored their adoption agreement terms and had both cats fully declawed. The day this couple surrendered the two cats, workers placed them in cages near each other, but one was hissing at the other from the stress of a public venue. Someone else in the rescue leadership decided to separate these two siblings who had zero history of anything but friendship, based on the hissing at the event. Each went to different foster homes with experienced foster moms.

I was called upon for behavioral concerns shortly after these two cats went to their foster homes. Both cats were terrified and, in turn, used their teeth as protection since they no longer had their claw defenses. As such, both foster homes were scared of the cats. One of the cats absolutely refused food and water and after more than 30hrs had not even gone to the bathroom. I came into that foster home to assess and did some energy work on the kitty. I felt intuitively in that session that it had been a wrong choice to divide these two cats. They needed to come back together. Both foster families wanted these cats out of their homes quickly because of their violent use of teeth when approached.

After I left that home, the kitty did calm enough from the energy session to come out of hiding to eat, drink, and use the box. The foster mom relaxed a little, but as she had a toddler, she still wanted the cat removed as soon as possible.

I pondered where to place these two kitties so they could remain together. They really needed a perfect foster home, willing and able to give both cats peace, time, space, and a lot of patience. I prayed about what to do for them, and then a married couple popped into my mind. They had wandered into an adoption event a few weeks earlier and talked with us. Unable to have children, they instead had a dog and a few cats. Though interested in fostering, they weren't sure if they should but left us their number just in case. I called them and fully explained the situation with these two big, beautiful girls that had not been socialized correctly as kittens, declawed, removed from their safe home, now terrified, and lashing out with teeth. They needed a home together to feel safer. This couple agreed to take on these foster kitties.

I gave the couple a lot of tips to help them with the rehabilitation of the cats. Grateful to be back together, the girls snuggled closely for safety. After several months in this home, the cats finally started opening up to the couple and allowed petting, began to play a bit, and ate treats from their hands. But the girls still hadn't braved exploring the home past their bedroom door. After we had brought in a few potential adopters to this couple's home, they decided that no one else would know better than them how to love and care for these intensely fearful and shy cats. They adopted them both, a happy ending to a rough situation.

If you have a shy kitty, work on having her feel safe with you and the family. If she can play and pounce in your presence, eat calmly, let you pet her, sit with you, and make biscuits and purr, well, these are the best parts of having a relationship with kitty. She doesn't need to hang out when the kids' friends come over. She doesn't need to sit calmly when the delivery guy rings the bell. Nor does she need to endure the chaos of cleaning house or putting away groceries.

The coming instructions in Chapter 8 will be vitally important to follow to help kitty feel more confident in your presence. Your steadiness, compassion, and genuine love will allow your cat to feel safe. With your shy kitty you have to remember that feeling safe is her highest priority.

Story Example: Shy & Stressed Kitty

I had a fluffy feral kitten that came to me at about seven weeks of age having already missed a big chunk of the window for socializing with humans. She proved a stubborn holdout in the taming process. She loved to hiss a lot. Her looks were so dirty, she obviously wanted to kill me with her thought waves. Still, she was an adorable kitten. I began to pull her away from the other kittens several times a day for an hour or so. Fearful, she would hide a lot in this new space. Eventually, she started coming out of her shell—head bonking my knees, hands, and face. Little gal purred so loudly and intensely, she drooled. I finally gained hope for her adoption when she began to sit in my lap and enjoy being petted.

A large family adopted her. Normally, I would not have arranged this type of scenario for a shy kitty. However, I knew the mother and father personally. The mother was intelligent, capable, and intentional in her parenting. She had two teenagers and two young ones. Her oldest struggled with anxiety. We arranged the adoption of this kitten for the oldest child as a project to continue to nurture and help kitty feel safe and loved. I gave them a four-page document of instructions.

The teen was delighted with the project and new furry friend. This teen took the instructions seriously, and her mother followed up and ensured kitty was doing well. It took effort and time. The husband terrified this fluffy baby because she hadn't been around a man before, but he made such an effort to be slow and gentle around her that she eventually warmed up. After several months, they sent me a follow-up picture of kitty sitting on the back of the couch with the whole family in the room. She joined them of her own accord. They were all pleased to see the work paying off.

❀ *Fluffy baby playing in the kitten room before adoption.*

Here are some instructions on how to help a very shy kitty blossom in your home. The earlier on in the relationship you start these steps the better. If you have done the opposite of any of these suggestions in the past, it may take longer for kitty to begin to trust, but press forward and rebuild the bond.

Tips for shy cats:

- To develop a stronger relationship, enclose kitty in an area of the home where you spend a lot of time but that isn't too busy or loud. A master bedroom and bathroom area usually works well. Make sure this space provides for all of her needs including litterbox, food, water, beds, toys, elevation, and intentional hidey holes.

- Do your best to control hidey holes by creating them yourself. Have a clean and organized room and place a few cave beds or cardboard box "houses" around the room so she has darker, secluded spots to retreat to. Block off hard-to-reach places like under dressers or large beds.

- Have levels that lead up higher out of reach, especially if children or other pets ever come into this space.

- Build trust by going slowly and allowing kitty to dictate touch and interaction. Present yourself as willing to interact many times each day by getting down on her level with your body on the floor. Lay down or sit down. Make visual contact—slowly blink at her. The softening and blinking of the eyes tell her you pose no threat. You are neither a predator nor are you prey. Look and blink but never stare.

- Use a softer speaking voice with those softened eyes.

- Use treats and toys to lure kitty out of hiding. Never grab or reach for the kitty as this will create fear and distrust. If you offer your hand, lower it and extend a single finger (soft, not pointing). If kitty chooses to rub against your finger, this is a good sign. Praise gently and offer treats. This interaction needs to happen many times to build trust before you initiate any other touching. Reaching over the kitty's head to touch the body is not going to help unless kitty already trusts you. For now, let kitty dictate all touching.

- If you have kids, intentionally parent them in their interactions with the cat by helping them understand how to build a bond of trust. They need to know if they ever do anything to upset or scare kitty, they damage the trust.

- After you have established good touching and she feels safe with that, you can begin to put your hand under her as if to lift her up. Start slowly, allowing her to get used to it. Eventually lift off the floor an inch or two (from your seated on the floor position, not from towering over her). Set her back down immediately. Do this a few times. Give desirable treats and praise to help her associate this action with good things. Eventually you can lift her into your lap—she will likely run away immediately. That is okay. We want her to realize she has a say in this. Working toward more time in your lap or being held is the goal. Don't ever force it. Control is not trust. Kitty may or may not warm up to you holding her, but do your best not to make being picked up or held a scary thing.

- Playing with kitty builds trust and strengthens the bond. Never roughhouse, and only use toys as an extension of your hand and body. Offer treats at play time, just a few bites.

- It's a good idea to work on sound and activity desensitization with kitty in the smaller space. Do this by playing a TV or radio at low volume and slowly increase volume to a normal level. You can play sound effects on your phone or computer like blenders, vacuums, doorbells, children playing, and more. Start by playing softly. Give kitty treats for remaining calm or indifferent to the noises. You want to slowly build up the noises in the safe environment over time and give treats for staying calm as they get louder. If kitty runs and hides, back the volume down a few notches and slowly build it louder over the next few days or weeks. You want to build the volume threshold to the level the item would be in real life. This activity could take weeks or months, so don't go from volume one to volume ten in a single day.

- Eventually you open up the door to allow exploring. Offer praise and treats when she joins you in other areas of the home. Never push or force progress but embrace her timing and effort.

🐱 With a shy or scared cat, you always need to make an effort to slowly introduce new spaces, new noises, new people and not thrust it upon kitty. Do this with sounds and smells before any visuals. Take your time. For instance, if your young-adult brother is going to move into the home, ask him to record himself talking and laughing and to mail you a sweatshirt and t-shirt with his smell on them (unwashed). Use these tools to help kitty adjust in the weeks before your brother arrives.

OVERWEIGHT CATS

Social media glorifies overweight cats. "Chonky" cats seem funny in videos and memes, but the reality is not comical. Obese cats function at a lower level than normal cats. They cannot jump up anymore or groom themselves properly; they are more prone to litterbox concerns and at higher risk for chronic health complications like diabetes. Ideally, your cat would never get overweight, but commercially produced food (especially cheap kibble), living indoors, insufficient physical activity, and mental exertion combine for more cats becoming hefty.

There are many ways to prevent your cat from becoming overweight, and there are ways to help them lose weight. Let's go over prevention tips first.

🌸 *My parents' cat, Minnie at 9.5lbs in 2018. Minnie at 13.5lbs in 2024.*

Prevent Kitty from Getting Overweight

Body Types

Understand your cat's body type and healthy weight range. I have six cats, and one, Gigi, would be considered overweight, but she is not obese. Though Gigi would be healthier if she lost a pound, she functions normally as a cat and weighs in around 13 pounds with long legs and body. Trixie, with smaller bones and stature, weighs about 8 pounds. She is in perfect body-fat range. I have a male cat, Beaux, who looks overweight because of all his fluffy fur, but when shaved, he is pretty near perfect. He might lean toward "stocky" or "solid," but he isn't overweight. He has larger bones and a bigger build and typically weighs about 14 pounds. At 9.5 pounds, Prim is my only kitty underweight, not dramatically so, but about a pound too light. What is your cat's body type and ideal weight?

Body Shapes

Going by weight alone is not enough. How can you tell if *your* kitty is too heavy or too thin? You can reference great "Feline Body Condition Score" charts online. I recommend you look at the 9-scale versus the 5-scale because it's a bit clearer. On the 9-scale range, you are usually okay if kitty is a 4, 5, or 6. If kitty is truly underweight, you will want to slowly increase her overall caloric intake until she reaches a healthy weight and then maintain that caloric rate along with normal activity output.

Diet of the Small Wild Cat

The toughest part about keeping a cat fit is managing the right nutritional balance. Domestic cats are obligate carnivores, which means they survive on animal protein and fat and not carbohydrates. When prey is readily available, the small feline in the wild will hunt and eat on average 6-9 times a day. Their prey is usually small.

In the wild, a cat's diet consists of less than 8% carbohydrates. This comes from grass they may nibble on, or it comes from the stomach contents of the prey they eat. Commercial cat food diets, particularly dry foods, can contain high percentages of carbohydrates, as much as 50% carbs with lower quality brands. Cats are not meant to eat this high amount of carbs even if their bodies can technically digest them (cooked carbs that is). I will not call out brands of cat food to avoid and ones to use. However, I can teach you some basics in reading cat food labels.

Understand Pet Food Labels

Currently pet food nutrition labels list by percentages for both wet and dry food. Note at this time: **pet food companies are not required by law to list carbohydrates** on their labels. To get a true gauge of the protein, fat, carb, and ash content, first remove the percentage they dedicate to "moisture." Let's say a dry food label lists the moisture content at 10%. Start by subtracting that 10% from 100%, which would total 90%. Now look at the protein percentage which, let's say, is 30%. Divide the 30 by the 90 to get the actual percentage of protein in the food. In this case that would equal about 33%. Now let's look at fat. Say it's also 10% on the label. Divide 10 by 90 and get 11%. Now look at the ash (add up fiber, ash, and the list for phosphorus, phosphates, magnesium, calcium, and include these in the ash content). Let's say Crude Ash is listed 3% and no fiber is listed. Say the label lists 1% of phosphorus, .5% calcium, and

.5% magnesium. This totals 5%, so divide that by 90% and get 6%. Now add up protein (33), fat (11), and ash (6) to get 50. This means the bag of dry food consists of about 50% carbohydrates. If you feed your cat her entire allotment of calories for the day using this food, she is eating 50% carbs compared to the less than 8% carbs a day God intended your cat to eat.

Cat foods, dry in particular, are utilizing more and more plant proteins as protein sources in the food. Recall that cats need to derive protein from animals. Plant proteins and animal proteins are not identical and this can impact digestion and nutrient absorption in cats.

"Grain Free" labels have become more popular when buying commercial cat foods because of their association with carb content. Potatoes, however, are not a grain and pet food companies use them as fillers along with peas, garbanzo beans, and other starches, then label it "Grain Free." These are carbohydrates, too. Though perhaps slightly less harmful than rice, wheat, soybean, and corn for kitty, it is deceptive and another argument in favor of reading food labels.

In general, avoid any food that lists carbs in the first 3-5 ingredients. Especially avoid foods where carbs appear first or there are 3 or 4 listed in the first 5 ingredients. Avoid foods that tout chicken "meal" or other meat "meals" as the lone protein in the first 3-5 ingredients. "Meal" translates into all the bits (not really meat) that have been highly processed and turned into a flour of sorts—like beaks, feet, and cartilage. Avoid products with phosphates and carrageenan as much as possible because of health hazard concerns. Look for foods with true meat in them listed in the first 2-3 ingredients. Look for cat food where deboned chicken or any meat comes first on the ingredients label.

In our culture, pet "nutrition" derives less from science and more from profit and ease. Do your best to meet the ideal obligate carnivore criteria when choosing cat foods. Feeding a balanced and safe raw diet is the ideal for our cats but not always attainable, especially in large multi-cat homes. I cannot afford to provide this to my own clowder. Instead, I go for an all-wet-food diet with dry kibble as treats/snacks and freeze-dried raw protein as toppers. I choose higher-end brands of wet food (some are human-grade) and the dry food is 8%-25% carbs per one cup serving. Additionally, I mix in bone broth for more water content or human baby food to enhance protein in wet foods.

Something Fishy

Be savvy about how much fish you feed your kitty. The pet food industry usually uses as cheap a source of fish as the manufacturer can find, which likely means farm-raised on grains, or if from the ocean, possibly containing heavy metals like mercury from rising toxicity in ocean waters. Fish foods are often higher in fat, fats that older cats have a harder time digesting. The fish flavors often contain very high "ash," or phosphorus and calcium, because they use the fish bones as a "meal" in these foods. In general, feed fishy foods just a few times a week and try to get higher quality foods when choosing a fish flavor— flakes of real meat over pâté. If your cat has had urinary crystals, exercise even more caution about feeding fish flavors, particularly dry foods.

Variety = More Balanced Nutrition

Consider keeping a mix of food brands in your cat's diet. Sticking to one brand and one flavor really limits the nutritional variety for kitty, not to mention the flavor variety. I hear cat owners often say something like, "My cat only likes dry food, and she only likes this one brand, so that's what we feed her." Would you do the same for your child? Would you only ever feed her chicken nuggets, french fries, and white bread or would you do your best to sneak in other more nutritious options while your child grows and develops her palate? Feeding cheap dry food to your cat and nothing else is akin to feeding a human all junk food. Expect weight and health problems as the outcome. In a perfect world your cat should eat 55-70% real animal proteins, 25-35% healthy fats, 10% or less of carbohydrates, a bit of vitamins/minerals, and zero ash or "meat meal" byproducts.

Story Example: Cat With Kidney Complications

I recently consulted with a woman because of kitty's late-night vocalizing, but kitty was also losing weight. With this fact and many other red flags for illness, I recommended an immediate vet visit. In my appointment, I learned that for a long time the cat had eaten a single prescription brand wet-food, specific for urinary issues. In our conversation I tried to persuade the guardian to give the cat a bigger variety of brands of wet and a small amount of quality dry food (which the cat loved) to balance nutrition. The cat mom didn't seem interested. Regardless, I submitted extensive comparative research on nutrition for different brands of wet and dry foods in support of geriatric cats with urinary complications in my modification plan for the kitty. Indeed, the vet later diagnosed kitty with beginning kidney failure and wanted the guardian to switch to a different wet food, but same prescription brand. I asked her to please review the modification plan on dietary suggestions. When she did finally review, she thanked me multiple times for helping her understand. She started adding different brands (some that I recommended) into the cat's diet and kitty was not only enjoying some new options but gaining back a little bit of weight. While it didn't negate the kidney failure, kitty's levels were in some ways improved at the next blood workup.

Without talking brands or showing actual labels, this is what I presented to her:

- The veterinary-prescribed urinary diet wet food contained high levels of carbs at 30% (not good considering kitty received no other food), normal levels of fat at 22% (too much fat is not good for geriatric kitties with health difficulties), okay amounts of protein at 42%, and very low levels of ash at 3% (good for cats with urinary stress). Truthfully, this food alone is not a great diet for a cat.

- A wet food I recommended had 50% protein, 36% fat (high for geriatrics), about 12% carbs, but very low in ash at less than 1% per serving.

- Another wet food I recommended consisted of 67% protein, which is great, about 4% carbs which, is pretty perfect, low in fat at 11%, but higher average in ash at 17%.

- The last wet food I recommended was great for protein at 62%, low fat content at 15%, about 10% carbs, and average with ash content at 12%.

- I recommended a high-quality dry food comprised of 67% protein (good quality), 19% fat, 8% carbs, and 5% ash/fiber.

Feeding all five of these foods each week balances out nutrition when using commercial foods. Overall weekly kitty receives 58% protein, 21% fat, 13% carbs, and 8% ash.

Drinky Drinky

Water intake is important for keeping a cat healthy. In the wild, when eating prey, a cat's food contains about 70% moisture. This is partly why the domestic cat doesn't instinctively drink a lot of water. It's important go the extra mile to lure kitty into consuming more water. Here are some ideas for doing that:

- Feed wet food every day, at least twice a day.

- Add a bit of water to the wet food (2 tablespoons per can) to make it even wetter.

- Buy water fountains. I recommend ceramic or resin materials as they are least likely to add flavor to the water. Metals and plastics tend to "flavor" water more.

- Understand that in the wild, it's not healthy to drink water located next to dead prey. Instinctually, many cats prefer to drink water situated away from their food. So, place the fountain or bowl across the room from food bowls.

- Use a water bowl with a crystal gem pod. I recently ordered one. The stone energizes the water with its healing properties. Whereas my cats opted to drink from the running fountains over a still-water bowl, they now first choose the still-water bowl with the gemstones inside over the fountains.

- Keep a still-water dish someplace close to the bathroom or kitchen sink to easily remember to dump and freshen daily or even twice daily (if tap water is safe).

- Keep all water fresh. Change it out daily. For larger fountains, add fresh water each day and completely dump and refresh one to two times a week, cleaning out the filter.

- If kitty likes to drink from the sink directly, allow for that. Toilets...only if you keep it really clean and don't use those chemical tank cleaners. I do not allow toilet drinking in my own home because it's unsanitary.

❀ *Skippy loves all fountains for drinking and play.*

Story Example: Dehydrated Kitty

A veterinarian asked me to help a client whose kitty was struggling with a few issues. The kitty had litterbox concerns, panicked itchy attacks with rippling skin, severe dandruff, and would not groom herself. The cat's owner gave her a single brand of dry food—one of the cheaper brands. The food and water bowls were those plastic self-dispensers sitting side by side. I asked how frequently she refreshed the water in the container, and she said that since the cat hardly drank water, she almost never changed it. I suggested that the woman buy a ceramic fountain and place it across the room from the food bowl. I also told her, despite her insistence that the cat didn't like wet food, she needed to start getting more moisture into the cat via pushup type of wet food treats like Churu or by offering broths. I explained that the lack of hydration would or could be a contributing factor to the litterbox misses, dandruff, and the lack of self-grooming. The guardian implemented those water and diet changes quickly. She saw the kitty drink water for the first time and kitty devoured broth. Over a few weeks the dandruff decreased, and kitty started grooming. The rippling, itchy skin attacks likewise decreased. Her litterbox problems resolved themselves as well (potty setup needed adjustments too, which the guardian completed successfully).

What if Kitty is Already Overweight?

Maybe you like to indulge your furry friend with lots of treats, maybe kitty has eaten a low-quality diet for a long time, or maybe the cat's lifestyle has been overly stagnated.

Here are a few of the many reasons why you do not want your cat overweight:

- Weight encumbers kitty's lifestyle with not being able to run, jump, or play as well. Limited movement is especially a concern for kitty's longevity if going outdoors.

- Lowers immune function which leads to more frequent illness.

- Higher risk of diabetes, liver failure, kidney disease, heart disease, and high blood pressure.

- With extra weight, arthritis is more likely to present along with joint degeneration.

- Chances for urinary tract strain can increase with kidney stones, infections, and crystals.

- Litterbox concerns increase in probability from both the higher risk for urinary diseases as well as arthritic pain or increased awkwardness getting into or out of the box.

- Higher risk for bowel complications with constipation, which could lead to litterbox misses.

- Inability for kitty to groom themselves well, including the bottom area. You may see kitties rubbing dirty bums on the floor, fur may mat, and dandruff will increase.

- Should your kitty need urgent life-saving surgery, overweight cats run a higher risk of life-threatening reactions from anesthesia.

- On average the cat loses two years of her lifespan.

In a book like this, giving instruction for weight loss is essentially moot because each cat and her circumstance is unique. I suggest you work with a cat behavior expert with nutrition experience or a pet nutrition coach to create a good plan for you and your cat's individual circumstances. Before starting, verify the weight-loss plan with a vet, as they can help confirm the ideal body weight for kitty and the correct caloric needs, and most importantly perform a health check prior to starting a diet. However, I caution against going with a commercial *diet* cat food which the vet office often recommends. At least I strongly urge you to analyze the food content yourself before committing to a low-calorie cat food and make sure kitty receives quality nutrition from a variety of sources. As I stated in the case above, cats need quality protein, low-carb diets. You need help from the vet to figure out the correct caloric intake and feeding schedule, and then aim for that with your food choices and portions. Don't forget to factor in exercise. If you plan to increase activity as kitty starts to feel more up to it, make sure to let the vet know and compensate the calories as needed.

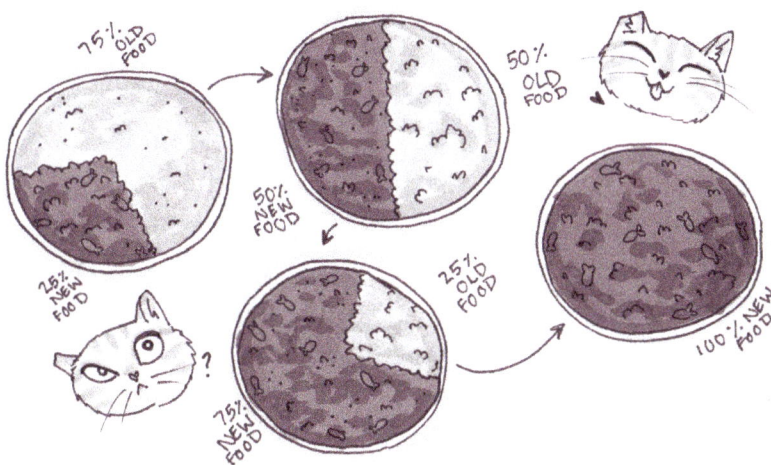

You can generally take weight loss for kitty slowly to help her not feel neglected as far as food goes. Ensure she has plenty of activity, enrichment, affection, and praise. Make sure all family members are on board with kitty's diet program. The program works better if a single person monitors and feeds kitty so as not to accidentally overfeed. If you are adding or changing foods to kitty's diet, don't give up if the cat rejects the food the first time you put it down. If she doesn't like it, you simply need to slowly incorporate it into the rotation by mixing it with food that kitty already likes. Here's a little chart to help:

Kitty will not love every food you offer, and if you repeatedly feed her the same one, even a yummy flavor, a cat may burn out on it. It's okay for you to feed not-so-favorite foods, especially healthier choices. As long as kitty eats the food, you are good. Do not leave wet food down for more than half a day. If you put it down in the morning and by evening the cat hasn't eaten it, throw it out. Dry food can stay down for a few days. Be sure that kitty gets enough overall calories.

Monitor kitty's weight on a regular basis. Because she likely only needs to lose a few pounds and human scales don't register small increments of weight loss very well, I suggest you buy a baby scale to keep tabs on kitty's progress.

DOOR-DASHING CATS

In the US, most rescues and some shelters require adopters to agree to keep their kitty indoors only. Interestingly, many rescues and shelters in the UK refuse to adopt to those who will not allow the kitty indoor-outdoor access.

There is always ongoing debate on safety versus quality of life/emotional wellness. Some argue that outdoor cats are destructive to the ecosystem because of their penchant for hunting birds, squirrels, and chipmunks (funny that these arguments rarely lament mice, rats, voles, or insects).

On page 269 we discuss deciding what is best for your cat—indoor only, indoor-outdoor, or outdoor only. I'll help you, if choosing to let kitty outdoors, do so as safely as possible.

When you have a cat desperate to get outdoors, and you don't want that, it can cause a great deal of worry. First of all, take some precautions for your door-dasher cat prior to beginning to train kitty. Some ideas include:

- Spay or neuter your cat. If a sexually intact cat has no mate in the home, no wonder she always tries to escape! Fix her, allow a few months for hormones to change in her body, and most likely your cat will stop trying to get out.

- Microchip kitty and provide a collar with your address and phone number on the tag. Just in case kitty gets caught on a fence or bush, purchase a breakaway collar, one that snaps open under pressure. You could invest in a GPS tracking collar, so if/when kitty gets out, you have an easier time locating her.

- Double up your exterior doors. For instance, if you come in through the garage, make sure the big car-entry door closes completely before entering the door to the house. Add a storm door or screen door to the front door. Not that it is easy, but you can squeeze into the one door and mostly shut it before opening the front door, closing the storm door quickly. However, these precautions become moot if your door-dasher kitty catches on to your tricks and makes her escape all the faster.

- Randomly select which doors you come in and out of every day. That way kitty doesn't know which door to wait by. Kitty is smart. She knows the daily schedule really well, and if you come home at 5-5:15 pm every day via the front door, she is there waiting at the door by 4:55 pm.

🐾 Before you leave the home, secure kitty in a section of the home that doesn't have access to an exterior door. Offer kitty all the bedrooms and bathrooms and put up a cat gate (like a baby gate but much taller) in the hallway. If you need to leave kitty for hours at a time, make sure this area of the home fulfills all her needs, like a litterbox, food, water, toys, activities, and bed.

Okay, How Do We Get Kitty to Stop Trying to Escape?

You can try several options to dramatically reduce the impulse. If kitty is already fixed, but desperate to get outdoors, she likely has a few reasons for that.

🐱 Kitty is super bored! She sorely needs something new to explore, to find something to hunt, or in general, to expend her energy.

🐱 The house is really chaotic with little kids or boisterous dogs, music or TV playing loudly all the time, or it is dirty and unorganized. The stress is too much, and kitty might crave alone, quiet time to decompress.

🐱 The litterbox is too dirty for kitty, and she may know that the great outdoors can provide unlimited "clean" places to go potty.

You ultimately need to decide what is best for your kitty in regard to accessing the outdoors. She may need more stimulation than you can provide indoors. You can certainly make life more interesting and diverse inside, but you have to actively work on keeping the indoors appealing. Yard fencing, catios (enclosed cat patio), and leash training are safer options for more outdoor time and you can train kitty to safely familiarize herself with the outdoors and then come home when called. (More on this on page 270.)

🐾 *Trixie in the front yard flower bed.*

If you want kitty to stay safely indoors, and I totally understand that desire because so many dangers lurk outside, let's talk about how to keep kitty from trying to dash out the door via environmental enrichment and training.

Environment

If kitty stays busier inside and expends more energy, she is far less likely to seek the outside. To accomplish this, guardians with door-dasher cats need to spend effort and possibly money to make the home environment more engaging and fun. Here are some ideas on how to upgrade your environment for a cat likely in need of more physical and mental stimulation. I keep explanations brief here because I will expand on them later in the book.

- Set up cat towers near windows for kitty to look outside. Allow kitty a view of the world. A place that gets sun at some point in the day is even nicer. (Note: If animals outside stress kitty, nix this plan.)

- Set up "Cat TV." I generally do not mean actual TV. Watching a screen for hours on end is bad for our brains, so it's not healthy for cat brains either. If you and kitty enjoy playing a game together on the tablet, for five minutes one or two times in the day, it won't hurt either of your brains. If your cat actually likes watching fish or birds on TV, then YouTube offers videos expressly for this purpose. Ideally what I mean by "Cat TV" is to set up some bird feeders near a window where kitty can easily view, or buy a real fish tank and fill it with fish. Ensure you have a secure lid on your tank.

- Stop free-feeding or using timed feeders and move to puzzle feeders for any dry food or dry treats. These puzzle toys, especially the more challenging ones, make the cat work for her food. This helps release both physical and mental stress.

- Create an upper-level playground near the ceiling for kitty with shelves, bridges, and boxes.

- Provide healthy greens inside for chewing on, like grass or catnip.

- Buy a cat exercise wheel. You will need to train kitty to use it, so if you merely set up and walk away, in all likelihood it won't get used.

- Make sure to have several planned play sessions with kitty during the day and evening. For an active indoor cat, you might need three 10-minute play sessions during the day. These need to be good hunting games where kitty can run, crouch, pounce, stalk, and attack prey.

- Have interactive toys for kitty, and swap them out daily with other toys. That way kitty doesn't become bored with the same old toys.

- Build a catio, large or small, for kitty to safely go outside.

Training

If you have enriched the environment and kitty still insists on running out the door, start clicker training and harness/leash training. Here we will touch on the concepts; on page 237 there is additional training details.

For clicker training, begin with the basics of loading the clicker with a high-value reward (usually a treat if food motivates kitty). Once kitty knows the click will produce a treat, move onto teaching kitty to target—following an object to a new location or touching the desired object. When kitty accomplishes the task, click and immediately reward. Your ultimate goal is to teach kitty to sit and stay several feet away from any exterior door. She needs to learn that sitting and waiting in her spot brings more reward than running out the door. You will also want to target train to "walk" leading kitty from one spot to another. As you clicker train, harness and leash train separately so that eventually the reward of sitting and waiting would be going out for a walk with you.

For harness and leash training, slowly desensitize kitty to wearing both. Start by placing the items down where kitty can see them. Reward kitty for sniffing them. Next briefly place the harness on kitty, starting with simply stepping into the harness leg holes. Then reward. You can utilize the clicker here if you'd like to reinforce the desired behavior. You click immediately when kitty has done what you wanted. Next allow kitty to wear the harness for just a few minutes, take off, and reward. Build up the length of time wearing the harness. If your kitty acts as though she cannot move while wearing the harness, get her to engage with a fun toy while wearing it. Help her to recognize that she can actually move around in the harness. Remove and treat. After kitty is comfortable walking around in the harness, next attach a short leash. Allow kitty to drag it around the house. Watch over this process and untangle the leash as needed. Remove and reward.

Build up the cat's time and tolerance with dragging the leash before you pick up the leash. Once kitty is well trained on these items, begin to explore outside while leashed. Kitty will likely not walk with you in a straight line. Allow her to explore in the yard with sniffing and rubbing her scent on things. Eventually, combined with your "sit," "stay," and "walk" clicker training, you will use the target to lead kitty to walk with you on the sidewalk in short increments. Remember to give rewards for accomplishing each task.

With all cat training, keep sessions short—no more than ten minutes at a time and typically one to three times a day. If training with treats, and doing so several sessions a day, be sure to consider reducing food amounts so that kitty doesn't gain weight. If you are not successful with training attempts, reach out to a feline trainer for help.

OTHER BEHAVIOR CONCERNS

Over Vocalizing

While this behavior can certainly cause frustration, potentially there is much to decipher to understand why the kitty is talking to you (or to the air) so intensely. First off, did you adopt or buy a breed of cat known for being talkative? Some breeds that are loquacious are Siamese, Bengal, Sphynx, Oriental, Japanese Bobtail, Burmese, and Maine Coons. But you do not need a full-bred kitty to get a chatty Kathy.

The "meow" is noted in scientific studies as a form of feline communication kittens use to get help and attention from their mother cat. Adult cats in the wild really don't "meow" to other cats. They communicate in purrs, chirps, trills, growls, hisses, and yowls. Dominantly they communicate in smells. So why do cats meow at us? Because they know we are the provider, just like a

🐾 *Foster kitten meowing at me.*

mother cat provides for her kittens. So secondly, is kitty seeking attention? Interestingly too, the cat meow and the infant human cry create a similar reaction in the human brain—to help and comfort.

Story Examples: Conversations with Cats

My cat Prim is cute for many reasons, but one of my favorites is that she meows in her sleep and wakes herself up with the talking. She then sits up and looks around for me, finds my eyes, and continues to tell me about her dream. I will talk back to her, and she meows her way over and sits in my lap to get petted.

Prim's biological sibling Gigi has become more of a talker as she ages. She is now twelve years; I worry how much she might talk at fifteen or sixteen. Gigi mostly talks when she "captures" some object in the house. She drags it around in her mouth, meowing and trilling. She will go on and on until I ask her about her catch. She then prances into the room with her spoils, drops it, and approaches me for petting and praise. I realize that I reinforce this behavior by my response.

Trixie has struggled with over vocalizing. Hers results more from separation anxiety. When alone or isolated in another room of the house, she will yowl and yowl—cry and cry. The funny part is, she isolates herself and then starts her loud monologue of woe. Trixie's vocalizing is the loudest and most worrisome. I try not to reinforce it while she is in the midst of yowling and crying. I wait for an interval of silence in each instance, randomly pausing a different amount of time before I call to her—sometimes forty seconds, sometimes ninety seconds, sometimes two minutes. If I call to her, she comes running to me and the vocalizing ends.

New vocalizing from your cat can result from medical reasons. If vocalizing is new and not a standard mode of operation for your kitty, I strongly urge a visit to the vet for a checkup.

As kitty ages, she may become more vocal or louder. This is associated with perils of aging like hearing loss or cognitive dysfunction like dementia. If this is happening, retraining won't help. Find patience and possibly make new arrangements for kitty within the home. If your geriatric cat wakes you up at 2 am every night by yowling loudly downstairs, she may feel lost, confused, or alone. A solution might be that she sleeps in someone's room at night with a closed door and all of her necessities like water, food, and litterbox. Having things close together and having a person she loves nearby will help a lot. Assuming you can sleep with her, that is. If you can't, contact a behavioral consultant to help you figure out a good plan for nighttime.

Some cats over vocalize at night, waking the household, simply because they are hungry and don't have any food around. Timed-release feeders often resolve this nighttime issue. There is no harm in having food access for kitty during the night. Assuming you *do not* have an overeater, free feeding food in bowls or puzzle feeders work well. Your late-night yowler might also be bored. Making life more interesting for kitty at night definitely has value! Place interactive or puzzle toys out before you go to bed, but remember to take them up in the morning, so they remain fresh and interesting.

Waking You Up During Sleep

This one makes me chuckle a bit. The Internet is awash in cat owners complaining about the cat waking them up when they are sleeping. It ranges from sitting on the person's head, making biscuits on the body, tapping the face with paws, sitting nearby and meowing, or nibbling ears.

In the wild, the cat's natural busy hours occur between dusk and dawn. It's a great time to hunt apparently. So, no surprise when cats want your attention (or food) at 4 am.

For me, this concern is a lot about setting healthy boundaries on the part of the human. I cannot sleep with all six of my cats! Oh, my goodness, I wouldn't get any sleep. I can only sleep with two of the cats—Gigi or Honey. The rest of the cats are too wiggly and annoying for this light sleeper. Sometimes Gigi gets the zoomies about an hour after we've gone to bed, and she refuses to leave the room. I can get super frustrated with that behavior because I can't fall asleep. However, most nights she is an excellent sleeping buddy. Honey is good for cuddling, though she has been known to touch my face when I snore to make me stop. She also wakes up around 5 am and wants me to let her out of the room. This usually works out for me as I have to get up about that time anyway to go to the bathroom.

What are your sleeping needs, your bathroom waking patterns? Are you a light sleeper or a heavy one? Figure out how to function with the cat in your room (or not) based on your sleep requirements. You cannot indefinitely sacrifice good sleep so the cat can cuddle you during the night.

With waking you early in the morning hours for food or for play, take the counsel from the last section and get a timed feeder, puzzle feeders, and interactive toys—all outside of your closed bedroom door. If you need help figuring out a customized plan at night for your household, reach out to a cat behavior expert.

Bum Scooting

This conduct is comical and also unhygienic. If you haven't seen this behavior before, look it up on YouTube. Plenty of videos show bum scooting.

Causes for bum scooting vary but here are the main reasons:

- Kitty is obese and unable to reach her bottom to clean it, so it gets dirty and itchy.

  Solution: Clean kitty's bum every day with a warm water washcloth and help kitty lose weight safely.

- The cat has impacted or infected anal glands.

  Solution: A vet visit to expel the impaction or to receive antibiotics, more water in the diet, nutrition adjustments, possibly some fiber like powdered psyllium for creating healthier stools.

- She is allergic to something in her diet, causing inflammation around anus.

  Solution: A vet visit can help you decide if the problem is centered on inflammation and from there eliminating certain foods from the diet to find the inflammatory food.

- Kitty has parasites in the bowels like tapeworms or round worms.

  Solution: A vet visit can diagnose a specific parasite from a stool sample, but you can deworm by following instructions from over-the-counter medications or supplements.

Some theories suggest that bum scooting could be about territorial marking, but there is no scientific proof of this. It would certainly leave a strong scent behind for other animals to "read," but most likely this is a behavior meant to communicate that kitty has a medical concern.

Frequent Barfing

The constant clean up factor can make this behavior frustrating. Sometimes the barf is unbelievably messy and other times not so bad. My cat Prim, who may be struggling with some health concerns in her old age, now projectile vomits. She often barfs when perched up high rather than on the floor like most cats prefer. I will find runny, drippy throw up on the windowsill, running down the wall behind my bed, on the bed headboard, and on the bedding. It can take over an hour, with laundry time, cleaning up.

A cat may barf for several reasons. Let's go over the most common:

- **Hairballs.** It is absolutely normal to have hairball barf. Grooming will create a buildup of fur which can gather anywhere in the digestive tract from the esophagus all the way out to the anus. Typically, hairball barf happens when a lump of fur is hanging out in the stomach or esophagus and must be expelled. Cats will sometimes eat something like grass to dislodge this lump of fur to then be able to push it out.

- **Overeating/Eating Too Fast.** This is fairly self-explanatory and can be all too common. Kitty is overly hungry and eats really fast and/or eats too much in a short space of time.

- **Nausea/Illness.** Vomiting is a symptom of many illnesses or toxicities. The marked difference is when kitty refuses food and is especially worrisome if the vomit occurs multiple times within a few hours. This timeframe, along with the lack of interest in food should help you recognize it as a symptom of illness. Moreover, the more the kitty throws up, the more the vomit will reach a bile stage.

🐾 **Regurgitation.** This happens frequently when kitty has eaten plant matter or if kitty eats a foreign or non-food item like string. It could also occur if the body rejects the food for some reason, e.g., an allergy to an ingredient.

Increase patience with barfing, as it is an inevitable reality of having a kitty. Please never scold kitty for this natural and uncontrollable action. In multi-cat homes you may get more than your fair share of regurgitated items and furballs. In my home, I tend to clean up the barfs on hard floors immediately. However, barf on carpet often cleans up easier if you let it dry out over several days. I place a paper towel over it to keep people from stepping in it. When dry, it picks up easily. Then vacuuming any leftover bits takes up the majority of the dirt. I can then go over it with my Bissell using the pet formula cleaner to remove any staining.

To prevent concerns with overeating or regurgitation, you can try a few approaches, like improving the quality of diet, feeding less dry food, and feeding much smaller more frequent meals. Utilize puzzle feeders or lick mats to help slow kitty down. Place food bowls further away from each other in multi-cat homes so that no kitty eats fast out of stress.

To help with hairballs, regularly brush kitty to remove excess fur, so she consumes less in grooming. You can give a regular small teaspoon+ dose of a good oil or fat like coconut, butter, or olive.

If throw up seems too frequent or worrisome or your instincts say something is wrong, take kitty to the vet.

Overgrooming

This behavior can prove a challenge to overcome. From the offset I will suggest that with this concern, it is always best to have a veterinarian, a veterinary dermatology specialist, *and* a feline behavior expert looking at the details of your situation and health of the cat to find the right solutions for kitty.

What is overgrooming? Overgrooming occurs when kitty spends so much time licking herself that she creates bald patches in the fur, sometimes even leading to the breaking, bleeding, and scabbing of the skin. Why would a cat do this? Any number of underlying factors or a combination of several at once can cause overgrooming. It can be difficult to pinpoint all of the causes.

For a long time this has predominantly been viewed as a stress behavior (and it is still certainly a valid option or very often a part of the equation when trying to diagnose the causes). However, newer data suggests that in 76% of cases, physical or medical factors create or contribute to the overgrooming behavior. Between parasitic, fungal, viral, and bacterial diseases, a wide range of possibilities can cause overgrooming. Still more possibilities crop up with allergies and inflammation of the skin. Pain from ailments like arthritis or kidney stress can be a factor.

It is extremely important to go to the vet. A general practice vet can help with ruling out more common issues like standard parasites or fungus. Bloodwork can tell if kitty suffers from kidney or other organ distress. Often the vet can diagnose pain from arthritis or other injury with x-rays and physical exams. The vet may give a steroid shot to see if that reduces or stops the overgrooming for a few weeks (inflammation indicator if it stops or reduces). If these are ruled out or if inflammation is confirmed, seek a veterinary dermatology specialist to continue the search among possible bacterial, viral, or allergy causes. I urge you not to just accept a "behavioral" or "stress" diagnosis from the regular vet and jump to medicating with an SSRI (selective serotonin reuptake inhibitors), a pharmaceutical drug, without further discussing with a specialist.

Although no confirmed studies back this information at this time, anecdotally, more cats seem to be developing food allergies, in particular to grains, which shouldn't surprise us given the high carbohydrate content in commercial cat foods when they have almost zero dietary requirements for carbs. Using a grain-based litter could contribute to overgrooming. Some vets diagnose protein allergies to specific meats like beef, chicken, or all poultry. A common practice to diagnosing these food allergies is the vet prescribing a hypoallergenic food. This is a controlled study and can help more quickly identify what kitty may be allergic to. It may behoove guardians to go this route for a time to identify what food is the cat's nemesis. It's always a good idea to seek second opinions from holistic veterinarians on allergies to expand your understanding and options.

Additionally, I have personally seen several cats in the last few years have negative reactions to vaccine boosters that then lead to neurological concerns like symptoms of feline hyperesthesia or personality shifts. These are not standard reactions, but possibilities to consider with overgrooming.

While you wait to discover potential medical factors, you can certainly address ways to reduce anxiety and create a more calming environment because in about 25-30% of cases of overgrooming, there is a stress component. Start by looking for triggers in the home by asking yourself: Are there inter-cat conflicts, even subtle ones? Has someone new moved in? Did the toddler start scaring kitty? Did I start a new schedule and am gone more or home more?

Once you have some ideas on these triggers, an objective party like a feline behavior professional can help you reduce the intensity of those cues for kitty.

Grooming is a natural and necessary habit. ***Overgrooming is not.*** Whatever retraining you begin, make sure to work with a professional so that you do not accidentally reinforce the unhealthy behavior nor hinder or scare kitty from normal grooming needs. Remember, while overgrooming very often has a medical component, it might only be a stress response. Show compassion toward kitty as you both work through this.

With stress, incorporating alternative healing tools can support feeling better, like crystals, energy work, prayer, healing frequencies and more.

Be cautious about adopting a "compulsive" label for this behavior as that can seem impossible to reverse. It is rare to deal with a strictly compulsive behavior. What makes it compulsive? It has become so ingrained in kitty that no triggers cause the behavior; it just happens. In the majority of cases, definite physical or emotional triggers lead to the action.

Pushing Items onto Floor

The Internet sports so many humorous videos showing cats knocking items off of tables, counters, and shelves. I often watch them on mute, though, as so many cat owners swear at their cats when they do this (while videoing the behavior), and I get sad for cats when they are called ugly words or yelled at.

Cats, especially young cats, are energetic creatures, and often homes do not provide enough exploration, activity, engagement, or exercise to expend the energy appropriately. This behavior of pushing a glass of milk or a vase of flowers onto the floor is boredom rearing its head.

As related in many areas of this book, environmental enrichment can reduce this behavior. This includes having regular, scheduled playtime with kitty several times a day, offering kitty interactive toys, puzzle feeders, "Cat TV," more places to climb appropriately in the home, good scratching posts, and safe time outdoors on a catio or a leashed walk.

When you have a cat, consider "cat-proofing" to protect your valuables. Don't place an expensive crystal vase, a breakable family heirloom, or a fancy porcelain statue in a spot kitty can get at. Put up items you don't want harmed on accident by a bored or adventurous kitty. Develop your patience and love for kitty to help you refrain from anger when something does get broken or damaged from her play.

Potted plants are often a temptation for cats and fall into this category. Though kitty breaking ceramic containers certainly presents problems, other troubles with plants prove more worrisome. Please be sure to not grow deadly plants with cats in the home. They could chew on them. I speak a lot more on toxic plants on page 261. You can find tips and tricks online to help you protect your plants from kitties, but they don't always work—like placing forks in the soil or tinfoil around the plant. The safest route is to create shelving up high for your plants that kitty can't get to. If your cat has access to your plants, and is not an indoor-outdoor cat, expect that she will dig in them, chew them, knock them over, and possibly even go potty in your large pots. Please don't get angry at kitty! While annoying to us, it is an expression of normal cat curiosity.

I find indoor-outdoor cats often leave indoor plants alone. The constant access to plants and dirt outside makes potted plants in the home less novel. Don't toss kitty outside willy-nilly to save your plants! There is much to consider when letting kitty outdoors (page 269), and I hope you value the life of the cat more than plants. Try adding a kitty specific garden made up of plants like grass and catnip. You can provide safe plants for kitty on the catio or screened porch. These "yes" items will help in deterring them from the other plants indoors you want left alone. If you are an avid indoor gardener and have yet to find a positive way to safely keep kitty out of the plants, work with a behavioral consultant on training techniques.

SPIRITUALLY SPEAKING:
HOW TO BUILD CONFIDENCE & SAFETY

When kitties struggle with boredom, shyness, or quirky and annoying habits, we can struggle with how to best provide for their needs. The contents of this chapter up to this point have predominantly covered practical, scientific, physical ways to address the concerns. What more can you do though to improve the situation? What can you do to help yourself maintain or gain patience with kitty?

🐾 **Emotional Support for Kitty.** Try to see conditions from the cat's perspective. Try not to anthropomorphize (projecting your thoughts and feelings onto kitty) but instead understand why a cat might act that way. Cats get bored, stressed, lonely, scared, hurt, or sick which can lead to any of these types of behaviors we've discussed. Do not leap to "the cat is mad at me" or "the cat is getting revenge" or "the cat is being a jerk." This is simply not true. I've heard from owners, "The cat is so getting back at me for not giving him his treats. He looked right at me as he peed on the floor." They think this eye contact proves defiance or revenge. It does *not*. It is about communication and asking for help.

🐾 **Prayer.** Communicating with the Heavens, with God, is the best way to get direction, especially if you have figured out how you most clearly receive guidance. In these types of situations, you can pray for understanding or seeing the triggers leading to behaviors. You can pray for help to have more patience. Pray for the needed money to seek help and care for kitty.

🐾 **Angelic Help.** Speak to the Angels around you. Ask for their help in caring for kitty, to watch over her as needed. Ask for a healing Angel or a cat-expert-Angel to help bring to your mind ideas for addressing kitty's challenges. Ask to have the needed tools or person to cross your path—whether in real life or online. Answers might come as an email offering services or a video or book that appears in your social media feed. Angels can send these to us.

- **Crystals for Kitty.** Look for the right crystals to support the needs of the cat. With such a variety of topics covered in this chapter, trying to list the crystals for each would expand beyond the scope of this book, but in general some of the best crystals for any ailment are clear quartz, selenite, rose quartz, moonstone, black tourmaline, citrine, and amethyst.

- **Supplements for Kitty.** Try stress-reducing supplements like flower essences or tools like FFPs especially in the instances of overgrooming, door-dashing, vocalizing, shyness, and chewing. Nutritional supplements may also help kitty to heal (consult with holistic vet).

- **Energy Work.** I always advocate the tool of energy work to help in cases involving stress, illness, and fear. Removing the trapped energetic baggage clears the way for more successful and lasting healing from a concern.

PURRRITO WRAP UP

Your cat may display her stress in many ways. From over vocalizing, overeating, door-dashing, overgrooming, and more, she is merely expressing that she needs your help to feel safer, healthier, and engaged. You now have numerous tools and ideas to help resolve the concerns. If for any reason you struggle to find the right solutions for your cat and situation, reach out to a feline behavioral expert. One of the joys of cats is their unique personalities and quirks, so find the humor and endearment in your circumstance with your feline friend to help you remain grounded and hopeful.

In the last three chapters we have reviewed the most common behavioral concerns for cats. I hope you feel empowered and enlightened on both the physical and mental care of cats as well as emotional and spiritual care. Once you have gotten a head start on solving behavioral concerns and feeling more love for kitty, dive into creating a truly special bond with her in the next section of this book.

PART 3

Cat-Life Purrrfection

❀ Honey
using a
puzzle feeder
to get a snack.

CHAPTER 8

Creating a Loving Bond

Okay, we've gone over how to reflect on ourselves and begin to change. We've also completed the chapters on understanding a struggling kitty when he has behavioral concerns. When we modify how we provide for and interact with our cat, kitty will most likely forgive, adapt to the new arrangements, and transform into a better pet.

No relationship is ever consistently perfect. When I have done something that scared or annoyed my cats, like clipping their claws or accidentally stepping on them, they flee from me, very upset. Still, within a few minutes they return to my side and seek my love. They either forgot the little unpleasantness quickly or forgave easily. They recognize that ultimately they can trust me. In the first chapter, I explained the acronym **BOND**. Everything you need in kitty-care boils down to "**B**e **O**bservant, **N**urturing, **D**edicated." When you are intentional in your awareness of the cat each day, you offer love, compassion, respect and freedom, and when you are reliable and loyal, a bond will inevitably form.

If our cat has learned in the past to expect truly negative behaviors from us, like corporal punishments, the changes he needs to make in order to trust again will be much slower. Kitty's long-term memory has held onto those incidents of past harms because it threatened his very survival. We need to remain patient with both kitty and ourselves throughout this journey.

Change is possible. For clarity, the goal here is not to be "perfect" but to work toward becoming "purrrfect." Life often repeats negative situations or circumstances, likely because God hopes we will learn to see the circumstance differently and grow. Kitties can really help us in this progress, repeating unwanted behavior until we learn to address their needs with compassion, hope, positivity, and grace.

Story Example: Repeated Experiences Until We Change

I make mistakes daily in my life and sometimes still with my cats. But I can recognize my progress by the caliber of mistakes I make and how I respond to them. Here's a super quick, non-cat example from my own life to help illustrate what I mean. Police have pulled me over for speeding more than a dozen times in my life. My stomach always dropped, feelings of defensiveness and justification arose, I'd get angry at the cops for their "ego-driven" behavior, and I'd bemoan the ticket and fear the amount. About two years into doing consistent energy work, I got pulled over for speeding. When the flashing lights popped on behind me, I had been singing a happy song. I glanced down at the speedometer, giggled, and said, "Whoops!" I didn't feel any anxiety or fear. I felt light, protected, and open to the experience. When the cop walked away from my window, I called out in genuine care for him to be safe that day. What a dramatic shift in mindset for me! And you know what? He let me off with a warning that day, and I haven't seen any flashing lights in my rearview since then. That was eight years ago. Sometimes the Universe provides the same type of experiences over and over until we learn to see it differently and can react differently.

I have mentioned energy healing throughout this book. Now is truly the time to pursue that for yourself and for your cat. Using one or more of these varied tools can lighten much of life's burdens. Once the weight begins to lift, we see more clearly what else we can do to become even healthier. Healing through energy work allows us to connect to God, Angels, and Spirit more readily, which then leads to easier love and connection with kitty. We appreciate that we have limits and begin to utilize healthy boundaries. We become far more tolerant of our cat because we better accept ourselves.

Our healing tends to come in waves, or maybe better stated, like a roller coaster with ups and downs. The longer and more we maintain higher ground before dipping, the better. We want to ultimately witness, as we look back, that we backslide either a shorter duration or not as deeply and that we keep climbing higher each time we rise. And with enough healing that we *do* rise, again and again.

As we grow and change, so will our kitties. Cats are emotionally and spiritually sensitive and will absorb our improved vibrations and emotions. Like us, kitty will grow and move forward (and likewise have possible backslides) on this journey of changing.

❀ *Life's ups and downs.*
Keep reaching for the next
highest point of spiritual health.

Now that we are in a good mindset to do so, let's get into how to create that loving and healthy bond with our feline friends. This plan covers the physical, emotional, and mental needs of the cat. As a heads up, we will discuss spiritual ideas for kitty's best life and greatest bonding with you at the end of the next chapter, *Going the Extra Mile.*

STABILITY & PREDICTABILITY

Cats love a predictable life. Predictability equals safety for cats and if yours feels safe, his trust in you increases. He will be calmer and more loving. An easy way to provide predictability is feeding, playing, and scooping the box at the same relative times every day. Life doesn't need the strictness of a train schedule, but if you are, say, someone who lives in flux a lot, and you have a cat, it's important to compromise by offering him regularity in his daily life. Create daily anchors that he can rely upon—like when you wake up or go to bed.

Meeting the cat's daily physical needs creates solid predictability for kitty. He is relying on you. If the cat feels secure by having plenty to eat and drink, peaceful sleep, exercise and activity, and a clean, safe potty, then he will have far fewer behavioral concerns. Like humans, if basic physical needs are not met, cats will become very stressed. Ticking this one off the list should prove pretty easy.

Recapping from instruction given throughout the book, the basics include:

- **Food**—feed several times a day. Each cat is different, but generally they need food more than twice a day. Put down wet food at about the same time each morning, afternoon, and again in the evening. Additionally, offer dry food in small amounts once or twice a day in bowls or puzzle feeders. If you work during the day, you could put out a time-release feeder.

- **Water**—keep water fresh and bowls clean. Get a drinking fountain. Place water away from feeding stations because kitty will more likely partake this way.

- **Sleep**—allow kitty several great sleeping options throughout the house. Kitty beds, heating pads, sunny spots, igloo beds, and your bed are all great options. Try not to disrupt kitty's sleep very often, especially avoiding sudden loud noises like turning on the vacuum in the same room when they are in a deep slumber.

- **Activity**—bored kitties can struggle, so keep life stimulating. Offer cat trees, perches, catios, toys, interactive play time with you, bird watching, and more. You can rotate a collection of toys in and out to keep them more interesting.

❀ *Playing with Beaux.*

🐱 **Potty**—to keep kitty happy, meeting this need is a must. Scoop the litterbox daily, make sure the cat likes the shape and style of box, use litter that kitty prefers, clean it our every few weeks, and make certain the location feels safe. Provide enough litterboxes; one for each cat plus an extra and at least one on each level of the home.

When changes happen in the cat's life like rearranging furniture, moving homes, or a fellow cat mate passing away, likely kitty will be out of sorts for a few days or weeks until he can adjust and feel safe again.

Create emotional stability for kitty. He needs to know you will be there for him and love him no matter what. Kitties can struggle with separation anxiety, so communicate with him about your plans. For example, if you go on a long trip, tell him about it. Find the best possible care for your cat and when you return home, take time to reestablish a routine along with a loving and safe connection. Be patient with kitty if he developed any negative behaviors from his stress over not seeing you for so long.

Most cats do not do well with changes, new people, or new environments because they value predictability. **Cats must have time and space to acclimate to new situations.** You can help them by remaining patient and taking time to introduce them to new changes, persons, pets, or environments slowly and purposefully. If you have guests over for the weekend and the cat hides, don't get worried or think that kitty is angry at you. Kitty has no need to socialize with the newcomers who stay briefly. Bonding to you is the goal, not creating a fearless super-cat.

UNDERSTANDING & COMPASSION

Cats have spirits. They have minds. They have feelings. **When you show understanding and compassion toward them** in everyday ways, they recognize this. When my cats accidentally fall, miss a jump, or do something clumsy, I don't usually laugh at them, and I never mock them. I ask them if they are okay with a sympathetic voice. Cats know when people ridicule or mock them—they may not understand the words exactly but know the tone and intent. They are sensitive creatures, so be kind.

When my cats show signs of throwing up, I don't fuss at them. I offer supportive words like "I'm so sorry you have to barf" or "Are you okay?" Am I bummed that I have to clean up yet another vomit? Yes. Absolutely. However, taking it out on them is moot. Would I yell at a human if they had to throw up? No. Instead, I do what I can to reduce barfing frequency by how I care for kitty (page 200).

If you must disturb a sleeping cat for some reason, speak with a soft voice shifting him out of the spot. Try not to startle the cat with loud, unexpected (to him) noises, like blaring music suddenly, vacuuming in the room he was asleep in, or flipping on the garbage disposal while he sits at your feet in the kitchen. If you do have to make noise, forewarn him. I often tell my cats, "Okay, I'm turning on the vacuum now," and I stand next to the machine for a few moments, giving them time to dash away if they choose.

Increase your understanding by learning the wild side of your cat's nature. **Knowing his innate biology will shift your perceptions of cats and can greatly impact your expectations of him in your home.** Jackson Galaxy does a great job in his book, Total Cat Mojo, with describing the "raw cat" and his needs. Essentially, you don't want to "uncat" your cat, but instead, heighten his raw cat. Toilet training cats is one way humans try to "uncat" cats.

What are some ways to appreciate the cat? Well, for starters, don't hate the claws. Claws are vital to cats. Having intact claws helps them with balance, agility, confidence, power, safety and territorial marking. Support the cat by keeping claws trimmed, offering great scratching surfaces, and not encouraging play where kitty uses claws against you.

Another example of appreciating cat biology would be understanding his senses. Knowing about the feline strengths and limits will help you better care for him. Consider the cat's eye—his eyesight is vastly different from our own. He has a wider peripheral view. He has far fewer cones and more rods than human eyes, which means he cannot interpret color like we can. He sees in blues, yellows, and grays. On the other hand, he has far superior vision in low light or darkness because he has more rods. How might this impact your life with kitty? Understanding that he can't see red tones or colors mixed with red, like purples, might impact your toy choices. It may help you realize that red food dyes in some dry cat foods are meant to appeal to you and not to kitty (and these artificial colorings are not healthy to consume).

🐾 *These images, created by Nickolay Lamm, illustrate how cats likely view the world.*

The cat's hearing range is different from our own in that we can hear tonal pitches in a slightly lower range than cats, and they hear tonal pitches we cannot in a much higher range, better for hunting bugs and mice. Their hearing is more sensitive than our own, hearing sounds softer in volume. This is how they know someone is approaching and dash away from the front door ten seconds before someone rings it. Because of their higher-range hearing, having sonic pest control in your home will likely bother the cat.

The feline's sense of smell resembles a dog's rather than ours. Though not quite as powerful as a dog's nose at 300 million scent receptors, a cat has 200 million receptors compared to the 5 million of a human. This is why cat experts plead with owners to not use perfumed litters, candles, and chemical diffusers in their homes, most especially near the cat's litterbox.

RESPECT

Show respect by showing restraint. Kitties really appreciate the freedom to set the terms and boundaries with regard to petting, touching, holding, picking up, and carrying. This is especially important at the beginning of your relationship. Let kitty come to you. Here is where children frequently mess up, creating aloof cats from too much unwanted handling. Building trust at the start, by containing your affections, opens the door to more genuine affection down the road.

When you speak to your cat **use a soft, kind, and respectful voice.** Some cat experts object to using a "baby talk" tone with cats. I wonder if they view it as degrading? As a way of talking down to the cat? I don't view it this way, nor do I think or feel like this when I use a gentle voice with my cats. You can use your real voice to speak to your cat, but keep the tone one of kindness. I have witnessed many rescue workers, frankly, a bit hardened by life's trials, use voices full of anger or impatience with the animals. It's disheartening to watch. Yelling or swearing never helps when addressing animals. This simply puts them further on edge and doesn't resolve the concern at all. It is not healthy to intimidate animals (or people for that matter) with harsh language. It's a harmful form of control that ultimately reflects a person's own fear and low self-worth. Kitties value being shown respect by the way people speak to them, the tone of voice, and the choice of words.

Felines are quirky and humorous beings to have in your life. **Enjoy the laughter that comes from observing your cat's funny antics.** Cats really like bringing laughter into our lives because one of their spiritual roles is to help us be happy. Mutually enjoying each other's company is a sign of respect.

Story Example: Funny Games

My cat Gigi and I had the funniest game the other night. I stood on one side of the bed, and she was on the opposite side on the floor. Using a wand toy, I tossed it slightly over the edge of the bed and dragged it back toward me. This wild-eyed, ears-askew cat face kept popping up over the mattress with paws whacking intensely at the attached fish, over and over for a good eight minutes. The whole time, I chuckled to myself, charmed by how adorable and silly she was being. It lightened my heart on a tough day.

A word of caution: if you laugh really hard *at* the cat and the cat in that moment is hurt, embarrassed, or scared, this doesn't build comradery between you. Laughter should be mutually shared in a positive or surprising experience and not at the expense of the other.

Pay attention to his physical body and wellness as a way of showing kitty your respect. Monitor how much he eats or does not eat, the amount of water he drinks (too much or not enough), has he peed today or not, is his poop healthy or does he have runny diarrhea? Your cat cannot verbally tell you he feels sick and tends to hide illness well. Don't let symptoms like goopy eyes, pus from a wound, sneezes, coughs, intense personal scratching, or reduced appetite go untreated. When petting kitty, develop as much trust as you can to regularly go over every part of his body and look and feel for any abnormalities. He may have a tick, a skin rash, wound, or a cancerous growth, and the earlier you discover it, the better. One big sign of a sick kitty is hiding. If you usually see him around and suddenly he just wants to sleep in the back of the closet all day, he is likely very ill. Take kitty to the veterinarian as soon as possible when sick as well as keep annual wellness checkups.

Lastly, respect the cat's will. When holding your furry friend, if he wants to get down, immediately allow it. If you see that kitty becomes annoyed or overstimulated by something you are doing, stop. Children and young men really struggle the most with respecting boundaries with cats, thinking they are bonding by roughhousing or manhandling. Overall, forcing a cat to do something they don't want to (except for their highest good, like taking medicine) shows a lack of respect. Another way people push their will onto a kitty is forcefully wanting an "adventure cat," but, because they are creatures of habit and put a premium on personal safety, most cats do *not* want to go adventuring. Yes, you can create an adventure cat buddy, but many cats or kittens will resist this pressure and become very stressed. I talk more about this on page 238.

RELAXED & BALANCED

Okay, this one I had to relax into. **Don't get upset at the cat for making your home dirty.** This may not be an issue for folks who have different priorities than a spotless house, which makes "relaxed" an easier part of being "purrrfect" for them. Other people love a clean home. For me with six cats, it's not possible to live in a truly clean home, as much as I try. Countless times, I will get done cleaning up one cat mess and boom, they leave another one. For instance, I have a blanket on the foot of my bed that Beaux has recently claimed as his prime barfing zone. Luckily, it is easily washed, but some weeks I wash it three times. I have literally just finished spreading it back on the bed and within a few minutes—barf! At those times, I have to think about the positive to stay relaxed—at least he didn't barf on the sheets.

With messes, it doesn't help to yell, clap hands, scold, hit, spritz water, and certainly never rub a cat's face in it. That's all pointless and some is abusive. This is where relaxing comes into play. **Getting upset at kitty frequently strains your bond.** However, you do not need to give up and live in a pigsty. Cats, too, like a clean home. Only sadly, they can't help with chores! Keep patient with kitties as you clean up barfs, pick up hair wads, trim pulled threads from furniture, wipe up poop smears, and more. Now, certainly if kitty has going-outside-the-box concerns, spraying concerns, and intense scratching of furniture, work on resolving the causes of stress for kitty and refocus them through reward training to behavior you appreciate.

Cat owners should not allow their homes to become filthy and smelly. Good guardians need to keep a balance between clean and relaxed. I have seen cats pulled from truly grotesque homes, and the poor babes are so relieved to be groomed, have their nails trimmed, go to the vet for medical issues, get ear mites or fleas treated, and finally have a clean litterbox. Again, cats like clean homes, and they deserve help from you in keeping themselves clean and healthy.

Another aspect to try to **relax around is property destruction.** I'm not recommending that you should live in a zero-controlled environment where the cats can do whatever they want and ruin all of your belongings. What I hope to relay is that getting stressed or uptight in general if furniture gets a bit scratched up, loops of carpet get pulled up, or a vase shatters isn't healthy for the overall bond. You have many methods to help train kitty and curb any destructive behaviors as I wrote about in Chapter 7. Here, I am encouraging overall balance. Embrace some Zen qualities the next time kitty starts digging in the plant. Distract him with a fun game of birdie-flying-on-string instead of yelling.

❀ *Getting in the Zen Zone.*

Lastly, another area people might need to relax into are inter-cat relationships or the cat's relationship with other species of pets in the home. When a quarrel begins to unfold with a hiss or a growl, **be the calming force.** Use a sweet, kind voice and stand in between or nearby the "arguing" cats. I typically say, "It's okay. Everyone is okay. Let's be nice to each other. Be nice." Over time, the cats learned my expectations in those moments. Now they defuse and walk away.

POSITIVE REINFORCEMENT

Use a lot of positive rewards to reinforce the behaviors you like. If the cat does something you like, in that very moment praise him with "good boy!" When you walk by the cat and he is watching you, tell him that you love him, or tell him that you think he is cute. Use petting or affectionate touches to reward and reinforce your verbal affirmations. Give out treats in the instant your cat does something sweet like head bonk you. Or give them out when kitty scratches on his post along with a verbal "good job" or "thank you."

Using these happy and loving rewards will take you a long way in your bonding, most especially if you avoid any yelling, scolding, or other types of aggression. Cats are trainable but a bit different from dogs in that they aren't looking to please you by obeying. However, **they want to feel good and loved, which motivates them to repeat actions that result in any type of reward** and lessen actions that get them ignored.

❀ *Rewarding Beaux with a yummy treat. (Photo credit Rachel Beecher)*

SPACE & FREEDOM

Allow the cat a lot of space and freedom in the home, as cats need a good-sized territory and a sense of belonging. Designating one room or solely the basement area or something along these lines is not healthy for kitty and will not result in strong bonding. Cats need to own their space, know it well, and feel secure in it. Kitty's confidence declines typically when left alone a lot or isolated away from their people. If

❀ *One of my foster kittens with a broken leg needs confinement for healing.*

you have aggression distress between animals in your care, then divide spaces merely as a temporary solution while you work to resolve the stress between them via a reintroduction.

Circumstances may arise where kitty needs temporary confinement to a small area of the home. If ill, wounded, needing short-term separation during a slow introduction or reintroduction, a taming process, throughout a move, or while fostering then it's best to confine kitty for the process. **Do not crate a cat on a regular basis as you would a dog.** Do not plan to live long-term with kitty only having access to a single room in the home. This confinement harms his inherently curious nature and love of play.

Side Note: "The Cat Room"

Having a designated "cat room" with *all* the cat stuff in it is not a good idea for your forever cats. Unless *you* spend the bulk of your own time in that room, don't expect them to remain in it or even use the items placed there. A multi-cat environment where all the resources are in one location will likely create tensions and a few cats may bully others away from resources like litterboxes or food bowls. A single cat space like this *is* ideal for foster cats or kittens who merely stay for a few months, as it's generally best not to let fosters free roam with your other pets.

Next on the list of freedom: make sure to **welcome kitty to be near you.** Greet him with love and attention when you come and go or when he comes and goes. For example, when one of my cats walks into the room I say, "Hi baby!" If kitty reaches out to you by placing his paw on you, stroke him and softly blink. If he talks to you, talk back to him. If he jumps up to be with you, be gracious about it. If you are busy and can't hold him, create a space nearby where he may remain close but not on you. If you work from home, place a shallow box with a towel in it near your computer (a heating pad amps up the allure). Place a cozy blanket next to your body on the couch. If you have to reject his desire for attention, do so with kindness.

ENRICHMENT

When cat behavioral consultants talk about enrichment, they want guardians to bolster the cat items in the environment as well as the time spent to help kitty stay engaged and active. **Play with kitty every day and offer new opportunities to explore as often as you can.** Indoor cats especially need you to play interactive hunting games. Cat professionals call it "the prey sequence." Use a toy as an extension of your body and manipulate that like an object of prey for the cat—a mouse, snake, bird, insect, or fly. (Remember, never offer your hands or feet as "prey".) Let him stalk, chase, pounce, bite the toy as many times as he wants for about ten minutes a few times a day.

Individual playtime is ideal, because not all cats (especially young ones) are good about taking turns. In the wild, cats hunt alone, not in groups. Some cats are good at taking turns, but if you have one that won't, play with him first and then place him in another room and close the door. Give him treats and make sure the room doesn't feel like a punishment. Then you can go back and play with the others.

Offer additional toys that are interactive via battery operation or toss around simple toys like soft mice or jingle balls to roll around. Pick up and swap out toys each night. Having a variety of toys to rotate in and out helps them to not become boring.

A strategy I learned, in regard to catnip toys, is to let them "marinate" in the herb. Get a secure lidded box and scatter loose-leaf catnip inside. Then place your catnip plushies in here. Occasionally add fresh, loose catnip. I use a decorative cardboard box with a latch lock. It stays under the coffee table, and every now and then I **invite all the cats to a "catnip party."** I have enough soft toys for each cat. I love watching them roll around and get a bit loopy over the catnip! I stay to monitor as catnip can create aggression in some cats, and I have a few like that. So, I police the party and watch out for any warning signs like growls or swats. After the party is over, return the toys to the box for more marinating.

As far as offering new items to explore, you don't need to go into debt to do this. You can accumulate them over time and swap them in and out of use. You can DIY (Do It Yourself) toys, forts, beds, cat trees as well, keeping costs low. Just ensure that whatever you make is safe for kitty. Honestly, simply allowing the cats access for one or two days to that newly unpacked Amazon box is great fun. You can add a new item of cat furniture every now and then and that helps kitty, too. These **creature comforts** make him feel like he really belongs in the home with you.

❀ *A catnip party.*

These items, like cat trees, window perches, igloo beds, tunnels, heating pads, wall shelves, sky bridges, catios, and more, help the cat stay engaged and happy indoors. Don't make the mistake of hiding the cat toys in far unseen corners and in dark basements. Kitty won't use it very much. Remember, a happy cat is a social cat, and he will want to relax in the rooms and places where you hang out. **I have cat décor and resources scattered in every room** of my home. In my master bedroom/bath I have two cat trees, a litterbox, a food station, a water station, a heating pad that is always on, a horizontal scratcher, a cat bed under my bed, and a cat tunnel. I spend a lot of time in this space; hence the cats

❀ *Honey finds joy in her new "canopy bed" AKA water bottle wrappings.*

do, too. I have a big cat tree, small hammock, cardboard kitty couch, horizontal scratcher, and cat fountain in my living room. The den has a puzzle feeder, two cat beds, a heating pad that is always on, a deep window ledge for cat rumps that I had installed when I remodeled, and a cat tree. Eight months of the year the big back deck, safe for kitties, has two sleeping baskets, a fountain, fresh herb plants and grass to munch on, lots of bird watching, and bug hunting. The cats have feeding and water stations in the kitchen and dining areas and other litterboxes throughout the home.

Now, that all may sound like a lot to some or not enough to others, but, in general, provide cat paraphernalia in proportion to the number of cats. We shouldn't have one cat tree and four cats, but we could have one cat and four trees.

The main point with enrichment is to **keep kitty happy, active, curious, thinking, alert, exploring, and safe while doing it.** Bored cats often become overweight and sometimes the monotony leads to behavioral concerns.

AFFECTION

Show your cat a lot of **gentle physical affection**. Now, if the cat won't allow you to touch him right now because the bond of trust is non-existent for him, give it time and let him lead the pace. Simply be in the room with him doing quiet activities until he shows an interest in approaching you. When that begins to happen, gently offer the relaxed single finger I previously talked about (page 131) and let him choose to come forward and rub against you. Offer verbal praise or food treats for showing an interest in being touched by you. Slowly work into giving short and kind strokes around the face. Take plenty of time and be patient. Pushing or rushing doesn't create trust.

If you can pet kitty, **watch his responses via body language.** Does he appreciate the way you touch him? I have seen some rough petting sessions from people to their cat, and the cat's ears are back and his tail flips around in frustration. The kitty clearly does not like it. Even if the cat doesn't claw or bite you, you can tell if he *is* or *is not* enjoying the touch. Does he lean into it or pull back from it? Is he purring or silent? Does he slowly blink his eyes at you or stare intimidatingly?

For the most part, cats like soft touches and gentle massages and not aggressive or hard pets. Be tender with your affection. All of my cats love face rubs best. They allow me to pet all along the spine, base of the tail, and even the tail. Sometimes they also permit me to hold their paws when they sit with me, but not all of my cats enjoy this "hand holding."

I do kiss my cats. Now, not all appreciate a kiss. Sometimes they draw their heads back when I smooch them, especially if I make kissy noises, but some of my kitties lean into a forehead kiss. I hug my kitties. When they hop up on my lap, I pull their bodies into mine to give them "a squish," a short, gentle hug that they don't mind. I also occasionally tickle the top of their heads or the base of their tails. I call all of these signs of affection "teasing." My cats know that they are always an expression of my love for them.

🌸 *Skippy reaches out to touch me.*

Sometimes I get an annoyed "merh" complaint (while still staying put on my lap), but I think teasing in kind ways like this builds a relationship. **Find some gentle and harmless ways to tease your fur baby.** It has only served to strengthen my bond with my kitties.

If you want to have the cat trust you and create a loving bond, never tease or touch in a mean or negative way.

Recognize when your cat shows you affection, then praise him and return the affection. Cats will slow blink at you; a softening of the eyes typically translates that he trusts you and likes you. If he reaches out a paw to gently touch your arm, leg, hand, or face, he is communicating his friendliness toward you. If he purrs while you love up on him *and all the signs of his body language are good* and he reaches out to bite you, this is a "love bite." Usually, kittens raised by a mama cat bite this way fairly gently. However, orphaned, hand-raised kittens can "love bite" a bit too hard. Learn the difference between a love bite and a warning bite. One comes with purring and softened eyes, and the other often comes with swishing tails and wide eyes. If you get a warning bite, stop touching kitty immediately and give him space. If you receive a love nip, please don't reprimand kitty for showing love (even if it hurt). It can harm the bond if you do.

Story Example: Love Bites

Trixie and Skippy are my biggest "love biters," and I hand-reared both from ages four weeks and three weeks, respectively. Unfortunately, both of them have scratched my skin and caused a small amount of bleeding with some of their love bites. Trixie bites my chin and hands. Skippy only ever bites my nose. He comes to me and sits in my lap, then flips over so that I cradle him like an infant. He places one paw on my chest or extends it to my chin. He purrs up a storm. I often kiss his forehead, and he leans into it. He then wants to reciprocate by biting my nose. Over the years I have become wary of these bites and sometimes withdraw my face so he can't "kiss" me. The more amorous he gets, the more likely he'll kiss too hard, so I say, "Be soft," and he has learned what that means because he now offers fewer painful love bites. When he gives me a soft love bite, I say, "Thank you, sweet boy." If he bites too hard, I sometimes say "Ow!" without thinking, but I don't scold or punish Skippy. How sad to punish him for showing me love.

Other signs of affection include head bonks (some call them bunts), where the cat presses his head into your body for a brief moment. Some cat behavior pros say that this is solely about marking you with scent, but I believe it also clearly indicates affection because cats do not go out of their way to touch other animals or humans in this manner if they do not care for them. Cats will rub around your legs: sometimes to mark you with scent, sometimes to tell you he is hungry, sometimes to show affection, *or* a combo of all three.

Cats groom you if they like you. In their own culture, grooming others signals friendship or belonging and is called allogrooming. It leaves their scent on you and shows affection. My cat Beaux occasionally shows his love by licking my forehead or hands. I let him do it for a few moments before saying, "Thank you buddy, you are so nice to give me kisses," and then pull my hand or head away (and wipe off).

❀ *Beaux giving me a "kiss."*
(Photo credit Rachel Beecher)

MINDFULNESS & THOUGHTFULNESS

Thoughtfulness and mindfulness work nicely to help relationship-building and bonding with your kitty. How do you utilize thoughtfulness? **Talk positively about your cat and to your cat**. Don't make the mistake of thinking that he does not understand you. He may not comprehend every word, but he has learned a fair number of them. And if not understanding the words, he certainly picks up on the energy of the intention of your words and can sense the meaning in that way.

Words are tools of creation. Our culture did not teach this to us growing up. Sarcasm, meanness, revenge, name-calling, disrespect, swearing, demeaning others (especially women), and other negative themes have run rampant in our entertainment for decades. Because of this, many people think and speak negatively, completely unaware **the words we say and the thoughts we think create our reality.**

Story Example: "Tricky" Trixie

As a kitten, Trixie was *so* busy and really destructive. She didn't try to make messes, but boy she did. I started calling her "Shiva the Destroyer" or "Tricky" because of how I felt about her behavior. (Really, she was just bored in our little apartment.) Around this time, I started learning that words have power. As a result, I stopped using the negative nicknames. It took months to retrain myself, but I did. She still had to grow

❀ *Trixie, having clawed and chewed her way inside the chair.*

out of her wild phase of kittenhood, but changing the words, or catching my own negativity and making the effort to change, really helped *me*. It created more awareness of myself and allowed me to improve. I became more patient overall with Trixie for her curiosity and playful endeavors. I found the delight and humor even in the very moments of discovering her next "project."

Choose words intentionally when talking about and to your cat to help develop a more compatible relationship between you. Remember, the same applies even when kitty isn't in earshot. The words themselves can create what you don't want, so avoid complaining about your cat to others.

PURRRITO WRAP UP

To recap in list form, here are ways to create a healthy bond with your cat:

Stability & Predictability

- Cats love life to be predictable.
- Meet the cat's physical needs daily.
- A part of predictability includes emotional stability for kitty.
- Cats have to have time and space to acclimate to new situations.

Understanding & Compassion

- Show understanding and compassion toward kitty.
- Understanding feline biology will shift your perceptions of cats and can greatly impact your expectations of them in your home.

Respect

- Show restraint.
- Use a soft, kind, respectful voice.
- Enjoy the laughter, in a mutual way, that comes from having a cat with funny antics.
- Pay attention to kitty's body and care for him when ill.
- Respect the cat's own free will.

Relaxed & Balanced

- Don't get upset at the cat for making messes in your home.
- If you get upset at kitty frequently, it strains your bond.
- Kitty likes a clean house, too, so provide a clean place to live.
- Relax about property destruction.
- Be the calming force in your home.

Positive Reinforcement

- Use a lot of positive reward reinforcement.
- Cats want to feel good and loved and are motivated to repeat actions that result in any type of reward.

Space & Freedom

- Allow the cat a lot of space and freedom in the home.
- Do not crate your cat as you might a dog.
- Welcome kitty to hang out with you.

Enrichment

- Play with kitty every day and offer new items to explore as often as you can.
- Invite all the cats to a "catnip party."
- Offer creature comforts.
- Have cat décor (cat trees, scratching posts) and resources scattered in every room.
- Keep kitty happy, curious, thinking, alert, exploring, and safe in the process of these activities.

Affection

- Show your cat a lot of gentle physical affection.
- Watch the responses via body language.
- Find some fun and cute ways to tease your fur baby.
- Recognize the cat's signs of affection for you.
- Praise your cat if he shows affection.

Mindfulness & Thoughtfulness

- Talk positively about your cat and to your cat.
- The words we say and the thoughts we think create our reality.
- Choose your thoughts and words intentionally when talking about and to your cat.

As a wrap up to creating the wonderful loving bond, know you may sometimes still scold, or clap your hands, or feel frustrated on occasion with kitty. You will shift further and further away from these habits as you become aware of them. Having this happen intermittently while doing all the other lovely, good cat guardian, "purrrfect" things will not hinder the cat from knowing and feeling loved and remaining in a place of trust. You will undoubtedly create a healthy and strong bond. You and kitty can both change and grow together in wholesome ways. If you are mastering these instructions and want to do more, let's go the extra mile, to make life with kitty even more rewarding and fun.

CHAPTER 9

Going the Extra Mile

Where does "going the extra mile" come from anyway? It originates from the Bible where Jesus teaches that if someone compels you to go with them one mile, *you* choose to go two miles. The story clearly teaches selflessness and making the greater effort. In our modern language we use this phrase to express *doing more than just what is required*. So how does that apply with our kitties? In this chapter we expand further on our cat-human bond. What can we do to walk further down the bonding path with our cat to create an amazing life with her? How can we keep our relationship thriving over time?

CREATING A SNUGGLY LAP CAT

In the beginning of this book, I spoke of how I meet many people who long to have a lap cat. They have this idea in their minds that the majority of cats are aloof and will choose, instead of showing love, to chew up your hand when you try to pet them. These folks want to win the cat lottery by finding that supposedly rare snuggly cat. It could be that more cats are feisty rather than loving. However, this "feistiness" results as an instinctive response to defend themselves, because **when pet cats feel safe, loved, respected, and valued in their homes, they show great affection toward their humans.**

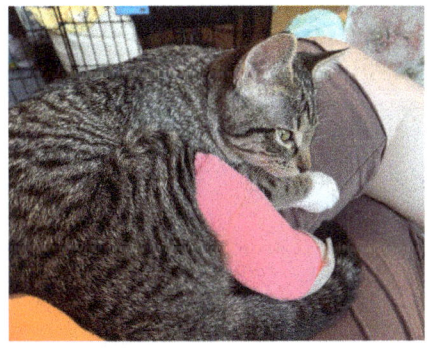

❀ *A sweet recuperating foster getting lap training time.*

No doubt, creating a lap cat is easier if you start off on the right footing with kitty. Still, I think you should have hope that your current kitty can at the very least improve her desire to snuggle as you make changes in the environment, meet more of her needs, and interact with her healthily. Instead of on top of you, she may choose to snuggle next to you on the bed or couch. Either way, **we want your cat to feel safe and loved enough to connect more**, to choose being by your side and even in your lap.

I've laid out some ideas here on how you can create or increase the opportunity for having a lap cat or a snuggler. Remember, though: if you have a stressed kitty or you have a strained relationship, fixing these concerns will need to come before working on lap time.

Here are my lap training recommendations:

- Start lap time training right away with your new cat and especially so with kittens who are more open to lap snuggles.

- When kitten is sleepy, place her in your lap. With an adult cat, pat your lap for her and make it clear she is invited to sit there. You can offer a treat for getting in your lap.

- Do not force or control the cat in any way. She needs to feel like she has a choice and is free to leave at any time.

- Find time *every day* for lap training. Cats form habits easily. But the more it is engrained in them at a young age, the more they will seek it out as a desirable sleeping spot.

- Be careful of how much you pet or touch the kitten or cat once she settles in your lap. Too much touch or movement can cause her to get down sooner than you want. Take the cue from your cat's body language because she will tell you if you can pet for several minutes or thirty seconds. Look for signs of annoyance like tail swishing, fur twitching, ears back. You want to stop petting well before these signs appear. If the cat truly wants to sleep, you have to be still.

- Allow for the kitty to stay and snuggle for at least 20 minutes. Listen to an audio book, watch TV, or read while kitty sits, purrs, and snoozes.

- The overall environment needs to feel safe and calm for kitty to seek you out and stay. If the cat hops up to cuddle, but your children come crashing unexpectedly into the room, the cat will likely leap down and run away. More than a few of these instances and your cat may develop the notion that sitting on your lap equals unexpected noise and commotion. So for better chances of success, plan lap time training at an opportune time for peace.

- Always tell the kitty "Thank you for snuggling me" when lap time ends.

- Once you have established the pattern, allow the kitty to sit with you when they request it at least 65% of the time. Otherwise, too much rejection may undo your training efforts.

These instructions may seem simple, and they are. It starts though with the cat feeling safe and respected, which may take more effort if you need to undo old habits. Lap cats are not rare. Cats even partially socialized with humans in the critical period of kittenhood who feel safe, loved, respected will still seek to be around you and show affection. Now, if your kitty was a feral (and still feral), the relationship will likely remain strained when it comes to touching and affection.

Story Example: Sickly Seven-Week-Old Kitten

I picked up a kitten for a rescue that a TNR group had found. They thought, based on her size, she was a three-week-old bottle baby kitten. When I peered into their boxes, I saw a tiny babe. I scooped her up, but with a closer look I realized she was over seven weeks old because her ears were big and once I cleaned her goopy eyes, I saw they had already lost the baby-blue color. She was very sickly, malnourished, and so dehydrated that she had gone limp. I rushed her to urgent care, and they started her on an IV. I picked her up later

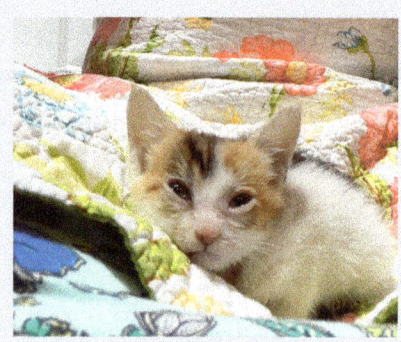 

❁ *First day with Cali and after ten days with Cali.*

that evening and brought her home. That first 24 hours she was so sick I could handle her easily. However, once she perked up, she hid from me. I spent a lot of time with her, helping her feel safe. She remained in my care for about eleven days, long enough to heal from her illness. By the end of our time together, she gladly and voluntarily sat in my lap for play and snuggles. I used the above techniques, and they worked quickly with such a young cat.

ULTIMATE PLAY TIME: *BE* THE MOUSE

So often cat behavior consultants will hear owners say, "My cat just doesn't like to play." Mhmm. Kitty most likely isn't engaging because the owners don't know how to play with her to get her interested or excited.

Kittens are playing machines. You don't have to do much to entertain a kitten or get them to engage in games. They have boundless energy to burn off, and they want to play, play, play! As your feline friend ages, you will need to do more work to get her to have fun.

The big thing to understand about adult cats and playtime is that they *play* by hunting and killing. Yes, they may still play fetch or happily swat around a little ball on the floor, but ultimately, they need to burn mental and physical energy in a good hunt to meet their needs every day.

Recall that in a multi-cat home, some cats won't get involved in the play unless they are alone in the game. If you have cats that will interrupt another cat's hunt

and take over, make sure to have the game in a location where other cats can't intervene. The domestic feline does not hunt in groups; they are solitary hunters. If you have three, four, or five cats, you can find playing one-on-one with each of them two to three times a day a bit overwhelming. If multiple teenagers or adults live in the home, assign cats to each person for daily play sessions to help shoulder the workload. If you are alone in creating hunt games for all cats, rotate playtime for each cat, playing every other day, or you can reduce each daily game from ten minutes to five.

Take time to review the movements of certain animals or insects the cat could likely kill. Watch how the mouse scurries and hides. See how the fly buzzes and lands. Embody how the bird flits and flies. **An engaging hunting session should involve the cat staring, prowling, pouncing, chasing, catching, and biting.** If you never let the cat catch or bite, it frustrates her. So, toys like laser lights can only go so far. Let the cat go through this sequence 3, 4, 5 times in a ten-minute game. You can rest in between rounds of hunting during the game. Timing-wise, it's especially rewarding for kitty if this game happens before mealtime or ends with a treat. If still unsure whether you are playing correctly with your cat, watch some good playtime instruction videos online.

Wand toys that you can manipulate at some distance from kitty make the best toys for hunting games: a birdie, snakey, lizardy, mousey type of toy. My cats prefer the toy Go Cat Cat Catcher for mouse hunts. They also like the long fleece snake-like wand toys. Fluffy feather wand toys are great. Most any brand should do. Ensure toys are safe and that if kitty pulls off feathers or the like, pick them up and throw them out to avoid choking or bowel blockage hazards.

I hope you have fun with kitty when playing! Remember, **it is a bonding activity and meets a core need of your cat.** Do your best to make time for this and enjoy your cat's charming antics.

CONTINUING EDUCATION

I think **learning about cats is fun!** The more you learn, the stronger your bond can become. The following list of ideas can help you continue having a fantastic friend affair with your furry buddy.

- Play cat board games! Some are for little kids and some for older kids/adults. Cat trivia games can definitely help you learn more cat-facts.

- Throughout kitty's life, check in to see if another great book about cats has been published that you must own. Reading fun stories about other cats can warm your heart, and there are tons of cat story compilation books, books about cat breeds, books on cat nutrition. Obviously, other books like this one can give you a lot of information to improve your understanding of cats.

- Learn more about animal communication. If you feel you have a gift there, you could become a professional animal communicator, not only helping your own cats but many others.

- Find courses online about cats or animal care and take them. I especially recommend ones that focus on developing more compassion and understanding like Fear-Free courses or The Trust Technique.

- Keep checking online for new and latest cat toys, trees, beds, and more. It's fun for both you and your cat to get a new cat item.

- Volunteer in cat rescue work, as this will teach you a ton about cats— relationships, dynamics, health, and more.

- Keep educating yourself on alternative healthcare options for kitty. You never know when you might face a cat illness, and it helps you feel stronger and more capable when you have a sure knowledge of other places to go for support even while still working with your vet.

- Go to a cat convention. Meet other cat-lovers and hear great speakers. Stroll the vendor booths to buy fun gadgets and trinkets for kitty. Maybe even get your picture with renowned cat whisperers or famous cats from YouTube.

TRAINING TIME

Training cats is absolutely doable. More people are recognizing this and giving it a go. As you know, felines are pretty different from canines, so while some training tactics cross over, some do not. Remember, dogs have been bred to be more obedient and reliant on humans; plus, they are pack animals seeking an alpha leader. Cats have none of those inherited traits, so **training them is all about making it rewarding for** *them.*

Clicker training works for cats as it does dogs. Marking the behavior you want or like with a click and then a treat helps solidify the action in the cat's mind. Adding praise and good cue words also helps build up the cat's training repertoire.

I will not spend a lot of time teaching you the mechanics of training in this book. Previous chapters share tips in regard to modifying negative behaviors. The same type of actions are useful in teaching a cat tricks, like shaking hands or jumping through a hoop. Set yourself up for success by obtaining a good clicker. I like clickers with a targeting tip (extendable pointer). Figure out what reward your kitty likes best. Food motivated cats are easier to train then those that are not. Give very small pieces of food treats, and remember, if you train more than once a day, reduce food a bit at mealtimes to compensate for treat calories. Make sure you seek additional instruction from competent training sources. Karen Pryor is well known for her training books. Seek out a cat training class or hire a cat trainer to come and help you get started.

Training your kitty is a bonding activity! **Cats that struggle with boredom, depression, anxiety, and other concerns will gain confidence with training.** You can gear training toward aligning kitty's behaviors with your will (e.g., not getting on kitchen counters, not becoming overzealous at mealtime, not scratching furniture, or willingly walking into the carrier) or toward teaching fun tricks (e.g., roll over, sit, shake, and jump). You can do both. Training sessions with kitty need to stay short. If they get bored or frustrated, they may refuse to train again. Five to ten minutes typically makes a good training session. Once or twice in a day is sufficient. Consistency is important. Make sure you carve out time to train at least three days a week.

❀ *My preferred clicker with pointer for targeting.*

ADVENTURE CATS

We have all seen amazing pictures and videos online of cats enjoying activities like paddleboarding, boating, hiking, camping and more. How adorable are those cats? Very cute. It is completely understandable to want that in your life too, especially if you are an outdoorsy, adventure-seeking person who happens to like cats.

Obviously, it is possible to train a cat to enjoy adventure situations. However, the reality is that **these are unique cats that had great training** and/or intense trust with their guardian.

Too many people, who do not know what they are doing, are now trying to turn their cats into those cute cats having fun outside with humans and dogs in all those amazing pictures and videos. And they are stressing out their cats.

Story Example: Looking for an Adventure Cat

At an adoption event a few years back, a young man showed up seeking a kitten to become an adventure buddy with him. He was so excited by the idea of taking his cat hiking and camping. He and his mother planned to both care for the cat as they lived in the same home. They arrived to pick out a kitten together. His mother fell in love with a tiny female calico, an extremely shy kitten. She came from a feral cat colony at about six or seven weeks old—barely living with a human family for six weeks.

I explained that this kitten would never become an adventure cat. He didn't seem to understand that because she missed most of the weeks interacting with humans in the *critical socialization period,* she would likely remain shy and skittish with any "new" situation, person, or noise. I told him that she could be a very loving and sweet companion in the home, but even with good training, she would not likely become the confident cat she needed to be in order to be outside in a variety of situations and feel no stress.

I encouraged him to go ahead and try harness/leash training. He might be able to go on walks with her, but that he needed to **watch her responses and body language and respect her needs for safety if she was telling him "no" to going outside** with cars and neighborhood noises. He *said* he would try to follow her lead and not force her into anything stressful. However, in the parking lot, he took her out of the carrier in the car and the kitten, in terror, jumped out of the open car window and fled. It took days for the rescue to trap her, but luckily she was safe in the end.

Story Example: Some Cats Say No to Adventuring

I had a foster kitten that my neighbor adopted, a sweet little brown tabby. She was well-socialized to me, but unfortunately experiences in her upbringing were very limited. What do I mean by that? We had a panleukopenia scare in my home when she was tiny. I had to sequester her and her mama and siblings to a single, sanitized room. Anyone entering the room, before the kittens could reach full vaccination protection, had to be clean—fresh clothes, washed hands, no shoes. While I spent a lot of time with the kittens, they didn't receive the socialization I usually give my fosters because they were stuck in one room with few visitors.

❧ *The little brown tabby I called Angel.* *(Photo credit Jim Grubb)*

This neighbor had a Bengal kitten already and wanted a playmate for the kitty. The Bengal was for sure the right temperament for an adventure cat. She loved being outside, gladly going on leashed walks and paddleboarding in her life vest. When they adopted this tabby from me, they tried to get her to do the same activities as the Bengal kitten. They thought my foster would adapt and learn to enjoy these adventures by example, but she never adjusted. It took my neighbor several months before she gave up on getting that kitten to be outdoorsy. She was always much too scared to have fun because as a kitten between ages two to nine weeks, she had so little exposure to anything new—not people, not noises, not outdoors.

If you want an adventure cat, you have to begin correctly. Give the experiment its best shot for success by looking for a kitten with the following traits and experiences:

239

- Raised with a variety of humans and animals around them, particularly dogs and children.

- Around humans from ages two to three weeks and beyond and handled daily for at least thirty minutes by trustworthy people.

- Raised in a good home that was safe and happy. Given a lot of verbal praise and positive physical touch. Children were gentle and not scary. Dog was loving and friendly.

- Has a confident personality. Not shy. Not easily scared. Interested in new things and people.

- Has spent some time, safely overseen, outdoors during the critical period of two to nine weeks old.

- Exposed to a variety of places in and around the house and locations outside the home (vet office, adoption events, car rides, the park) and showed no stress or little stress.

- Bonus: Has already begun harness training and clicker training.

So how do you find such a kitty? Get good at asking questions. When you go to the shelter or the rescue adoption event, bring this list. If you feel you aren't getting truthful or complete answers, then move on. Use prayer, asking God to lead you to the right kitten. Ask the Angels to create the right path, meet the right person, or show you a sign with the kitten meant for you and this role of adventure buddy you desire her to fulfill.

Sometimes certain breeds have the right generalized character traits, so then seeking a full bred kitty might prove right for you. Still, if the critical socialization didn't happen well in that 2–9-week period after birth, then no matter the breed, the kitten will not likely become a good fit for keeping calm in a variety of circumstances. So, drill the breeders, ask to visit them in the home to see the situation in which they are being raised long before the kitten is ready to adopt. A good breeder, one who truly loves the animals and who hasn't let the breeding get out of control, should be well-versed in correct socialization techniques. Some breeds known for being more social and active include Bengals and Maine Coons.

Other breeds with good characteristics might also fit for creating an adventure cat. Do your research, but again, don't rely on these characteristics. They will be moot if a kitten wasn't socialized correctly.

Another idea, which I am not necessarily encouraging but recognize it as a possible route for creating an adventure cat, is to foster orphaned kittens as bottle babies or mama cats with babies. You will likely have to raise many kitten babies to find one with the right temperament. When you act as the "mother" to a kitten, the bond of trust goes way up. Trust is important in training a cat to stay calm and happy in a variety of situations and around a diversity of noises and people. Bottle feeding neonates is hard work and requires a lot of sacrifice, time, love, patience, and money. This is not an easy route. Again, the temperament of the kitten is key. You may socialize the kitten in all the right ways, and they can still be naturally shy. Just as with people, cats' spirits come into the world with distinct personalities. I have raised nearly 50 bottle babies and another 30 kittens; only a few of those would have had the right temperament to train as an outdoorsy adventure cat.

Story Example:
Early Training Exposure Has Lasting Impact

Honey, now a forever cat of mine, was incredibly chill with all people as a tiny kitten, including small children and adults with disabilities. I thought she might be a great service kitty—one licensed to visit the sick or elderly in hospitals, hospice, or senior homes. I started leash training her early and taking her driving in the car with me. I took her into stores. I exposed her to a lot of noises and situations. I took her outside for walks on her leash. We rode elevators. However, when she reached about one year, she started biting, warning bites when she didn't get her way like with nail clippings or putting her down off my lap when she wasn't ready. She couldn't visit with others in a service capacity if she had any inclination to bite. I don't know if I spoiled her too much or if her "tortie-tude" started coming out, but

❀ Young Honey sleep training, I mean leash training at the store with my mom and also in my car.

I gave up the training and certification dream. I could have trained her to be an adventure cat because our trust bond is high and she is still, years later, chill with riding in the car, meeting new people, and loud noises, and she loves going outside. I'm not an adventurer myself, so that's why I didn't go that route.

Side Note: Adopting a Tiny Kitten Isn't the Way

If the previous information has led you to think that adopting a young kitten is the best choice for creating a feline adventurer, but you don't want the hassle of bottle feeding, so instead you think getting a kitten when it is tiny will fix that, here are some ideas to consider: this path will not get you the adventure cat you desire. Never take a kitten from the mother cat too early. It disadvantages kittens to lose the love, protection, and influence of their mother cat before ten weeks of age. Doing so can cause emotional damage to the cat that will prevent it from becoming the ideal adventure buddy. Preferably mamas and kittens should remain together for twelve weeks. Orphaned kittens are one thing, but purposely separating a kitten from her mother for selfish reasons is not okay. Also, be aware of your state laws. My state says it is illegal to separate a kitten from her mother before eight weeks of age or two pounds.

Story Example: Sometimes a Cool Adult Cat will Find You

Rarely, but sometimes, a confident adult cat will land on your doorstep. These cats are strays and not ferals. The difference? Strays are those clearly socialized by humans when little kittens. I love the UK story, *A Street Cat Named Bob*, about a confident, outdoor cat who landed in the arms of a man who didn't even know he needed a cat. The cat totally increased this street busker's income by tagging along and literally saved his life. Years ago, I fostered a little adult male cat from the neighborhood that I initially intended for TNR. I'd seen him around a lot and suspected he may have fathered the first batch of kittens I fostered along with their feral mama. I finally trapped him and took him to get neutered. Unlike most ferals, he stayed totally chill on the car ride. Turns out, he was fully socialized. He had some fight wounds that needed to heal, so he stayed in the house for a few extra days to mend after his alteration surgery. He was so self-assured and incredibly loving that I decided to adopt him out. Whatever room he walked into, no matter the circumstances, he owned it, so I nicknamed him "little jefe" (little boss). Years of homelessness made him oblivious to the "new" or the "loud" that drive most cats under the bed. He found the perfect home: a family looking for a confident cat,

🐾 *Little Jefe. Small, scarred from street fights, but proud.*

hoping to get one with a background that most other adopters would shy from—like living on the streets for years. They snapped him up when he demonstrated how chill he could remain in the pet store with a ton of new cats and people around.

Okay, you finally found the ideal adventure kitten or cat; now what? You must do several things. One, build the bond of trust between yourself and the kitten. This book contains numerous ideas and information needed to do just that. Second, start training the kitten. Your training needs to be all positive and reward-based techniques. Punishment and control do not work with cats as a training tactic and will sever bonds of trust.

Exposure is important at the earliest age. The first step for safely exposing kitty to a variety of situations is harness and leash training. Make sure the harness is comfortable, yet secure enough so the kitten can't squirm out of it. Keep the process rewarding with praises and treats. Refer back to page 195 for instructions. After you complete this first part of training, start coaching kitty to come to you and sit by your feet when you are standing and holding the leash. Mark the behavior of sitting by your feet with a click and a treat. Attach a verbal cue to it like "come" or "sit" using the language of your choice. Google has quick tools for looking up and listening to pronunciations of some basic words and phrases in a multitude of languages. Sit, Come, Stop or Halt, Drop It, Walk, and Run should be the basics you master with your cat before you go on your first big adventure.

Before taking your young kitten anywhere, expose her to a variety of sounds that she may hear when outside—dogs barking, wind, rain, thunder, waterfalls, car horns, car brakes, crowds, strangers' voices talking, yelling, laughing, and much more. Select the sounds based on the activities you want kitty to join you on. Start by downloading these sounds and then playing them back at low levels and slowly increasing the volume levels over time. As kitty is exposed, offer rewards. Remember to introduce your kitten to a lot of indoor sounds too, like vacuums, fans, appliances, music, TV, and more. Always give treats to associate the strange noises with good things.

Watch the kitten's body language—if she shows signs of stress, immediately take a step back by going to a lower volume and return to the last place she remained calm. Signs of stress include eyes dilated, ears back or flat, licking mouth, trying to hide. If you get to hissing, scratching, growling, or trying to run away, training is not going in the right direction for kitty at all. Desensitization helps train kitty, but if you overexpose or flood the kitten with something too scary, kitty may never bounce back. You have to be an attentive guardian and trainer, looking at kitty all the time to assess how she is handling this process.

Do sound training for several weeks, simultaneously with harness and leash training, and clicker training the basic commands. Complete one session of each daily, three to five days a week. Afterward, start taking kitty into new or different environments, a friend's home, the car, the vet's office (merely to stop in), the grocery store, or similar. Begin this in-person exposure when kitty is four to six months old. It's crucial to go on outing activities with the kitten frequently, up to four times a week. Make sure the kitty associates all of these experiences with positivity and rewards like treats, playtime, affection, and praise. Tiny signs of hesitation at first to something new is okay, but if kitty warms up quickly because she trusts you, you are headed in the right direction with your training.

Seek additional training advice or techniques from qualified experts. You may want to call a cat trainer or behavior consultant to get customized tips before you start.

When you choose to take kitty out of the home on adventures, pay extra attention to her health and wellbeing. She is at a much higher risk outdoors for *everything*—parasites, diseases, accidents, attacks from other animals, eating or drinking something contaminated or toxic. Remaining with you at all times reduces some of those risks, but keep your eye out for any dangers to kitty. After each hiking trip, check kitty for injuries to her feet and comb through the fur to look for ticks or other concerns. If you go boating or paddleboarding, make sure kitty wears a life jacket. When camping, keep kitty secured in her own fully zipped, closed playpen when you are not able to pay attention and when you sleep. Having a larger, loving, fully trained dog to help watch over and protect kitty when adventuring is a great idea. **Another trained cat or dog will always help guide the kitten in the process as she watches and learns from their example.**

CATIOS & AWESOME CAT FURNISHINGS

I don't know which cat expert originally coined the phrase "catify" in regard to making your home a cat haven. I believe the Internet gives credit to Jackson Galaxy and Kate Benjamin for the term "catification." Catify is now a fairly common term for cat guardians to hear. But what does it mean to *catify* your home?

It means you go a step beyond the norm and **make it clear that the kitty is a priority in your life by creating a home where she truly belongs,** a home where she has things that belong to her and is not just living in a home where you own everything. Catification isn't about spoiling, but about belonging, enrichment, activity, and health.

I love having a well-decorated home, a clean home. And with my first cat, I didn't catify for her. She was *okay* without as she didn't have any territorial competition with other cats, animals, or children. I can't even recall if I had a good scratching post for her. She did have a balcony to go out on and window ledges big enough to sit on to watch the outdoors. However, everything in the home, aside from a few toys and litterbox, belonged to me. I didn't make any space or any item "hers."

Over the years as I added cats into my life, I was forced to catify my home to help keep the peace, territorially speaking. Now, after learning so much about cats and loving my furry friends dearly, I happily catify my spaces. Does the decorator in me cringe at the cat tree in my otherwise well-designed space? Yes. But we make the same compromise when living with anyone we love as we don't always like their favorite chair, throw pillows, or paint color choice. Make room for kitty in your home and help her belong.

I have seen carpenters or builders, who are also cat lovers, create some amazing wall and ceiling playgrounds for cats in their homes. What cool set ups! So far, I have installed some floating cat shelves and beds on the wall, but the full playground must wait for a future date. Google phrases like "cat home renovation ideas" or "design cat walkways in house" and look at amazing photos to inspire cat playgrounds for your home.

Interior cat-construction changes are awesome, but pricey if you have to hire it out. Some folks have spent as much as $40K to catify the whole home with custom carpentry. However, consider if you will stay in that home permanently or if you might sell it in the future. If selling, catification like this may not work as you'll likely want to keep your home standard to appeal to the most buyers. However, adding something like a catio could work beautifully. **"Catio" equals a "cat patio" with secure walls for kitty's safety.** Catios are located on the exterior of the home, and depending on the size and if you buy prefab, make yourself, or hire out, you could spend as little as $500 or upwards of $5000. Upon resale of the home, large catios could easily be turned into greenhouses, extra storage spaces, or more traditional porches should a new home buyer not want a catio.

❀ *Pics of my catio space in the new home.*

I recently moved and had a catio built. I hired it out because of my limited tool ownership and carpentry skills. Due to my multi-cat needs, I wanted a large catio, and luckily the home I live in now already had an overlarge cement patio in the back yard as a foundation. The cats access it via a cat door from the family room. The space measures about 115 square feet and over eight feet tall. In nice weather, I can sit on the catio with my kitties. This safe outdoor space allows kitties more mental and emotional stimulation in their day and expands their territory.

Instead of a catio, you could **fence your backyard** with a tall vinyl fence. The slick plastic fencing makes it hard for claws to climb and the height makes it difficult to jump over. Make sure cats have no way to squeeze under or in-between the fencing panels. These critters can escape like little Houdinis, so be smart and prepared. If you have a large cat like a Savannah, a 6-foot fence will not likely do the job. Attach forty-five-degree angled netting systems to any style fencing to ensure kitty stays in the yard. Keep in mind that setting a cat loose in the backyard unattended may still have some hazardous or life-threatening consequences. You have to weigh out what is best for your kitty and your circumstances.

You can buy wall shelf systems pre-made as an easy way to catify your home interior. I purchased one of these sets from a carpenter in Ukraine on Etsy and hung them on the catio. The Internet offers a huge selection to choose from. Just be sure to check reviews before you buy. In this case, I only spent a few hundred dollars on the set and installed it myself.

Naturally, the nicest looking cat furniture costs more. For sure you can purchase cat towers covered in cheap brown or grey carpet and sisal rope for less than $150 each on Amazon or Chewy. The cats don't care what their furniture looks like and certainly do not fathom what it costs. **What matters to them is if it is comfy, safe, fun, and useful.** If you have the means to get custom-made cat furnishings that will match your home décor, then do it. It will make you happier to have the feel of their belongings blending in better with your own. I have noted that custom-made items like cat trees usually wear and tear a lot better than the cheaper, factory-made item. Your cost to buy a custom tree may run $1000 or so, but then there is the one at Home Goods for $80. You do what best fits your budget. You will more likely need to replace that $80 piece about every two to three years, depending on the use it gets. Often the sisal rope shreds and unwinds fairly quickly, looking bad. If the tower structure is still sound, you can remove the old sisal rope and replace it on your own. Simply hot glue it on by winding it tightly around the post. Sometimes I wrap the sisal posts in quilting-cotton batting and upholstery fabric. The fabric will shred significantly in six to twelve months, but again, not too hard to tear off and redo. These little upgrades cost around $50 dollars each time and will take an hour or two of your time. I have not yet needed to do anything to repair my expensive custom cat tree, other than clean it, and it's ten years old.

Side Note: Fancy Furnishings to Hide Kitty May Not Fly

Cat furniture that serves a dual purpose like a coffee table/litterbox can work successfully, but some cats hate single-entry, covered boxes, especially in multi-cat homes. Be aware of this if you plan to purchase high-end pieces to try to mask or hide the presence of the cat to visitors—your cat may refuse to use it. Try out a cheaper covered box first if you think you want to go this way in your home. However, know that many cat behavior consultants advise against small, single-entry, covered boxes.

Recall that earlier on I told you not to dedicate a single room, especially a distant space you never visit like a corner in the basement, to all things cat. When you do this—put all the cat equipment in there—you indicate to the cat that they don't belong in your world—that you are embarrassed to have her, that her belongings cause a burden, and other emotionally and mentally damaging subtext messages. **Cat resources and furniture need to be spread out in the home and in the highest traffic areas where you and the family spend a lot of time.** This is true integration and the highest showing of your love and respect for her.

As mentioned in a previous chapter, in a multi-cat home these tight spaces with all of the cat paraphernalia often causes territorial conflict and stress in the animals. Don't be surprised if cats quarrel more often, avoid each other, start acting out in the home with urine marking, or display redirected aggression. Often one or a few cats will "claim" this small area and thwart other cats from having safe and free access to resources.

Catifying your home often includes creating enrichment activities or "cat TV" in several areas of the home (page 194). If you have good window ledges in your home, adding a bunch of bird feeders in the yard creates that "TV" for her, giving her something to engage in and watch. You might get a large aquarium with fish for the cat to study. I have seen new aquariums online built to allow kitty up inside the aquarium (sans water exposure) and be surrounded by fishes. Plants on the exterior of the home near the windows that attract hummingbirds, bees, and butterflies help engage the cat. Some folks use actual TVs for entertaining kitties. Some YouTube videos depict hour long footage of fish, birds, and squirrels that some cats find entertaining. You can download games on tablets or other touch screens where kitties can "kill" prey by hitting it with their paw. Though fine in moderation, just like with your children, you don't want your cat in front of a screen for hours on end.

Have enrichment activity toys for kitty. A big running cat wheel works great for high energy cats. Cat It Senses has a whole line of toys dedicated to sensory playtime. With toys like this, you often need to pick them up and put them out of sight for a few weeks and then bring them back around. Keep playthings novel in order for them to capture kitty's interest for the long run. If you set up sensory toys and leave in the same spot, you will likely find it gets explored a lot in the first two days and then only occasionally looked at after that.

Scratcher posts are a high priority. Use both vertical and horizontal surfaces that are secure and won't tip or fall down when kitty uses them. Have a variety of surface types like bark, sisal, cardboard, fabric and more. Provide at least two or three favored scratchers for a single cat and then add another one or two for each additional cat in the home. I have more than ten in my home for the six cats. A lot of products are now designed to protect furniture and still allow the cat to scratch your couch or chair, like over-the-arm scratcher installations. Some might think this trains the cat to target all

furniture; however, if you designate the area as permitted and reward train them to those spots alone, then you can still successfully protect other furnishings in the home that are not covered.

I hope this section has your creative juices flowing and that you are excited about how to incorporate kitty into the home more fluidly and fully by catifying your spaces. It is fun for both of you, and it warms the heart to see kitty more relaxed and engaged in the home. Providing for her in this way goes a long way in purrrfecting your bond.

HOMEMADE OR RAW FOOD DIETS

Having a large cat or pet family can make a full raw diet (commercial or homemade) cost-prohibitive for the average person. Additionally, making all homemade pet food is time-prohibitive. However, I have done some study and certification on feline nutrition and want to bring it up as a valid way to increase your care and connection with kitty. I see **this as an excellent way to go *extra* with our feline friends.**

Normal commercial pet food companies overly process cat food, especially dry kibble, until little valuable original nutrition remains. These products contain, of course, a spectrum of quality ingredients versus not good ingredients, so learning how to read them is important. The same spectrum exists with commercially produced raw food diets. Reading the labels on all the foods you contemplate is an important step in taking better care of your cats.

Understanding which ingredients are most worrisome and how to decipher true nutrition, like removing moisture from the equation and deducing carbohydrate percentages, are important skills (page 187). In general, having a large percentage (listed higher on the ingredients list) of the following are not the best for kitty:

- Carbohydrates, especially from grains and soy.

- No quality proteins and merely meat "meals" (AKA flours made from unwanted bits of animals like beaks, feet, and cartilage cooked intensely and then ground into an ashy mixture).

- A large percentage of the protein in the food derived from plant content like pea proteins or other vegetables.

- Carrageenan, which is a thickening agent linked to health issues like cancer.

- High amounts of phosphates, phosphorus, magnesium, calcium. Some is good if a quality source, too much creates health concerns for cats.

Raw food diets create controversy in the pet-care world. **In the wild, cats obviously eat raw meat.** Their digestive system was built to process and gain the most nutritional value from meat. Some veterinarians may argue against it for our indoor companions because there could be a higher risk of bacterial contamination like Salmonella or E.coli on raw meats. It is possible for a cat to become sick because of these bacteria, but if you buy frozen or freeze-dried raw foods commercially, you should not have issues. If you make your own raw foods for kitty, make sure you educate yourself on how to handle and prepare meats safely and include all needed nutrients and amino acids. If you are careful where you purchase and how you store raw meat, the risk of bacterial growth is greatly

lowered. You can find book and recipe resources for feeding naturally, many of which are provided by holistic veterinarians.

A homemade diet is not necessarily raw. You can create cooked foods for kitty. These are better than commercially produced foods because you use human-grade meat products and ingredients (the same is rarely true in commercially canned cat foods) and you simply cook instead of pressure canning in intense heat or baking 4-5 times at high heat (like dried kibble), so your nutrient content will suffer less damage and have a higher energetic vibration. As with a homemade raw diet, please follow carefully constructed recipes by qualified experts like holistic veterinarians.

Side Note: Feeding Kitty a Vegetarian Diet

I've noticed an odd trend in our culture to try to put pet cats, obligate carnivores, on a vegan or vegetarian diet. On one hand I appreciate that vegans don't want to contribute to the slaughter of other animals by feeding their cats meat, but unfortunately they harm their pet's health by forcing them to fit into their personal moral worldview. While some studies show a cat *can* digest plant protein, there are no long-term studies to show vegetarian or vegan health ramifications for cats. God designed cats to derive their nutritional needs from meat. I too hope and long for a future where all animals are treated more kindly and fairly, but we can't expect to force our ethics onto animals, in the wild or in our living rooms.

If your cat has been eating commercial kibble most of his life, getting him to switch to a raw food diet will take effort and time. In Chapter 7, I wrote about overweight kitties. Refer to the chart there on how to slowly change a cat's diet (page 191). It can take months to successfully transition.

If time and/or money prevents you to from going this extra step, do not stress that it means you aren't a good cat guardian. Just **do your best to provide better quality foods by examining labels, feeding more wet food than kibble, and offering a variety of brands and flavors to get nutritional balance.** You could add good supplemental support to keep immune systems strong. Talk with a veterinarian about good supplements, probiotics, vitamins, and more. If your regular vet doubts these tools, find a holistic veterinarian to help you.

HEIGHTEN YOUR SPIRITUAL CARE

We've already gone over how to use spiritual tools to help our own healing and caring for kitty. So how can we take it a step further?

Here are a few ideas to heighten spiritual care:

- Pray for your cats on a regular basis. Ask God to help you discern their needs and meet them more fully. Ask for their protection in day-to-day living.

- Ask Angels to help you communicate with and care for your cats daily. If you can't get to them (say you are in the shower or going potty when a big cat fight breaks out) ask for the Angels to hurry in and help break up the fight and calm the kitties. There are Angels designated to help with animals, so don't be afraid to ask for help.

- Utilize crystals daily to help cats. If you have a cat with a chronic medical concern, have a set of crystals or a crystal necklace to use for them regularly. Use your intention with those crystals to help kitty be healthier and stronger.

- If your cat goes outside, shield them every time with a visualized energy shield to help keep them safe.

- Do regular energy work on your animals to help keep them emotionally balanced. Energy healers can work from a distance, so animals do not suffer stress from traveling or by the presence of a stranger. Some energy modalities you can learn yourself and do at home like EFT and Emotion Code. Use an animal communicator to help you know your cat better.

❀ *Angelic cat helpers.*

🐾 Pray over the food, supplements, and medicines you give daily to kitty. Ask for them to purified and safe. Pray that the cat's body will process them with ease and find them useful.

🐾 Learn the skill of energetic muscle testing to help you discern which foods, supplements, or treatments kitty will benefit from.

🐾 Remember to think of your cats with your spiritual mind, recognizing their will, emotions, energies, and needs.

As we embrace our spiritual nature and divine potential, tap into the Universal Knowing within us, and connect with God and His Angels, we will discover additional ways to care for our kitty and all our loved ones. **I know of no greater asset than the power of God.** To use this power, we need to be a kind person, a peaceful person, a compassionate person. Now, we won't always at the top of our game, so to speak, and will inevitably make mistakes that pull us away from a spiritual connection, but the beauty is, in the moment we *sincerely* ask for help to reconnect, we will get it. If we have pulled far away, it takes effort and time to get back to where we were. We can absolutely do it and progress even further into the light. Cats are often believed to be spiritual and sensitive beings, so they will truly appreciate our effort to remain in tune with God and His Universe.

PURRRITO WRAP UP

To recap in list form, here is how to go *extra* with your cat:

Creating a Snuggly Lap Cat

🐾 When pet cats feel safe, loved, respected, and valued in their homes, they are very affectionate with their humans.

🐾 We want your cat to feel safe and loved enough to connect more often by snuggling.

Ultimate Play Time: Be the Mouse

🐾 Remember, adult cats *play* by hunting and killing.

- An engaging hunting session should involve the cat staring, prowling, pouncing, chasing, catching, and biting.
- Playtime is a bonding activity and meets a core need of your cat.

Continuing Education

- Learning about cats is fun, so keep seeking new information.

Training Time

- Training cats works best when we make it rewarding *for them.*
- Cats who struggle with boredom, depression, anxiety, and other concerns will gain confidence with training.

Adventure Cats

- These unique cats have great training and strong bonds with their guardians.
- Watch kitty's responses and body language. Respect her needs for safety if she tells you "no."
- Exposure to the new is important at the earliest age.
- Having another trained cat or dog will help guide the kitten in the process as she watches and learns from their example.

Catios & Awesome Cat Furnishings

- Catification makes it clear that you consider kitty a priority in your life by creating a home where she truly belongs.
- "Catio" equals a "cat patio" with secure walls for kitty's outdoor safety.
- Fencing your backyard is a possibility for kitty to enjoy outdoors.
- Cats don't care about the style or expense of cat furniture. They just want comfy, safe, fun, and useful.
- Cat resources and furniture need to be spread out in the home and in the highest traffic areas where you and the family spend a lot of time.

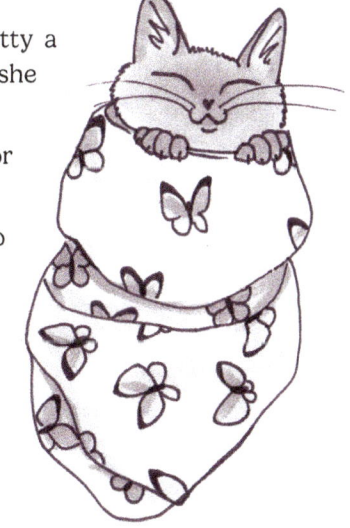

Homemade or Raw Food Diets

- This is an excellent way to go *extra* with our feline friends.

- In the wild, cats eat raw meat.

- If time or money prohibit a raw or homemade diet, do your best to provide better quality foods by examining labels, feeding more wet food than kibble, and offering a variety of brands and flavors to get nutritional balance.

Heighten Your Spiritual Care

- We can utilize spirituality to care for our cats.

- I know of no greater asset than the power of God.

As we wrap this chapter on going the extra mile, I hope you feel more excitement or possibilities with kitty. I want life to be fun with kitty, bringing you both joy and appreciation for one another. The final part of this book will reflect on additional important aspects of cat care. I pray the information there will give you confidence in offering the best home and life, through all circumstances and situations, to your furry feline friend.

PART 4

Elevating Everyday Care

❀ *Skippyjon getting some rest time in with crystals.*

CHAPTER 10

Making Life Safer for Kitty

Like parenting children, cat guardianship requires that we consider the safety of our animals. Humans go to great efforts for their children to "baby-proof" homes, screen babysitters, and find safe neighborhoods to live in. While there are certainly differences in effort, stress, and worry, we need to think about how to protect our cats and increase the security of the home and lifestyle we provide for them.

Sometimes, as both parents and pet guardians, we will make grave mistakes. I lost my cat, Stella because of my pride and lack of education on cats. I want to share her story as it illustrates my lack of awareness about potential harms to cats and my foolishness in not heeding Spirit when prompted to *not* do something. We need to have both temporal information and guidance from above to care for our cats successfully.

Story Example: Stella

With her white coat and black fur blotches, Stella looked like a Holstein cow. She was my first kitty as an adult. At thirty-one, I adopted her from my sister, Marcy, who had brought home two kittens for her family. One was an amazing cat, totally chill with her small children. Sweet Stella, however, found the very busy home so stressful that by the time she was nine months old she hid all day and licked bald patches in her fur (psychogenic alopecia).

In my home with no stress, Stella relaxed. She had a quiet life but still received lots of love and snuggles. I'd lived with Stella for about three years when I found myself at the grocery store around Easter time. I was admiring the pretty Easter lilies and despite my financial deficit decided to buy one for my apartment. As I placed it in my cart, I felt a distinct voice telling me to put it back. I thought it solely a prompting to remind me about not wasting money, so I rebelled against it and bought my lily anyway.

As an indoor-only cat, Stella tended to nibble on flowers or plants I brought in the house. At that time, I was oblivious to the concept that some plants cause toxicity, even death, in cats. She'd chewed on roses, tulips, succulents. Once I had hydrangeas in the house arranging flowers for a niece's wedding, and Stella got sullen and sick for a few days after gnawing on those. I noticed, but she bounced back so I didn't think much of it.

❀ *Sweet Stella at Christmastime.*

Well, of course she nibbled on the lily. I watched her do it. Clueless. Days passed, and she got sicker and sicker, to the point where she wouldn't eat and hung her head over her water bowl. It was two days before it finally clicked that something was really wrong and that it must originate from eating the lily. I frantically Googled "cats and easter lilies" and was horrified to learn that this plant caused kidney failure. I raced Stella to a 24-hour vet on a Saturday afternoon. The vet did bloodwork and found that her kidneys were indeed failing. I asked crying, nay begging, "What can we do? Anything?" He said she had less than a 10% chance of recovering but would need hospitalization and IV fluids if we tried.

I clung to that "less than 10% chance" and admitted her into the hospital's care. I went to my car and bawled. I prayed and hoped. The vet tried, but after a few days Stella was extremely miserable from water weight and the inability to urinate. Her kidneys had not improved. It was clear she wasn't going to heal. I had to decide to let her go. The vet kindly came to my apartment so that Stella could pass in a place she felt safe.

I learned so many things from Stella. I learned the pain of letting go of someone you love because it is best for them. I learned (and am vigilant to this day) that some things cause toxicity and death to pets. I also learned a gut-wrenching lesson of the results of not heeding the Spirit who told me point-blank to put the potted lily back. God tried to look out for me and Stella. I chose to be rebellious and prideful, thinking I knew better and could spend $7 dollars on the flower. That $7 dollars turned into a $1200 debt, and worse, the loss of my cherished kitty friend.

For years after her premature death, I easily wept about the situation and what we both went through. One night, triggered by something a sibling said about putting their pet down, I went into full-blown anxiety mode. Since I had done some healing, I had the ability to reflect and pinpoint why this panic suddenly arose in me. Having learned Body Code, I used it that night to release negative energies around Stella's loss. At last, I began to heal and become calmer about what happened. The guilt, heartache, and shame retreated, leaving behind a soft sadness for a sweet friend lost and gratitude for knowledge gained.

It feels stark to open this chapter with that story, but I wanted to spark a sense of vigilance within you to not have a similar heartbreak. This chapter is devoted to kitty protection, so let's discuss how we can make life safer for our feline friends.

TOXIC PLANTS

Many plants are toxic to cats. Some mildly toxic ones cause upset tummies or diarrhea, while other more deadly plants can induce organ failure. The ASPCA lists around a thousand plants on their database, and almost half are toxic; again, most mildly so, but it's vital to know which ones are fatal. I keep the ASPCA website available on my phone along with Google to check any plant items against cats' reactions to them. I do not bring vegetation into the home or yard unless I have researched it first.

Listing out the entirety of poisonous plants here is not possible and you have other, more comprehensive resources available online. However, here are a few common plants toxic to felines. Bulb flowers are generally toxic or deadly to cats; in particular, consuming any type of lily leads to organ failure. Foxglove is fatal. All rhododendron plants, including azaleas, cause death in cats. Common houseplants like sego palm or dumb cane are poisonous, the former lethally, the later causing severe irritation. Christmas plants like holly, amaryllis (bulb flower), mistletoe, and poinsettias are problematic—not deadly, but enough to make kitty sick. Hydrangea, if ingested in enough quantity, will cause illness and depression for several days. Eucalyptus, delphinium, carnations, dahlias, all common in bouquets, are bad for kitty. Cannabis, if kitty eats too much and depending on the form, can make him very sick, or he could possibly die. Tobacco causes problems too; cats become ill from chewing cigarettes.

Cats will nibble on plant matter for a few reasons:

- Their diet lacks water, and they believe they will get that additional moisture from plants.
- Curious cats like to explore their environments in very tactile, paws-on and mouth-on ways.
- They may eat to induce vomiting to help them feel better. Cats nibble on grass as a way to expel furballs.
- The cats' food may lack specific nutrients, and they seek to fulfill that deficiency in their diet via plant matter.

To support your cat's needs you can:

- Offer plenty of fresh, clean water around the house. Fountains typically help kitty drink more water.
- To avoid the destruction of houseplants or floral arrangements, play with kitty several times a day to expend energy in healthy ways.

🐱 Keep kitty brushed, especially during hotter months when fur shedding is high, to reduce hairballs. Providing safe grasses to nibble on is totally acceptable.

🐱 Serve a balanced and healthy diet. Feed more wet food than dry using a variety of brands with higher-quality proteins and fats, and fewer carbs. Enhance food with vitamins, probiotics, or other supplements you discuss with your veterinarian.

As a general rule, indoor-only cats tend to be more curious and excited about plants and flowers you bring into the home. Indoor-outdoor cats typically don't get wound-up over plants inside. I have four indoor-only and two indoor-outdoor cats. The girls who go outside don't usually bother a vase of flowers, but the other four can't leave it alone. Even though I bring in non-toxic cut flowers, I must put vases in hard-to-reach places or store them in a secure closet overnight so the flowers look nice for longer.

Here's a brief list of **safe** cut flowers you can bring home. Remember to check all types if the bouquet has a mix of flowers and greenery.

Roses ✿ Baby's Breath ✿ Daisies ✿ Zinnias ✿ Sunflowers ✿ Camellias ✿ Orchids ✿ Status and Stock ✿ Hollyhocks ✿ Lisianthus ✿ Snapdragons ✿

For a fun treat, grow catnip and other pet-friendly herbs and grasses in a pot for your kitties. Keep it out of reach for a week or so after planting to let roots take hold. I have a potted garden on my back deck in spring, summer, and early fall. This year I bought seven or eight catnip plants along with some grasses, safe flowers, herbs, and several veggie plants. I supplied catnip and grass so the cats would leave the other plants and herbs alone, and it worked well. I kept the cats from the deck for a week after I planted. Three months in, two of my cats decimated half of the catnip plants. Skippy and Prim have a catnip addiction and just can't seem to help themselves once they get started. The other kitties

❀ *Beaux sniffing the catnip on the back deck.*

munch here and there, rub on the plants, and walk away. Despite the cats constantly chewing it, which was the intent, the grass grew nicely.

TOXIC HUMAN FOODS

If you browse this topic online, you will find a bit of a mixed bag on particular types of foods. Certain websites caution people not to use specific foods, because in excess they can harm the small cat body. In small amounts though, cats will tolerate some human foods just fine. Some sites fully support a raw meat diet and others caution against raw meat (because it has to be handled, prepared, and stored safely due to potential pathogens). Some say absolutely no dairy products and others say some dairy is fine. From my research I'd put things in this order:

Totally avoid:

- **Grapes, raisins, and their stems** — can lead to kidney failure if ingested.

- **Alcohol** — any type can make a cat very sick, leading to coma or death.

- **Caffeine** — anything with caffeine in it like coffee, some teas, energy drinks, etcetera.

- **Chocolate** — if kitty consumes a small amount he will likely be fine, but large amounts can cause distress. Cats have no need for chocolate, so don't permit it.

- **Xylitol** — technically there isn't a lot of research on cats and this fairly new sugar substitute, but it has shown itself to cause serious toxicity for dogs, so avoid it.

- **Yeast** — raw bread dough or activated yeast can cause kitty's stomach to bloat and twist, becoming deadly. Avoid brewer's yeast. A bit of nutritional yeast is fine.

- **Night shade plants** — like tomato, potato, and eggplant, are dangerous when consumed raw. Potatoes and tomatoes lose toxicity to cats once cooked, but best to avoid it. Note that dry cat food companies commonly use cooked potatoes as a filler.

Avoid or use caution:

🐾 **Nuts** — macadamias are toxic. Nuts like walnuts, almonds, and pecans contain fats difficult for kitties to digest.

🐾 **Garlic and all types of onions** — if cats get a tiny bit via licking a soup broth or similar, they shouldn't have discomfort, but generally avoid.

🐾 **Citrus** — doesn't typically tempt kitty but avoid letting him lick up your custard pie dish or fish dinner remains if it contains citrus. Note that citrus like lemon is a common ingredient in nutraceuticals for cats, so small amounts medicinally are safe.

🐾 **Salt** — small amounts will not harm, but really large amounts cause serious illness or death.

🐾 **Raw meats and eggs** — if you are skilled at handling, cleaning, and using raw meats then your kitty may enjoy a raw-meat diet. The FDA and veterinarians caution that raw meats may contain Salmonella or E. coli bacteria and could cause serious illness if contracted. However, to say raw meat isn't safe for kitties (hands down) is odd, because in the wild they eat raw meat. Very fresh raw meat. Be careful with eggs as well because too much can keep kitty from absorbing biotin, a much-needed vitamin for skin and coat health.

🐾 **Dog food** — it won't hurt kitty to get some nibbles every now and then, but you cannot feed a cat a dog-intended diet because it lacks all necessary feline nutrients.

🐾 **Fat and bones** — avoid giving cats bones to chew on. They can pose a health risk if swallowed. A little bit of animal fat is an okay treat, e.g., a few pea-sized pieces of fat left over from your ham or steak, but do not feed fat often. Kitty has a hard time digesting too much fat like this.

Safe to use, but sparingly:

🐾 **Dairy** — a small amount of dairy as a treat, if kitty likes it, is safe. Given daily in large amounts or as a main food source? Not great. Letting kitty lick up some milk or cream (one to two tablespoons), giving him small bits of cheese, plain yogurt, or letting him lick your dinner plate that has butter or sour cream on it is fine. Never feed kittens cow's milk. Using goat milk products proves gentler on a kitten's tummy, so use fresh goat milk if you cannot get kitten formula.

- **Deli meats** — most contain a lot of preservatives and sodium. Use sparingly as a treat every now and then.

- **Coconut** — don't give a cat coconut water. Don't give them the fruit flesh. However, coconut oil does have holistic health benefits if used correctly. I use it on baby kitty bums for taking temps and on kitties with skin irritations or mild wounds. Kitties may lick a bit of it off your finger or spoon. Use a food-grade coconut oil.

- **Human canned tuna** — this is totally fine if given as treat, used to lure cats into a humane trap, or to tempt a sick kitty with a low appetite. I often recommend tuna water or chicken water, especially the low sodium kind or watered down a bit, for dehydrated kitties. Do not feed canned tuna every day.

- **Liver** — when fresh or cooked, it's okay as a treat every now and then, but not as a meal regularly.

- **Junk food** — plain corn or potato chips in little pieces, a few kernels of buttered popcorn, licking the ice cream bowl, and the like are okay on occasions. Make sure the snack doesn't contain ingredients dangerous to cats like caffeine, chocolate, high sodium, or xylitol.

Most cats really aren't that into human foods, but each cat is also unique. In my house, Skippyjon will eat about anything from a plate or bowl I set aside. I have to be aware of what remains on my plate, especially if I have raisins or grapes. I called the vet once because he ate pieces of walnut from my cereal bowl. Although, when it comes to cat food, he turns up his nose, preferring only pâté chicken or turkey. Prim will lick up my plate, too, if it has something like butter, cheese, or meat on it. She likes to eat any fatty flavor. She begs for corn chips or popcorn when I have that out. Gigi asks for half-and-half every night, an emotional ritual for attention. She stands up against the counter and meows, I scratch her head, she anticipates as I get a saucer and the pint out, and I pour out about a tablespoon. She sniffs it and licks a few licks, then walks away. Beaux and Prim finish it off. I don't give it to her every time she begs, just a few times a week. Honey and Trixie express no interest in human food. Well, Honey will lick my glass of milk if I'm not looking.

OTHER TOXIC SUBSTANCES

There are so many possibilities here: paints, glues, chemicals, cleaners, medicines, pest poisons. Know many substances can harm your kitty. Make sure your cat cannot access the places where you store these items. If you see your cat get into anything you aren't sure of, look it up. Keep the emergency vet clinic number in your phone as well as program in the ASPCA's poison control hotline. Don't delay in getting help as some of these substances may lead to death in cats.

Consider how many toxic items we have in our homes on a regular basis. In the US, our laws and regulations on known toxic substances are much more lax than in many European nations. Our government tends to put the profits of business above the individual safety of people (or animals). This is a sour side effect of "the American Dream." Don't get me wrong. I do see the value of the ability to raise oneself up in life via invention or business ventures, but sadly there is much moral corruption in massive corporations, creating harmful products for the public to consume. I cannot name products or companies, but many organizations, typically non-profits like www.ewg.org, will educate you on the toxins all around us. These toxins are not usually lethal in a single exposure or dose, but compounded over time, they can really harm our bodies. If they can harm the large human body, they most certainly impact the small feline body. Additionally, cats are at a greater disadvantage because they lack certain enzymes to help break down toxins in their livers.

All this to say, you and kitty might want to consider moving in a greener direction, embracing a more holistic lifestyle, and living an organic life. Cleaning products should derive from nature as much as possible. Certainly avoid using cleaners directly around kitty; shut her out of a room you are currently cleaning. Air out rooms before allowing reentry. Avoid perfumy and highly chemical items in your home like air fresheners, scented plug-ins, candles, fabric sprays. Stop using aerosol hair products. Be aware of toxic chemicals used in home building materials like drywall, paint, carpeting, or luxury vinyl. When you install or paint, avoid letting the cat in the area for a time. Air out the home significantly at these times. Use the old-fashioned tip of laying out a lot of fresh-cut onion slices to absorb toxins in the air.

Most of the time cats avoid things they find unpleasant. However, some deadly substances actually entice cats. Bleach gets many cats excited. It's like a catnip reaction, sadly to a fatal substance. When using bleach, keep kitties away. Store out of their reach. Never leave bleach residue behind when cleaning. Moreover, cats find anti-freeze or other fatty car fluids attractive. I rushed my cat Honey to the vet after she consumed power-steering fluid that was dripping onto the garage floor. The vet had to force feed Honey liquid charcoal, and gratefully everything turned out alright. Garages in general should be off-limits because we commonly store toxic items there.

Take care with your medications and supplements. Try not to drop any on the floor without immediately getting down and retrieving. Never give human medications to your cats! Specifically, aspirin and ibuprofen can prove deadly if consumed. Occasionally, you can use some over-the-counter meds to support cat care when they are sick, but never do so without consulting a veterinarian.

Let's quickly touch on the use of essential oils. On the humorous side, typically my cats flee from me when I put on oils. They really dislike citrus, floral, and tree oil smells. I find it humorous that a cat takes no offense to human body odors like poop or toots, but put on lavender oil and they bolt the room. There are exceptions. Stella always reacted in a semi-possessed way with wild eyes and nipping me whenever I used oils in the mint family (catnip is in the mint family). Honey loves the scent of clove oil and rubs all over me and tries to lick me when I put it on. Honey, if I leave the lid up, will stick her head in my box of essential oils and rub her face all over the closed bottles.

On a more serious note, essential oils run the gamut of quality from very poor to exceptional. Do some personal research to find brands esteemed as clean for human use. These need to be

❀ *Honey is my sole cat interested in oils.*

food-grade, or better, therapeutic-grade oils. You will need to dig even deeper to find oils marketed as safe for pet and even cat use. I have run across blanket statements that essential oils are bad for cats, full stop. To err on the side of safety, you can adhere to that. Up to this point, while I use oils daily on myself, I have shied away from using them with my cats because I know how sensitive their systems can be. When you have a truly high-quality brand of pet-safe oils and you have learned from an expert like a holistic veterinarian how to use them specifically for cats, using essential oils is possible. Until you educate yourself though, I recommend not attempting anything other than aromatherapy with a quality oil in a diffuser and make sure kitty can leave the area if wanted.

INDOOR VS INDOOR-OUTDOOR VS OUTDOOR

There are many concerns associated with cats living outside or being indoor-outdoor pets, hence the ongoing debate among cat lovers on the merits of indoor only versus allowing cats outdoor time. For those of us with pet cats, it can boil down to average life expectancies as the decision maker.

Indoor

An indoor-only cat, on average, will live twelve to fifteen years. Many live several years longer into their late teens or early twenties. Even though much safer, indoor-only kitties wrestle with the big concerns of boredom and obesity. An indoor-only cat not expending enough energy and/or eating a low-quality diet may become overweight, and this could lead to health complications earlier in life like diabetes or arthritis. However, indoor cats receiving good quality food and engaging in play long into their adult lives will likely stay healthy longer.

As already implied above, houses are not without their dangers. A kitty can have an accident within the home or consume a toxic substance, like my Stella eating the Easter lily. Nevertheless, if you keep your kitty inside, their longevity outcome increases substantially as compared

❀ *My outdoor upper deck with four kitties on it.*

to outdoor cats. Sans outdoor exercise and hunting, indoor-only fur babies must have activity and engagement.

Providing enrichment is the key. Refer back to page 194 for ideas if you need them. If you have the ability, create safe outdoor spaces like upper decks or balconies with no way down or build an exterior catio. Some people have built enclosures out in their yard, but you have to carry kitty from the house to the pen in a safe way like a carrier. Besides, kitty cannot come and go as they please in that scenario.

❀ *Foster kitten Cookie posing for photos on screened porch.*

At my former house I had a very large double deck off the back. The upper deck had no access down, and my adult cats were savvy enough not to jump down or fall off. The lower deck was screened in. Neither place was officially a "catio" because humans used them too, but the cats loved these spaces. In my new home, I built a catio.

Another increasing popular option for indoor-only cats is the "adventure cat." Refer back to our previous discussion if this is something you want to review (page 238).

Indoor-Outdoor

Speaking as a rescue worker, I would say keep your pet cats indoors. It cuts out a huge number of risks to a cat's life. Unlike indoor-only cats, the average life expectancy of an indoor-outdoor cat is about six to nine years. On average, this equates to six years less life than indoor-only kitties. There are more potential dangers outside. Cars, dogs, coyotes, racoons, mean humans, poisons, cat fights, deadly plants or insects, and potential exposure to cat viruses are some of the things your cat may face while outside. Young cats outside, especially under one year, are the most susceptible to early death. Possibly their immaturity keeps them from making wise choices that then leads to higher risk scenarios like running in front of moving cars.

However, speaking as a cat expert and guardian, there may be reasons for allowing a cat to be indoor-outdoor. You may have adopted an adult cat already used to going outside, and they dash out every chance they can get. You may have territorial tensions in a multi-cat home like I do, and more territory lessens stress levels. You may have a cat who gets depressed if not allowed outdoors. If you experience one of these or a similar reason, you may choose to do indoor-outdoor.

I am not encouraging this practice per se but want to give counsel on how to do it to the best of your ability, so the cat's risks go down when outdoors.

First of all, do not simply open the door and send the cat out. Do not force a cat outside that isn't interested. If you have physically impaired or immune compromised cats, do not let them outside. Consider the traffic around your home: Do you live in an apartment complex, in the city, or near a busy street? The higher percentage of cars, people, or roads close by, the more likely your cat will run into a tragic end. If you live in a quiet neighborhood with light traffic and nowhere near a busy road (like I do), the scenario for letting kitty outdoors on their own improves. Do you have good neighbors or rough neighbors? Are they pet lovers or animal haters who wouldn't feel bad about poisoning your pet? What are the HOA policies? City ordinances? If you feel you have positive answers to these questions, you may have less risk for your indoor-outdoor kitty.

Never send kitties that are not full-grown outdoors on their own. As I already mentioned, kittens really struggle keeping themselves alive outside. Being small makes them a target for even more predators, including owls and other birds of prey. They often make foolish choices when scared because they panic too much. They are still in the stage of life where they chew and eat things out of curiosity, including toxic or poisonous substances.

Once your cat is big enough and actually interested, introduce the outdoors slowly and with you right beside him. I recommend using a harness and leash. Let him sniff the outside in either your front or back yard. Spend time going around the whole house or apartment building. Allow the cat to explore slowly, to rub his face on things to mark his scent: house, bushes, mailbox, sidewalk, or trees. Do this many times over a period of weeks.

In the same timeframe you are wandering the yard on the leash, clicker train the kitty to understand his name and come when called. If you have an indoor-outdoor kitty you *want* him to come home when you call.

Once kitty becomes used to the environment outside on a leash and is comfortable enough to have been marking his scent, you can remove the leash and wander around with him. Do this new routine several times. Allow kitty to walk away from you and practice calling him back with a click and reward. Once kitty eats the treat, pick him up and carry him into the house. Eventually, kitty can go out on his own, once you feel he is fully trained, has marked his scent around the property, and acts calmly and safely outside.

❀ *Honey demonstrates rolling around and marking her scent on the sidewalk. See how she checks her scent?*

I recommend that you keep kitty even safer by not permitting him to stay out overnight. Call him in before it gets dark. The chance of danger increases exponentially for kitties after dark. In a few pages we will discuss ID tags. Make sure he has one on every time he goes outside. If you follow this guidance, kitty will be safer outdoors.

Side Note: Exterior Cat & Dog Doors

When it comes to putting in an exterior pet door, in general I don't recommend it because other critters can come into your home uninvited, and kitty can leave without your realizing. Outside access pet doors with microchip-reading capabilities, leading to a fully enclosed backyard, and with a timer or lock during night hours (after kitty comes indoors) are the safest option.

Story Example: Enlisting Heavenly Help

I have trained my two girls, Honey and Trixie, to go outdoors. Honey was two years old and Trixie five when we began the slow introduction to the outside and only because both expressed a lot of interest in going out. We do a routine of "one in, one out," meaning they can't be outside together unless I am with them. They squabble if they are both outside without supervision. Generally, they stay in the yard and almost always come home immediately when called. I don't give food rewards for coming when I call, but you may need to depending on your kitty. My girls do expect affection rewards though when coming home, and they receive praise like "good girl" and "so glad you are safe." Each gets picked up, petted, and kissed.

If my girls do not come immediately, I go back inside and ask my Angels to send them home, that I need them safely inside. All but a few times, the cat returned to the front door within five minutes of that request for help.

I'll say more on this in the next chapter, but I up the protection ante for my cats that go outside by shielding them energetically before they leave the house. What does that mean? It means I place, with my intention, an energy field around the cat that then acts as a shield for them. I always say a verbal prayer asking God and the Angels to protect them while outside, keeping them safe, for the highest good of all. I pet the kitties while I do this "shield placement," and they both enjoy the affection. I then tell the kitty I love them and to be safe as I open the door for them. Our words and intentions have real creative power, especially when combined with Spirit. I fully believe that this ritual increases their safety outside. However, I do this after doing all of the above safety measures, not in place of.

❀ *Trixie in the front yard.*

Outdoor

Outdoor-only cats that have people looking out for them on a daily basis have an average life expectancy of about three to five years. Some do live longer, for sure, but the many outdoor cats that just live a year or so pulls down the average. Their longer exposure to all the outdoor threats obviously increases their risk of experiencing traumatic or deadly circumstances.

Some cats at the shelter need outdoor-only homes or to become a working cat in barn programs. Typically, these animals either have not learned to use a litterbox reliably, are not overly friendly to people, or haven't lived indoors before. Sometimes, people need a cat for pest control on their property. Guardians still look out for them, ensuring they have plenty of food and water, and veterinary care if injured or sick.

Do not adopt a young, socialized kitten, and then drop him outside as an outdoor-only cat. That kitten could easily have found a good indoor-only home and remained much safer. Don't adopt an adult cat that has never gone outside, and then expect him to live outside and be an expert hunter. If you want an outdoor cat, get an adult cat with the right background, temperament, and skills to be outdoors. You do the same type of homebase training with a new outdoor-only cat, keeping him in the garage or enclosed porch for a few weeks or more as he accepts you as his new family, begins to mark the territory with his scent, and recognizes where the food comes from.

Stray or Feral Outdoor Cats

Neighborhood or community cats that have no particular human looking out for their needs have an average life expectancy of two to three years. The average lifespan is so low because of all the young kittens that die before they reach one year. Without a mama cat, or if mama has another litter quickly, kittens struggle to survive outdoors. They are too young or small to endure without constant protection and guidance. With no one looking out for them, life can be really hard and short. When I helped ferals in Georgia, one year coyotes decimated cat colonies everywhere nearby. At the start of my efforts, I had plenty of cats to help, but after two years, essentially, no more ferals came to the house to eat. Now, a big part of that proceeded from doing TNR, stopping reproduction, but part of that also resulted from how dangerous and precarious outdoor living can be on a small predator animal.

There are two types of community cats: strays and ferals. Recall we touched on the differences on page 31.

If you feel sorry for community cats, do what you can to support them and make their lives a bit easier. You can seek out a TNR group and become a member. Get training from them and learn from their experiences. Participating in TNR groups will get you access to additional tools and resources. Help by getting many of the cats in your community fixed or assist feeding a colony on a regular basis. This work really needs volunteers.

MICROCHIPPING & COLLARS

Microchipping is easy. A small device goes under the skin and has a unique identifying number. Should the cat be lost and then found, a vet office, rescue, or shelter can scan for the chip and find the owner information online. If your cat accidentally gets lost, having that microchip is the best chance of getting kitty back into your arms.

If you adopt a "free kitten," you will need to get him chipped when you go to the vet clinic for vaccinations or when you get kitty fixed. Sometimes shelters and breeders will microchip, so ask them upon adoption if that is included or not. If not, remember to get it done as soon as possible. Make sure to register the chip online under your name and contact information, and keep it updated over the years if your information changes.

Most rescue groups microchip their cats, so if you adopt from a rescue organization, kitty will likely already have one in place. Many rescues will not transfer the microchip data into your name but keep the information under their own organization. This is because, try as they may to find quality homes, too many adopters abandon pets. The rescue prefers that if the cat is left behind or lost that

their group is contacted to pick up the cat. They will reach out to the adopter on record and see if the loss was accidental or not. They gladly reunite pets or keep them if no longer wanted. If you adopt a cat and the rescue association keeps the microchip registered under their name, keep the group updated if you change your phone number, email, or address.

🐾 *Trixie, wearing her fifth collar and ID.*

Another key identifier is having a collar with an ID tag on it. Getting the right style of collar is important. You want to buy "breakaway" collars. A cat can easily get the collar looped around branches or other entanglements like fences. If they are wearing a breakaway collar, then with enough force, the cat can break free of the collar. Buckle collars, Velcro, or other styles will not break open to free the cat. Cats have strangled, starved, or become an easy target for a predator because of a stuck collar.

Breakaway collars unfortunately do get lost and must be replaced. Trixie has lost at least four collars over the last few years, two of them in the house, and I still have not discovered them! I learned to not buy $15 collars and $15 tags at the pet store. I buy them "in bulk" on Amazon to save money. You can get three or four breakaway collars for around $12. Personalized ID tags can be as low as $3-$4. Remember to check reviews on the product and provider before purchasing.

Story Example: Good Fit

Make sure that the collar and ID tag fit the cat or kitten appropriately. An adopter of one of my bottle babies came by my home for support when the kitten became ill. When I pulled her out of the carrier, she looked miserable. Not only was she sick, but they had put a very large, heavy bone-shaped ID collar on a three-pound kitten. How uncomfortable for her to wear! Nay, haul around. That tag was made for a 40lbs dog. If you place too heavy of a tag on a small cat, over time you can cause muscle and bone development stress. The ID tags on my adult cats are about the size of a quarter and weigh less than one.

Ensure that as the kitty grows, so does the size of the collar. Most collars or harnesses are adjustable and come XS-XL. Fit the collar tightly enough that it doesn't easily slip off, but also loose enough so it's comfortable to wear. A correct fit allows you to easily fit one to two fingers between the collar and kitty's neck. If a collar is placed on a kitten and never adjusted as he grows, the collar can cause slow strangulation or starvation of the animal. I once saw a trapped adult cat with a kitten collar embedded into the skin creating a raw, oozing, infected, and painful wound that required surgery to remove.

If you have indoor-only cats who show no interest in dashing out the door, then you do not need to put a collar and ID on the cat. It is more comfortable for the cat not to wear one. However, you may have other reasons for placing a collar, like wearing one with a jingle bell because the cat frequently start spats. With the warning sound, he is less stealthy.

Side Note: Jingle Bells

Believe it or not, the jingle bell has actually created some controversy. On one hand, it has value and on the other, could be a hazard. Mostly, I say it belongs in the good category with indoor inter-cat disputes and as a subtle warning device when a kitty unnecessarily hunts outdoors. However, it appears anecdotally that some larger prey animals have begun to associate the small jingle bell sound as an audible presence of potential prey, putting the cat in danger.

GPS collars have a tracker embedded in the collar or in the ID tag. These collars cost a lot more, and it may be harder to swallow if the cat loses it. However, if you have a cat that runs away or wanders too far from home, you may want to invest in this type of tool. At this time, embedded microchips do not come with GPS included.

MOVING

If you plan to move, invest in a collar and ID. The event of moving, the weeks of preparation before, and the disorganization for weeks afterwards are very upsetting to cats. They are territorial creatures of habit, and the chaos stresses them out. Prior to starting your packing, place an ID collar on your cat. I strongly recommend your first step in the moving process is to set up one or two safe spaces in the house for kitty. Have all of his needed belongings in one space and keep him in that zone while packing up other rooms. Wait to pack that safe-space room until last.

On the day of the move, have an off-limits bathroom to everyone but you. Have everything removed but litterbox, food bowls, a few toys, and a cave bed for the cat. Place kitty in here to hide out during the ruckus. If your cat gets super stressed, take it a step further and secure him in a zip up enclosed play pen or large dog crate so he can't dash out the door when you open it and hide in an unfindable place. You can cover the crate with a large blanket to help kitty feel more secure.

When you travel with kitty to your new home, make sure you have a secure carrier. If traveling more than a few hours, the crate should be large enough for the cat to have a small litterbox, a bed, and food bowls. If you choose to let the cat loose in the car on a really long trip, *never* open the car doors until you have secured kitty inside the closed carrier, crate, or securely on a harness and leash you are holding. If you cannot rely on your children to keep this rule, then *never* let the cat out of the carrier or crate until safely inside your new home. (Be sure to check state laws on animals free-roaming inside moving vehicles.)

Story Example: Cross-Country Moves

When Gigi and Prim were kittens, I moved across country, over two thousand miles. I let them out of the carrier to roam the car. At this point I could easily scoop them into the carrier and lock it when I had to stop for food or gas. I had a small litterbox on the floor of the backseat and food and water dishes on the floor in the front seat area. When I moved back the other direction two years later, I no longer felt comfortable letting them both loose in the car while I drove because they were

🐾 *Gigi and Prim as kittens on our long road trip.*

278

too big to scoop up easily and Prim had become even more skittish. I invested in a big crate that held them both. It took up almost the entire backseat of my sedan. They could sit upright, stand up, and walk around a bit. I had a small litterbox and food bowl in there, along with a bed. I kept it covered in a blanket. We stayed in pet-friendly motels along the way where they could get out and roam in the room.

Once you arrive at your new home, first thing, set up a safe room or play pen for the cat—a secure and closed location. Once the busiest part of the move is over, allow the cat to have one room in the house to settle into. Try to have some familiar things for him like his favorite bed and cat tree set up. Like when you first adopted, give the cat time to acclimate to the new noises, smells, situation. Don't just set the cat loose into that crazy mess. Help him adjust to the idea that this is his new territory. He needs to settle in, start scent marking by rubbing his face and head on wall corners and floors. He needs time to relax a bit in that safe space while you work on settling the rest of the house, unpacking, and moving things around. Note that if you are renovating anything while living in the home, it will take even longer for kitty to adjust because of the noises of construction and strangers coming and going, so keep him in that safe space for as long as needed.

After things settle down, slowly allow the cat to explore more spaces. Shut all exterior doors. You do not want a panicked cat to dash out the door and become totally lost and not have his scent anywhere around to figure out where home is now.

If kitty was previously an indoor-outdoor kitty, do not merely let him go outside; keep him indoors for several months. He needs time to establish this house as his new territory and new forever home. Once you do let kitty outside, leash him up and go with him. Follow the same steps as previously written in this chapter to help kitty acclimate to and claim the outdoor space before letting him out on his own.

If you have an outdoor-only cat and you move, please keep kitty inside for several months on an enclosed porch, in the garage, or in secure place where he can't escape until things settle down. Allow the cat to begin to claim this new space as his home. Before letting him outside on his own, follow the same outdoor introduction steps previously given in this chapter. Watch kitty closely when outside to be sure he associates the home as his new territory before letting him loose. You can see this when he begins to feel calm, curious, and mark the corners of walls, the bushes, or roll around on the sidewalk or grass leaving scent.

FINDING YOUR LOST KITTY

For loving and dedicated pet guardians, losing kitty can be devastating.

Story Example: Losing Trixie

When I first bought my home, I rented out my basement to a few younger women. Six months later, I had a roommate move out. Her parents came to load up and haul her things. Unbeknownst to me, Trixie had gotten into my garage that morning, and when they opened the main door to load their truck, she ran off because she was afraid. I had no idea until late in the evening when I locked up and fed the cats. I realized I hadn't seen Trixie all day. I searched high and low inside the house, three times. No Trixie. I finally texted my roommate's mother to ask if she had seen Trixie that day. She had. She saw her dash under their truck and cross the street but didn't say anything to me because she knew (at that time) all my cats were indoor only and assumed it was a neighbor's cat.

I was so worried! I immediately prayed for help getting Trixie back home. I went out with a flashlight and looked around for her, but no luck. I looked outside for her three to four times a day every day she was missing. On day two I created "missing cat" flyers and went door-to-door to all my neighbors. While I *did* feel sad and stressed, I also felt a calm assurance. When I had prayed about her that first evening, I felt that everything would turn out okay, that I needed to have faith that she would return.

Still, I did all the labor I could do to help reunite me with Trixie. I didn't simply sit back and assume I didn't need to participate in the process. Since her scent was not placed around the yard, I put her litterboxes outside in both the front and back. I made calls to all the shelters, even the one two hours away where the moving truck went, and gave Trixie's description to all. I called the rescue organization I adopted her through to give them my updated information in case they were contacted. I continued to pray for her. I asked that Angels protect her and help her find her way back home. I requested that my family members pray for her safe return. I spoke to many neighbors every day. By day five, I admit I worried that my feeling of assurance had been wrong. Had she found anything to eat? Had she found a water source? Did someone take her? Was she injured?

On the sixth day, in the morning, my sister called to cheer me up. As we chatted, I felt prompted to go outside to the front of the house. I was still talking while sitting in the yard, and then I heard a few tentative meows. I stood up and said, "Trixie?" She ran out from the side of the house and literally leapt into my arms. I was so grateful! My sister cried with me over the phone for her safe return. Though a bit dehydrated and exhausted from a week of stress, Trixie was safe. I am grateful that I trusted in God and the Angels who protected her until she found her way home.

Story Example: Miracle Returns

Not all lost pets come home, but sometimes families get a miracle even after months apart.

My sister, who is raising her granddaughter, has three cats, a dog, two bunnies, and seven chickens and married to a man who would prefer a no-pet life. Zuri, her granddaughter, about six years old at the time, loves animals. She had excused herself from the dinner table one evening and gone to the front yard while the rest of the adults around the table chatted. She came running back in, "Nana, Nana! Can we keep him? Can I feed him? He looks so hungry!"

When questioned what she meant, she explained that she was petting a cat in the front yard, but he looked so hungry. Her Nana said, "No. We can't feed a stray cat. Your Papa will leave me if we have anymore animals!"

Disappointed because she wanted to help the kitty, Zuri went back out to at least keep him company and give him some love and friendship. She came back into the house a few minutes later and asked, "What does 'Xavier' mean?" Her Nana asked her what brought on that question and Zuri replied it was written on the kitty's tag.

When my sister heard this, she went outside to see the cat and look at the tag. The kitty did look a bit worse for wear. She looked at the tag and called the number engraved there. The family answered, and when my sister said that she found their cat in her yard, they were overjoyed! They had moved to the area a few months earlier, and their long-time cat bolted in the move because of all the chaos. They immediately hopped in their car and drove to my sister's house for a joyful reunion with the family pet they thought was gone for good.

I hope your beloved kitty never gets lost, but if so, let's talk about a few tips for finding him again.

Social Media

Use social media, if you can, to find your cat. When I lost Trixie, I did this as well, though I didn't really have any local neighborhood contacts. Having people wishing you well, praying for you and the cat, or sending up good vibes has power. It comforted me to feel heard and supported. Having friends on social media who live close by means they can also watch for your kitty and help spread the word to their contacts. You could send a social post to the local rescue groups and shelters to either re-post or be aware in case they get a cat in that looks like yours.

Local Shelters

Call all the local and county shelters. They should ask for details. Sometimes they will take those over the phone or will ask you to email information, along with a recent photo and microchip number, if kitty has one. You really want to do this task, especially if your kitty is not microchipped. Cats without identity are put up for adoption or euthanized after short holds. Make sure to describe any distinguishing features about your cat. For example, Prim has a tiny brown dot in the middle of her pink nose and Honey, has a small scar on her right ear. Shelters are typically busy, so call back a few times a week to check in as they may not remember to call you. If you are reunited with your cat, inform all of the shelters that your kitty came home safely.

Flyers

Use flyers to get the word out. It should include the clearest picture you have of kitty, some details on the cat (e.g., shy, friendly, never been outside), date kitty went missing, and all of your contact information. If you can, instead of just leaving at the door or on a car, ring the doorbell and talk to people. This gets them to care a bit more, so they want to help. Several of my neighbors called me after receiving my flyer by hand to say they were thinking about us, asking if she'd returned yet, and offering comfort.

Microchips/Collars

It comes in handy if kitty already has ID when lost. If you have an indoor-only kitty who accidentally got out, he may not be wearing a collar. At the time she got lost, Trixie did not have a collar, but she was microchipped. As I recommended above, if moving, make sure to put a collar on kitty for several weeks before and after the event. If you don't have a microchip, get one implanted before you move, as a safety net.

Contact Local Rescues

If you have already done this on social media, that is great. Additionally, you may want to email information to the rescue and call them. It gives them a heads up should someone bring in a found cat that looks like yours. Again, if your cat isn't microchipped, stay on top of following up so that your kitty doesn't get adopted out to someone else.

Search for Kitty

I am sure you will search for kitty. Looking at dawn or dusk may give you the best chance of finding him. Cats tend to be more active at those times; however, a stressed and scared cat may simply feel safer moving around in the dark. Note that tromping around may scare your kitty into silence and hiding. I recommend using a flashlight and calmly calling out the cat's name. Hopefully, he will recognize your voice even through his panic.

Scent-Heavy Objects

If kitty never spent time in the yard and didn't have the chance to scent mark his territory, you can help him find his way back home by placing scent-heavy items outside of the house. This includes used litterboxes, bedding, cat trees, and more. Place in both the front and back yards near the house. I put a litterbox next to the garage door and one on the lower back deck. Also, put out water and food. Use strong smelling food like canned tuna. Even if kitty is too scared to reveal himself, he may come close for food.

Live or Humane Traps

You can set live traps around the house or in any area where you spotted your kitty. You can buy these online, at the local farm supply store, or see if the shelter will loan a few to you. Set them up with entry facing the least intimidating direction, place highly scented food like tuna at the back of the cage, and cover the outside of the cage in a camouflage blanket (colors like green or brown). Make sure that nothing interferes with the trap door snapping shut. Check the traps twice a day and refresh the food especially if cold enough to freeze, or if so hot the food spoils faster or attracts insects.

Prayer & Spiritual Help

Include prayer right at the beginning of this process. Ask God to send inspiration on what you should do to find kitty. Pray for the cat to stay safe from harm, evil, or accident until you can be reunited. Request Angels that love you and serve you to help kitty cat find his way home. Seek for calm and comfort. If kitty has been gone a long time, ask to know (intuitively) if you should keep looking, keep hoping, or mourn the loss.

Invite good friends and family to join you in prayer. If your friends don't pray, you can ask them to send out good thoughts and hopes for you to find your kitty. You can fast to support the effort as well. Fasting is a way to sacrifice something that is hard for you to go without (food), and it conveys more urgency and humility to the Heavens that you really are serious about receiving help. Fasting can have the ability to soften you and therefore be more attuned to Spirit. Have faith that fasting will bring you closer to God and remain open to seeing and accepting a miracle.

USING CONNECTION TO SPIRIT TO PROTECT CATS

As spiritually minded people, we should develop our inner-knowing or intuition. We need to find a place emotionally and mentally where we can tap into Spirit to receive answers and be confident in what we receive. It is not an easy place to obtain. If you are there, amazing! Do everything in your power to remain in that peaceful, loving, and happy space. I admit to attaining such peace and losing it, several times in my life. But I can say with confidence I am much happier when close to that sensitive and quiet place where inspiration comes readily.

For me, I have to let go of frustration, anger, and judgement. I need daily activities to help me focus on spiritual matters, like prayer, meditation, scripture reading, listening to uplifting podcasts or books, listening to spiritual music, saying positive affirmations, doing energy work or tapping, etcetera. Several hours of every day concentrated on being positive, loving, and hopeful keeps me focused. This world has a great deal of negativity all around us. Try to pinpoint some of the most discouraging and peace-negating aspects of your life, and change them or avoid them. For me, I left social media. It helped me feel less anxious and stressed because of all the debating and unkindness there. Social media can be a place of support, too, but the negatives outweighed the positives for me. Also, for me, watching dark TV or movies —depressing stories; hopeless endings; plots centered around violence or murder; women or children portrayed poorly or being abused; unhappy, angry, vengeful, vindictive, or selfish main characters; lustful situations—these messages deter my connection to Spirit. I found music, too, influenced my spiritual state. A lot of popular music today has negative lyrics and are too simple in their melodies with intense, low-resonating repetitive beats; this does not increase our intelligence or support positive thinking.

Sometimes toxic relationships keep us in a state of negativity and conflict. I worked with a rescue as an interim director, and it was one of the most negative and conflict-ridden experiences in my life. The work was utterly draining and devastated my connection to Spirit. Relationships, whether personal, family, or work, are not always easy or even possible to escape. Figure out a strategic plan to shift these unhealthy associations and balance them better in your life. Maybe you can find ways to reduce your time with them. Your plan to cope better and change yourself might include a weekly therapy or energy session, daily prayer and meditation, journaling, or other productive ways to reduce stress and frustration.

Again, having daily time, two or three hours a day if we can manage it, to focus on positive and peaceful thoughts and feelings, will help counterbalance challenges in our lives we cannot change or control. We can do this by: Ensuring our getting-ready-for-work time includes healing music or positive audio books. Carving out time for prayer two to three times a day. Getting up early and doing a thirty-minute meditation. Making sure to find time to read from religious texts each day. Writing out affirmations and posting them near a mirror or on a bedroom wall. Saying them out loud morning and night. Recording and then playing them on our phones as we commute to work or school. Selecting a needed mantra, and saying it over and over silently in our mind all day long. Shifting our thoughts to include God as often as possible throughout the day—simple "I love You God," "Help me with this God," or "I am so grateful for Your support in..." phrases will help us stay connected to Him and to Universal Power. Visualizing Angels helping us and asking for them to support even our little needs to make the day better—like finding good parking spots, keeping us safe when scared, or helping kitty to come home before dark.

If we struggle with an addiction to things like recreational drugs, alcohol, prescription meds, or sex/pornography, connecting to Spirit will be very, very hard to accomplish. Something about altering our state of mind or turning to oblivion or pleasure in harmful or selfish ways disconnects us from Universal Power. That isn't to say that our Angels won't still try to help us or that God isn't worried and longing for us to make healthier choices, but it does mean we are cutting ourselves off, making it difficult to attune to spiritual impressions and whispers. If we want to lead a spiritually informed life with real connection to God's power, we must be clean of toxic and highly negative influences. The journey to sobriety often travels a long, hard road, but worth the effort. We can't do it alone and should seek quality help. Surround ourselves with people who have overcome and know how to help us do the same.

How does all this advice relate to becoming a better cat parent? Well, it certainly helps us to be a happier, healthier human, and everyone we live around will benefit from that. However, I do want to illustrate the point further via a story. It is not only about having that connection to Spirit, but having the wherewithal to heed the impressions and do so without fear. It takes practice to trust our impressions. I have found listening to this guidance leads to receiving more wise guidance. Conversely, ignoring prompts leads to fewer and fewer prompts. This skill indeed helps us protect our cats and make better choices in their care.

Story Example: Tat Tat

My niece Rachel was selling her home in Wyoming, and she didn't want the presence of her cat or a litterbox to deter potential buyers. Plus, she hoped to avoid stressing her kitty with moving, packing, and unpacking. She thought it best to send pets out of the home during this process and bring them back once everything settled down. She called and asked me if I would cat-sit Tat Tat for a few months until they arrived back in state and moved into their new home.

While talking with her, I heard a distinct voice in my mind say, "If he comes to your home, Tat Tat will die." Though a bit shocked by the thought, I shook it off. I justified that I am excellent at caring for cats. "Why on earth would he die in my care? He wouldn't," I silently retorted to myself. So I said yes, and Tat Tat shortly thereafter arrived at my home. In his own home, he was

❀ *Tat Tat in my room watching the outside world*

normally a very chill cat. Suddenly being dropped into my home with four other cats and his family nowhere to be found, he became depressed, and living in my storage room probably didn't help. He hid most of the day and wouldn't eat. After several days, I had to force-feed him. His depression went on for weeks. He did eventually pull out of his sadness and began to explore my home.

At his own home in Wyoming. he had been an indoor-outdoor kitty. A "cat about town." A strong, but fixed, tom cat. At my house he mostly avoided my cats who just hissed at him. He began to lounge comfortably in odd places like on top of the microwave. I was happy for him that he had settled in.

At my house I have a very large second story deck with no stairs down. My cats had been using and loving this outdoor safe space since we moved in the year before. The first time I let Tat Tat on the deck he disappeared! When I realized he was gone I went out and called for him. There he was on the roof of the house! How did he do that? No clue. My other cats had never attempted such a feat and still not to this day, five years later.

I gratefully coaxed him safely down, but the deck became off limits to him. Toward the end of his several months' stay with me he became restless, wanting to explore more. So, I went outside in the front yard with him. He was a good boy, exploring slowly. He started marking his head and cheek scent on the walls and corners of the house and garage. Good sign! He would be able to find his way home. We stayed for about fifteen minutes, and I took him in. The next day, I decided to let him out again, and I took a short walk around the block with the intent of bringing him in afterward. He wasn't in the front yard when I arrived back home. As I walked into my house

(you can see straight through the glass door to the balcony), I saw two of my cats keenly watching something below. I went out to look over the edge, too, and Tat Tat lay motionless on the ground below.

It had only been fifteen minutes. I stood there for a moment in shock. I had barely seen him prancing happily in the yard not long before. I had to force myself to shake off the shock and run down and around outside to check on him, but he looked dead. When I arrived, he was gone. His neck appeared broken.

I sobbed as my mind raced. What had happened? I could merely surmise that he had climbed a tree and tried to jump to the deck and somehow slipped. Hit his head on the railing? Cats skillfully right themselves before landing, so why hadn't he?

"If he comes to your home, Tat Tat will die," I was warned. I talked myself out of it in that moment on the phone with Rachel because how would I explain that to my niece who needed my help? Whom I wanted to help. "Sorry, I can't because I just had this impression that if I take him into my home he will die." I feared sounding foolish or like I was making up a lie to avoid the job. I didn't want to disappoint my niece who asked for a reasonable favor. But ignoring the prompting led to the loss of her cherished pet, one so good with her young toddler children.

Poor Tat Tat passed away only days before his family would be ready to take him back home.

You can see by this story I still waffled with listening to and heeding impressions I received. My Stella had lost her life because of this, and now Tat Tat. I want you to do better. I hope you will follow through with your impressions, even if they seem odd or unlikely. You never know. You will not likely be sorry you followed the counsel, but may find yourself sorry you didn't.

Not all the promptings or intuitive messages you receive will be literal life and death situations, but some might. Learning to heed them all the time is our surest way and the safest path for the cat in our care. Sometimes, when I go to let Trixie or Honey outside, I just don't feel good about it that day, so I keep them inside. Sometimes the messages I receive deal with what the cat needs to feel happier in my home, like a new cat tree or toys.

PURRRITO WRAP UP

Taking care of kitty takes forethought. Life has many potential threats like toxic plants, foods, or chemicals, encountering dangers outdoors, or getting lost in a move. Using the tips from this chapter will reduce risks for your furry friend. We are responsible for their welfare, so we should put dangerous items out of reach, train outdoor cats to come when called before nightfall, and keep them in up-to-date IDs, among other efforts to keep them secure. Additionally, we can use our spiritual tools to preserve our kitties safe from harm, accident, and evil by enlisting the help of God and Angels. Listening to promptings from Spirit can literally save the lives of our pets.

CHAPTER 11

Preparedness for Kitties

When we think of preparing for a natural disaster, we might put together 72-hour kits for our family. Some might go further with evacuation plans and where to meet if the family becomes separated during a disaster. However, we often forget to make plans for our pets in the event of an emergency.

After Hurricane Katrina hit the gulf coast in late summer of 2005, I saw a documentary called *Left Behind Without a Choice*. It covered the attempts of animal rescue workers to get into areas declared off limits by government organizations because of the devastating hurricane damage. Eighty percent of the city of New Orleans was still under water days after the storm ended. Officials did not allow rescue volunteers in for weeks and in some areas, more than a month after the storm. Watching the footage of that documentary broke my heart, witnessing all the tragic ways animals died—mostly by drowning or starvation—because no evacuation plans existed for animals. Humans had designated shelters, but those shelters did not permit animals. They had to be left behind. While I do value human life over animal life, the loss of lives is a stark and terrible contrast: nearly 1400 people lost their lives due to the hurricane, whereas estimates for the loss of domestic pets ranges between 50,000 to 70,000. In the end, over 88,700 animals were unaccounted for after the storm.

Forty-four percent of the population refused to evacuate before the storm because they didn't want to leave pets behind. Many of the human lives lost resulted from their desire to stay behind and help furry friends make it through the storm. Those who did stay to care for their animals and survived needed rescuing in the first few days afterward, and at that point, were forced to leave behind the animals they loved. Many other pet owners who did evacuate tried to do their best to prepare a pet to survive the storm and thought they would return home in a matter of days, not knowing they would not return for months

❀ *New Orleans after Katrina hit.*

or, in many cases, never return. Because of the dire circumstances, sadly their "best" wound up ultimately harming their pets. I can still sense the anguish and heartache those pet owners must have had knowing that their beloved pet was dying, and they could do nothing to help. Animal rescue workers found pets on the brink of starvation; closed in bathrooms where food was long gone and water toxic from sewage and molds, weeks and weeks after the storm had passed.

Gratefully, the horrors of all the tragic ways animals lost their lives in this particular catastrophic event changed the law. The Pet Evacuation and Transportation Standards Act (PETS Act) of 2006 now requires cities, counties, and states to include evacuation plans for companion animals. As part of your preparation for your kitties, find out what your community's plans are for animal evacuations in the event of an emergency.

Ideally, when evacuating, you take your pets with you. Prepare ahead and ensure you have all the tools and equipment needed to do so in a quick, drop-of-a-hat way. If you have farm animals, have a plan in place for them as well.

Remember, natural disasters often extend beyond the one or two days they may physically rock your community. Consider potential long-lasting fallout and timeframes it might take to get back home after different types of disasters. Wildfires or volcanic eruptions leave behind smoke and ashes that make the air unbreathable for days or weeks. Large-scale earthquakes create rubble and rescue efforts potentially making your home inaccessible for weeks or months. Hurricanes and floods can damage sewer lines, unearth graves, or create toxic molds that may force governments to shut down areas for long periods of time until appropriate clean up happens.

Obviously, some disasters occur out of the blue, and all you can do is deal with the outcomes. Other emergencies give you a small window of escape. In those instances, what plans do you have for your family and pets?

72-HOUR KITS

Every member of your household needs a 72-hour kit, a standard grab-and-go backpack or bag for emergency evacuation. "Every member of your household" should include pets. Online resources are available with information on what to include for the needs of the humans and pets in your family. You can buy ready-made kits or make your own. I suggest making your own, so it is personalized for you and your pets' needs. Have a bag for each kitty, or combine in one bag, but each cat needs her own supplies.

Suggested items for each kitty's 72-hour kit:

- **Water** — Three days of water. An average-sized cat (10 pounds) needs about 7-10oz of water a day.

- **Food** — Three 2.5-3oz wet food cans and three cups of dry food. Pack light weight food bowls (plastic in this instance, though I never recommend plastic for regular use).

- **Bedding** — Blanket or small, soft bed that smells like home and has her scent on it.

- **Potty** — A small litterbox, scoop, three to six plastic bags, and a spade. I suggest the disposable metal baking pans available at the grocery store. Place scooped dirt in the box when you arrive at a safe location (hence the spade) or carry something lightweight like shredded paper. Also, pack pee pads for in or under the box, just in case your small box causes overspill from adult cats. Don't pack heavy litter as it will weigh you down. If you use dirt on location, make sure to administer de-wormers as soon as life gets back to normal. Expandable travel litterboxes are available to purchase, as well.

❀ *Supplies laid out for you to see.*   ❀ *All packed up and ready.*

🐱 **Carriers** — A secure carrier for each cat. If you land at an animal-friendly shelter, but it requires your pet to remain kenneled at all times, think ahead on how to make your pets comfy for three-plus days. A tiny carrier that your adult cat can't stand up or turn around in is not comfy. I suggest you have a medium to large carrier *and* a lightweight fully enclosed pet playpen that folds and carries easily. The playpen should be large enough for all cats, bedding, the litterbox, food, and water bowls. The stress may cause otherwise friendly and bonded cats to quarrel, especially in tight quarters. Have a large, lightweight blanket to cover the playpen, making it more cave-like.

🐱 **ID Tags** — Each needs a collar with ID tag. Most indoor cats do not need to wear collars. However, in an emergency situation, have a collar and tag in the go-bag or otherwise on hand. The ID tag should have pet's name, your phone number, and address. Leashes with a harness help you contain a cat outside of the carrier; this works best if you have previously leash-trained your cats. *Do not* rely on a leash and no carrier with an untrained and stressed-out cat.

🐱 **Toys and Treats** — Include a few favorite toys and treats. Cats are creatures of habit, and this upheaval will be *very* stressful for them. Help them feel a bit safer with treats and toys. If you have multiple cats in a kennel together, don't pack catnip toys if it creates aggressive behaviors. You don't need that in stressful scenarios.

🐱 **Medications** — Remember to pack any medications she requires. You may have to add this to the kit on the fly—but don't forget it!

- 🐱 **Pheromone Spray** — A spray bottle of Comfort Zone or other pheromone spray can help relax cats. You can spray a bit on a blanket or on the playpen itself 10-30 minutes before using.

- 🐱 **Proof of Vaccinations and Ownership** — Carry a file folder of copies or originals of vaccination records, pet ID cards, adoption paperwork, and microchip numbers.

If you foster cats or kittens on a regular basis, you should have a ready kit for that scenario. I often have orphaned bottle babies or orphaned kittens, which means I need a bag with items like formula, organic baby wipes, bottles, bottle warmer, water, a heat source, carrier, towels, playpen, and baby or kitten food.

Remember to revamp your 72-hour kits annually to replace expired foods and meds in the kit.

In a situation where you need to find pet-friendly housing because shelters for the emergency do not permit animals, plan ahead by plotting out potential distances you might need to travel to find safety in various emergencies. Keep a list on hand of motels/hotels in those areas that permit pets.

In emergencies, cell towers often go down or the Internet is not available on your phone. If money tends to be tight, save up cash and stash in your 72-hour kits for the cost of shelter if you have to stay in a motel/hotel for several days. It's a great idea to keep an old-school road map in your car.

WHAT IF YOU AREN'T HOME WHEN AN EMERGENCY EVACUATION HAPPENS?

Prearrange with a good neighbor, a close-by friend, or family member to come to your house to rescue your fur babies if you cannot return home during a disaster. Where possible, pick someone who loves animals and will go the extra mile to save your furry friends. Prearrangement on this is very important because, again, in emergency situations like an earthquake, you may not be able to call through to anyone due to busy phone lines or downed cell towers.

If your selected person also has pets, make a pact to take care of each other's pets if the other is not home when an emergency happens. Swap house keys.

Make sure they know where you store your emergency supplies, and vice versa. Preferably, your schedules are not the same because it's not likely to help much if you both typically work during the day away from home.

Prearrange where you will meet up so that if you can't get through on the phone you still know where and when you can try to get your fur babies back. Give plenty of lead time like twelve hours after the disaster evacuation. Plan on a meeting spot not likely to be impacted by typical disasters in your region. Have a backup spot, just in case.

It's best, if possible, for this person to know your pets well. They should know your pets' names, how many you have, where they typically like to hang out or hide in the house. If your pets like this person, or better yet trust this person, the designated rescuer can likely get them to safety more quickly. Have this person around often so your pets gain that trust.

Animal Notification Stickers

Another safety item you should have is a pet notification sticker or sign to place on your front window or door. These stickers let rescue workers know animals reside in the home. Stickers should be vinyl decals that you can write on. For extra precaution, put stickers on all exterior doors. Have extras to change out the decal if you lose or gain a pet over time. Look for a sticker that allows you to write the number and types of animals on the sticker. Include your emergency phone number.

Carry in your wallet a pet notification card, especially if you are single and live alone. These cards help emergency workers know that you have pets at home that will need help if you have been critically or fatally injured in an accident. I include on my card that I frequently have bottle baby kittens that can't go for more than 3 hours without care. Include on that card the name and contact of your emergency pet helper or the rescue group where you foster.

SHELTERING THROUGH A DISASTER

Designated Shelters for Disaster Evacuations

If your city evacuation plan requires owners to drop off pets at designated shelters, identify ahead where they are located and arrive prepared with the following items:

- **Cat ID Information** — A collar with ID tag and the pet's microchip information.

- **Proof of Vaccines** — Emergency shelters may require copies of up-to-date vaccine proof, especially rabies. I suggest the 3-yr rabies shot, so you don't have to remember to renew it as frequently. Also, if you shy from over-vaccinating kitty, be prepared for rejection from shelters, unless you can provide a recent Titer Test showing immunity.

- **Full Contact Information** — Home address, address of where you are staying during crisis, cell phone numbers, and email. Include one to three other names and contact information of people who can act on your behalf in case the shelter cannot reach you.

- **Picture Information Sheets** — Include a paper with multiple pictures for each of your cats, list any identifying physical markers on each cat, personality traits, and a brief history (age, approximate weight, health history, meds required, special concerns).

- **Hard Carriers and Kennels** — Have on hand extra-large hard carriers or metal kennels that fold up to take to the shelter for your cats. Often, others are not as prepared, and the shelter or rescue may run out of crates and kennels, so supply your own. A soft zip-up playpen is okay in a pinch for this. Permanently affix your personal information to each crate or carrier.

No Animal Shelter Options

If government officials force you to leave your home and there are no local plans for animal sheltering, you may need to pay for a pet-friendly hotel in a safe area, or maybe family lives close enough yet out of the storm's path and will allow you to bring your pets. If you have to leave animals behind, *and I emphasize that this should be an absolute last resort*, do your best to prepare for the kitties based on the type of disaster they are about to endure. In hurricane or flooding situations, put cats on a mid or upper floor with high perches in a room with no windows or few that you have boarded up (for hurricane, not flooding). Put large self-dispensing food and water containers that have several weeks' worth of food and water on something high like a countertop on that upper floor. If a tornado, put them in a secure spot like a basement area with cement walls and higher perches (in case of some flooding from pipes breaking) and no windows or boarded windows (to prevent glass shards). Do the same with self-dispensing food/water containers high off the ground with as long a supply as possible. Include many places to go potty as you won't be around to scoop, and ensure the room has air flow. Unplug all electrical items. Have safe hidey spots for kitties as they will be scared. Make sure your animals are previously microchipped and that you have taken recent photos of them. Carry with you proof of ownership you may need should rescue groups or shelter workers evacuate your cats, and you need to claim them later.

Shelter at Home During Storm or Natural Disaster

If permitted to stay and you choose to "shelter at home," please keep your pets close with you and as safe as possible. They will be scared like you. Animals often know a weather or seismic event is in the works, so keep all pets inside once you hear of a projected storm. If you've let them out per usual because the storm is still hours away, the changes in air pressure may spook your cats with their keen senses and they could choose, because of fear, to hide outside during the storm.

Prep for flooding by putting supplies onto higher surfaces. Prep for hurricane and tornado by boarding up or shuttering your windows. Have emergency items at hand like flashlights, battery operated radio, water, and food. Make sure to select the safest places in your home to ride out the storm. Choose interior rooms or basements depending on the disaster heading your way.

Prep the "safe room" by first putting all your cats in it while you bustle about the rest of the house making other provisions. You may choose to put them in secure carriers or playpens within the room. Your urgency with preparing might upset your kitties, and they may dash out of the room or hide because they know something is wrong. You may not be able to find them if you wait until the last moment to gather animals in the safe room.

PREPARING FOR PERSONAL DISASTERS

In the event of a fire in your home, a pipe bursting, or a tree falling through the roof, what is your family plan? What is the plan for your pets?

A fellow animal rescuer once told me of the plan she came up with as a teenager to save the cats that slept in her room in the event of a fire in her house. She planned to shove them in pillowcases, tie those in a knot, and toss them out her first story window. Now, whether the plan was sound or not, at least she thought about what to do, just in case.

We don't want to dwell on or obsess over worst-case scenarios. Overthinking about negative possibilities can actually attract more negative experiences into our lives. However, thinking about them briefly, in order to plan for a "what if" moment so that everyone in the house is safe (including pets), I believe, is using wisdom and not negative thinking.

What will be your plan in the event of a fire breaking out in your home? You often have seconds to get everyone to safety. If you have a family, you can assign anyone mature enough to oversee a pet each. Help them understand that going toward the fire to save a pet is not safe and only firefighters should attempt that. If the pets are in areas of the home not yet engulfed in flames, how do you safely get them out? Grab a blanket or sheet and wrap the cat up in it so that they cannot see what is going on around them and hurry out the door or window. If for some reason a carrier is right there, grab it too. But don't worry about getting the scared cat into the carrier right now. Leave them bundled in the blanket and once safely outside, transfer the cat to the carrier. If your vehicle is accessible, place pets inside the car and safely secure there while emergency workers do their jobs. Don't risk your life by running back into the house to save pets and inform emergency workers when they arrive.

In times of emergency, having a solid bond of trust between you and your cat is key. Cats can panic like humans when something scary or tragic happens. If the animal runs from you and hides in a difficult to reach place, you waste precious seconds. Clearly, an animal in fear, even if they love and trust you, may still run away and hide, but having them see you as a savior versus an additional threat is very important. If you've been prone to any negative behaviors toward your cat, this is a moment where you may not have the outcome you desire because of a distrusting relationship.

After the Disaster Tips

Everyone will be reeling from the event, including your furry friend.

Help her feel safe & secure after a disaster by:

- Limiting her space to a single room.
- Separating from other animals if she displays aggression toward others.
- Keeping the room darker.
- Allowing her great places to hide or burrow.
- Trying to get back to the "normal" routine as soon as possible.
- Showing extra patience and gentleness because of her trauma experience.
- Considering the need for energy work on her if displaying long-term anxiety or fear.
- Taking the pet to see the vet if she does not get back to normal behavior as expected.

LONG-TERM PREPAREDNESS

"Preppers" can sometimes be the butt of jokes. However, there is wisdom in being prepared for the unexpected.

Some good reasons for having a long-term stash of supplies include:

- As a wealthy nation, the US has had plenty of access to products if we have the means to purchase them. However, during the recent pandemic of 2020, we all witnessed supply chain difficulties on certain products and longer shipping times for online orders. Pet food and pet litter were included in this supply chain and shipping issue. I remember waiting 2-3 weeks to get litter that I usually got within 2 days. Economists have warned of future supply chain problems.

- If you belong to one of several of the world's largest faiths, you likely believe in a future with apocalyptic-type of events or recreation events, in which case it would be wise to store up items like food, water, and medicines to better survive such events.

- Another more common concern is having a long period of unemployment. Preparedness allows you to keep your pets during this time. Often in rescue work we see cats or other pets relinquished because of a loss of income. The pet owner no longer has funds to buy pet food or pay for other essential pet care.

In any of these situations, having a store of supplies at home, ready to use, helps ease stress.

Store Food & Water

Have at least a three-month supply of food, litter, and medicine conceivably for a time of food scarcity or reduced finances. A longer supply is even safer. Even if you currently make homemade cat food or provide a raw diet, it is important to store either all your ingredients, freeze-dried foods, or commercial cat food. It can be pricey to go out and get a full six-to-twelve-month supply of items for your pets in one go, so I suggest a plan to build up your supply slowly by buying extras every month. Buy one or two extra boxes of litter, cases of wet food, or bags of dry food each month.

To know what you need, first calculate how much commercial food you would utilize in that timeframe, whether 3, 6, or 12 months. For me, I have six cats and want a 12-month supply of food on hand. I feed in total about 8 ounces of wet food twice a day. I need either three 5.5-6oz cans or six 3oz cans every day. For a year's supply I need either 1,095 large cans, 2,190 small cans, or a mix of the two. Most cases of cat food come in 24 cans. If I need 1,095 cans, I require about 46 cases of canned food. I typically go through about four 7lb bags of dry food in an 8-week period. If I divide 52 weeks by 8 weeks, I get roughly 7. That means I need about 28 6-8lb bags of dry food. Buying larger weight dry food bags saves money. Cats could also eat a bit less then these projections if you choose to ration in a time of need. Also, calorie dense foods call for smaller servings.

Chart for food you will need on hand for a single 10lb adult cat:

Approximate Servings	3 Month Supply	6 Month Supply	12 Month Supply
Dry Food (1/2 cup/day)	5lbs of dry food	10lbs of dry food	20lbs of dry food
Wet Food (1 2.5-3oz can/day)	92 cans of wet food	183 cans of wet food	365 cans of wet food
Water (6oz/day)	5 gallons of drinking water	9 gallons of drinking water	18 gallons of drinking water
Litter (1 box/month)	3 boxes of litter	6 boxes of litter	12 boxes of litter

If you only store dry food, store twice as much per cat as the chart recommends. Remember to store additional gallons of water to make up for needed moisture (extra 2 ounces/day). If you only store wet food, store 2 times as much per cat as the chart recommends.

Keep in mind dry food is bulky to store and wet food more compact. But dry food stores easily once open and wet will not if you don't have electricity or another way to keep it cool. Use your available storage space wisely. Once you have your supply, simply keep buying what you need regularly and rotate out the older food into current use and put the new at the back of the food storage. Foods all come with a "best by" date, but the writing can be tiny and sometimes hard to see. I recommend labeling foods with a dark permanent marker as they come in. Write the best by or purchase date nice and big on the case. It's easier to see when swapping out older foods for new foods in the rotation.

Side Note: Sharing is Caring

Should the worst happen in our communities, I recommend fostering community unity to work together for survival. Our mental prep: visualize ourselves helping those directly around us in hard times by sharing what we have. In a time of crisis, if we show love, kindness, respect, and compassion to others, we perpetuate and attract positivity for ourselves and the community. If we are giving and supportive, the likelihood of others returning help when we need something increases. We create a stronger unity by helping our near neighbors. In regard to pet food, if we can afford to, store a bit more than needed, so we can share with the other pets around us whose families didn't know to prepare.

Store Basic Pet Medical Supplies

Medical supplies are wise to have on hand if you can't access a vet and your pet becomes sick. These items give you basic options to support your kitty in a time of crisis. You can easily purchase online and most without a prescription. I want to reiterate; I suggest this for times of crisis only. If all is well and you can get to the vet for diagnostics, you should go that route.

List of recommended items:

- De-wormers. Get broad spectrum coverage and one specifically for tapeworms. Have enough on hand to do several rounds of treatment for each cat.
- Flea and parasite control like traditional flea meds, collars, or shampoos. Dawn dish soap and flea combs if you can bathe kitty. Mineral oil for ear mites.
- Diagel and psyllium supplements for cats with bowel problems like diarrhea or constipation.

A broad-spectrum antibiotic like Clavamox for potential secondary infections with flus or wound infections. These can be stored on the shelf until mixed, but then need refrigeration. Albon is good to have on hand for diarrhea bugs and doesn't need refrigeration. (Prescriptions needed and unless you know your vet well or work in rescue you are less likely to have these to store.) Eye med drops or gels like Terramycin for eye infections like conjunctivitis. Make sure you also store a reference card on dosages if you can't get online to look it up.

Cat vitamins and human-grade probiotics (refrigerated). L-lysine. B12 subcutaneous (sub-q) injections (prescription needed). Immune support supplements for cats.

Wound-cleaning supplies like iodine, sterile bandages, fur clippers (battery powered for times of electrical outage), rubbing alcohol to sterilize instruments, scissors, sterile needle and sutures for wound closing (this may be impossible without anesthetic, but for serious wounds, it would be nice to have the option), and soft or plastic e-collars.

Activated food-grade charcoal for toxic consumption emergencies. Mix with water and force-feed to kitty if they consumed a toxic substance. Have dosage information on hand. Be aware cats do not like this and may gag or aspirate if not delivered effectively.

Sterile needles and cat IV fluid bag, like Lactated Ringers (prescription needed), for administering sub-q fluids to seriously wounded or sick cats. Fluids can be the difference in saving lives. You must be trained by someone to do this safely or know someone close by who has experience. It is possible to over-hydrate, so know the correct amount for kitty's weight. Keep your fluids sterile so they can be of use the next time around.

Unflavored electrolytes for humans. Buy portioned flavorless dry packets to mix in water or unflavored bottles of Pedialyte. Good to have this to force-feed to a sick cat to keep them hydrated. If you can't do number eight on this list, please keep this on your shelf. They do not last long after opening and need immediate refrigeration.

- High-calorie foods or highly tasty foods for sick cats like Royal Canine Recovery, Hill's AD, Gerber chicken or turkey baby food, canned tuna or chicken in water. Also keep on hand a calorie-dense gel for cats and kittens. Mix these items with electrolyte water to pass easily through a luer slip tip syringe to force feed.

- Colloidal silver has anti-bacterial, anti-microbial, anti-viral properties. I recommend the brand Sovereign Silver or Argentyn 23. Both are produced by the same company; they just contain different parts per million (ppm) of silver. I prefer Sovereign for cats because it's a smaller dose of silver. If you are not familiar with using this tool, make sure to download uses and dosages prior to any disaster event and store with supplements. Colloidal silver must be stored carefully so as not to cause oxidization of the silver in the suspension. Do not keep colloidal silver anywhere near electromagnetic energy (e.g., appliances or computers). Store at a consistent room temperature and in a dark place. I recommend an aluminum box to block electromagnetic frequencies (EMFs) and store in a basement. Quality colloidal silver is not cheap, and you don't want it spoiled. You can use it both topically and orally. If you google for information on this item, the Internet may bombard you with a lot of material stating colloidal silver is ineffective or dangerous. If this worries you, ask any professional in the alternative healthcare realm, and they will tell you colloidal silver is a valuable tool and perfectly safe in the right doses with a quality product.

- Anti-fungal and anti-bacterial shampoos help kitties with skin infections like ringworm. Treating skin infections quickly is important as they can progress rapidly, so keep this type of shampoo on your shelf.

- Natural cat supplements produced by companies like Amber Naturalz, NHV, or others a holistic vet may recommend are great to have on hand. Should kitty become ill, these will help support the feline body to heal itself. You can find a variety of supplements for kitty ailments like urinary tract stress, liver and kidney support, and sinus infections. I keep many of these products on my shelf and use them regularly. Note that products suspended in alcohol makes them viable longer once opened but calls for more caution in usage. Products that suspend in glycerin and water are safer but creates a shorter shelf life once opened.

- A variety of syringes (with and without needles) in different sizes. These come in handy for administering colloidal silver, electrolytes, sub-q fluids, and liquified food. I keep on hand a 1ml/cc, 3ml/cc, 10ml/cc and a 20ml/cc. I have both luer lock tips (for bottle feeding tiny kittens with a Miracle nipple) and luer slip tips for giving meds and fluids. With needles, 20-22 gauges are typically what I use. Butterfly needles work great for wiggly patients and tiny kittens. When using needles, you need training from a reliable source like a veterinarian.

- Additional items to store might include Diphenhydramine for pets for bad stings or other allergic reactions, pill-popper covers, regular Neosporin for surface wounds or inflamed skin, thermometer, tick-removal device, and prescription pain meds for cats like Gabapentin (with dosing information).

I want to reiterate that I am not a veterinarian, but I am a holistic healing enthusiast with a lot of personal experience healing sick kittens and cats. Research any products you put on your cat medicine shelf. Keep dosage cards and all appropriate use information stored alongside medical items. Reference multiple ages and weights in your documentation, so you know the right dosage for your kitties. Keep books on hand for healing home remedies for pets, especially those written by holistic veterinarians. **Include your vet in discussing what you should store and deciding dosages for your specific cats.**

PREPARE IN THE EVENT OF YOUR DEATH

All of us have known members of our families or others in our circle of friends who died unexpectedly or tragically. Because we never know when it may be our last day, we should have a last will and testament. Sometimes we think of wills as only necessary for the wealthy, but it is an opportunity for us to spell out our final wishes to our surviving loved ones. It's important to include our final hopes and requests for our pets so there is a plan for their future. If we have a life insurance payout, earmark some of those funds to help transition pets into new homes. Those expenses might include getting up-to-date on medical care, providing food, or as an incentive to a poorer relation or friend who would take in our pets and treat them well but can't really afford them. We should notify family members ahead of time our wishes for pets and what the will states regarding them.

Consider naming specific people to inherit one or more of your pets or designating one person among your family or friends you trust to take on the task of rehoming your pets to good people. If you do not have anyone like that to call upon, prearrange with a rescue group that in the event of your death, they will take your kitties in to rehome. Offer the rescue a donation as part of the final settlement of your estate to help the organization be less stressed about taking on the responsibility. Again, having funds set aside to aid in this transition will help the pets receive the care they need for quality rehoming. I would suggest about $1000 per pet as a minimum. You can stipulate in your will, in whichever scenario you take, that if all the funds are not required for the medical care and rehoming of the animals after your passing, that the earmarked funds go back to family or donated to a cause you care about.

When pet owners fail at making these arrangements and having it all in a legal document, it is not uncommon for family members who do not care about animals in general or do not care about our pets in particular to be careless or thoughtless about what happens to the cats. Pets of the deceased too often wind up unceremoniously kicked to the curb to fend for themselves or dropped at a shelter that may or may not be a no-kill shelter, because those remaining do not want the bother of finding new homes for our fur babies.

One last thought for this topic of preparing for our animals in the event of our death. Please let us not plan to have pets euthanized and buried or cremated with us unless our pet is terminally ill or otherwise truly unadoptable. It is gratuitous to take their life prematurely for the sake of our own emotional comfort or because it seems like the easiest thing to do.

Story Example: Why Not to Euthanize Pets Upon Death

When I bought my condo, it previously belonged to an elderly woman who had passed away. Gertrude lived alone with her little dog, Bean. While renovating the condo, I met another elderly woman in the neighborhood who walked her dog every day. Her dog always wanted to come into my garage or yard. One day, this woman, Francie, told me that the dog she walked was in fact the same Bean who lived in my home for many years. Francie and Gertie had been best friends. Francie told me that Gertie had requested Bean be put down and buried with her when she passed on. But Francie couldn't bear that idea and instead kept Bean. I was so glad for that doggie that Francie made the choice to disregard her friend's wish in this instance. Bean lived another five happy years. How sad if her life had been cut short unnecessarily.

SHIELDING & OTHER TECHNIQUES TO USE IN DISASTER EXPERIENCES

Everything I have shared thus far on preparedness is temporal advice. Now, I want to share more spiritually based practices and ideas that can tie into caring for your pet in chaotic times. Some people believe that tragic things just happen, and nothing can be done to prevent them. I can understand that perspective, but I have a different view. I believe that several things will help spare us from some of the hardships in this life as well as give us strength to come through the difficulties we do face with more peace, purpose, and hope. I have included below a short list of things we can do every day for ourselves (and for our pets) to help us navigate around unnecessary challenges and pain. I elaborated on many of these ideas in Chapter 4.

- **Use Prayer** — Pray to God for protection for yourself and cats, that you will only have experiences for your highest good or the highest good of others.

- **Ask for Angelic Support** — Speak to the unseen Angels all around us and ask them for help in an emergency. They are waiting for your requests.

- **Use Energetic Shielding** — Place protection around those in your home who are vulnerable and can't shield themselves, like pets and children.

- **Keep a Positive Mindset** — Positivity begets more positivity in your life, reducing negative encounters.

- **Be Grateful** — Gratitude helps us focus on others, be of service, and remain humble in trying times.

For this chapter, I want to go more in depth on shielding, a daily practice I use with my indoor-outdoor cats. I spoke on this briefly in the previous chapter. The practice of shielding is about energy and intention. Everything in this world is made of energy and has a vibration, including our emotions and thoughts. Energy shields can have the power to protect someone from the unseen realm *and* the physical realm. Place shields with a specific purpose. The intention is always about protection.

I learned to create a shield like this: visualize a shield in your mind's eye, asking for it through prayer or intention. As an example, again, each day when one of my cats that goes outside during the daytime asks to be let out, I stroke her gently down her back and say, "Okay, let's put your shield up. We are asking God and the Angels to protect you while outside. I want you to be as safe as you can be. Be nice to the other critters. Come home safely. I love you." Then I visualize her shield—its shape and color—around her body as I open the door.

Use the shape and color of the shield that pops into your mind the first time you create it. If your mind's eye sees the shape and color shifting over time, allow that. My cat Honey has a salmon-colored shield with flecks of gold, with pointy tips all around her. My cat Trixie has an emerald-green shield the shape of an oblong gemstone with facets at the head and tail ends. Primrose has a rounded rosy, pink shield. Skippy a baby-blue square. Visualizing the shield this way with intention helps strengthen it.

In times of emergency, if you have to place your beloved kitty at the shelter, place a shield around her before you leave. Each day you are apart, pray for the shield to stay up, protecting her. If there is a fire and you can't find kitty, draw hope for a miracle by asking God to shield the kitty from the fire and smoke until rescued by firefighters. If a storm stresses your kitties in a multi-cat household, place shields around them with the intention that they will feel safe, guarded, and calm.

An aspect of strengthening the shielding intention is to offer gratitude. Every time I let one of my two girls back inside, I say a silent prayer of thanks for her safe return. I also verbalize to the cat, "I'm so glad you are home safely."

If you do all the above faithfully and believingly but you still have a tragic experience with a disaster or some other hardship, take comfort by trusting that something in the experience will help you learn, grow, and become a better human *or* something from the event will help someone else involved to learn, grow, and become a better human. Experiences, both the good and the hard, give us wisdom and knowledge; they can soften our hearts and humble our minds, and they can bring us closer to God. We have our free will to decide if a painful experience will strengthen us or weaken us.

PURRRITO WRAP UP

Hopefully, this chapter energized and inspired you to work on your plans for your pet's preparedness. Have your 72-hour kits ready, know the community evacuation plans for pets, prepare ahead for a friend to help evacuate your kitties if you are not home during an emergency, get a pet notification sticker for your front door or window, have all your medical paperwork and vaccines or Titer Test up-to-date and ready to go, know how you will safely shelter at home for certain emergencies, and make a plan for your pets in case you unexpectedly pass away or if you are getting older. Additionally, make your needed spiritual preparations and utilize those skills to help protect you, your family, and your pets.

CHAPTER 12

Holistic Health & Medical Care for Kitty

While not a veterinarian myself, I am qualified to discuss this topic. With all the rescue work I have done, I have experienced a myriad of health issues in felines, from mild to deadly. I have interfaced with more than thirty different veterinarians over the years and been an at-home-care nurse for so many of my cats and fosters. Because of my own interests and background, I have always gone beyond merely the prescribed meds from the vet with each sick kitty. I try to fulfill the full spectrum of my cats' needs when they are unwell—a body, mind, spirit approach.

As someone who feels called to be a healer, I put a lot of focus and effort into my ailing kitties. After dealing with more than forty feline health concerns and diseases over the years, I have learned the following: be persistent in getting the needed veterinary care for each cat; make efforts to hasten healing via alternative methods like energy work and therapeutic frequencies; keep cats in a clean environment while healing; provide good nutrition and supplements; access prayer, fasting, and Angelic support to bring comfort and miracles; and most importantly offer love, tenderness, attention, and time.

This chapter does not focus on instruction on what *you should do*, but rather, I hope, on points to consider, offering ideas and sharing stories to help you make the best decisions you can when your pet is ill. *You* are the best advocate for your cat's wellness. Who else is with the cat so consistently or who notices the details of his life? Find the professionals who will hear you and truly do their best to care for your feline friends.

HEALTHY HABITS INSIDE YOUR HOME

First, I want to start with the benefits of doing your best in regular everyday life to offer a healthy home for kitty. When we consider the well-being of the whole system (physical, emotional, mental, spiritual) we improve overall wellness, thus reducing risks for ailment and illness. Strive to have a balanced home life where one focuses on meeting the needs of all energy bodies—both animal and human—in a holistic way. Balance can be hard to come by, so it takes a continuous awareness and effort to make little changes for the better.

In general, our US culture really stresses caring for the physical body and is beginning to improve its awareness of the mental body, but on the whole, our culture does not contemplate or care for the emotional and spiritual bodies very well. Addressing one's physical needs alone misses the mark.

So, with cat care, how can we consider the whole being when taking care of kitty and creating our home environments? Let's go over some suggestions. (On bolded items, I will share personal experiences with each.)

Physically:

Nutrition quality
Supplements that support immune health
Exercise and play
Toxicities we bring in the home/how to reduce toxins
Muscle testing to clarify needs
Annual vet checkups and bloodwork as cats age
Safe, clean, and comfortable litterbox
Quality sleep

Mentally:

Puzzles and challenges in play
Training with rewards
Consult with a cat behavioral professional when concerned
Speak powerfully on behalf of kitty with positive language
Learn more of each other's communication styles
Vibrational frequencies and healing sounds
Continuing education on cats (for ourselves)

Emotionally:

Quality over quantity of life/what is best for each individual cat
Awareness of stressors and triggers/reducing them
Positive rewards of affection, praise, and sometimes treats
Animal communication sessions
Compassion and patience
Energy healing regularly
Crystals to help balance

Spiritually:

Daily prayer on cat's behalf
Seek support from Spirit and Angels
Personal revelation or messages and signs from Spirit to help understand cat's needs
Shielding cat for extra protection
Intentional in our actions and thoughts in our care of kitty
Fast for extra help when needed

Story Example: Supplements That Support Immune Health

When I first took in five-month-old foster kitten Hero, he was suffering a great deal with many ailments. He was malnourished to the point of suffering from rickets, something the vet said he rarely saw. Hero had a bacterial skin infection. He had an eye infection. He suffered from prolonged diarrhea with mild burns around his anus from dirty fur there. He had chronic sinusitis with intensely huge boogers sneezed out all day long. And with his medical visits, the vet diagnosed him with Feline Leukemia Virus (FeLV). This disease weakens the immune system, which explains why, combined with lack of nutrition, he struggled all at once with so much sickness.

The vet and I decided on an intense protocol to get Hero stronger. He started immediately on an antibiotic for his skin issue and an antibiotic ointment for his eyes. The vet wanted me to test out a new immune support supplement on the market to be given daily. I provided Hero with high-quality foods including daily Gerber baby food in chicken and turkey. On top of this plan, I added a few additional supplements. I gave him a feline liquid multi-vitamin, L-lysine, colloidal silver, and probiotics every day.

Hero progressed nicely within a few weeks with weight gain, eyes cleared up, skin infection abated, rickets resolved, and diarrhea stopped. However, his giant boogers persisted. We continued on the supplements for months. He grew from 1.5 pounds to 6 pounds in four months and became active and playful, curious and cute. At about the two-month mark of my care of Hero, I researched online about how to resolve or reduce chronic sinusitis and boogers. Some veterinarians were finding success in reducing the sinusitis with long rounds of antibiotics. I discussed this with my vet, but he worried that a long round might make Hero more resistant to antibiotics that he might need in the future due to his FeLV diagnosis. I weighed the pros and cons and decided to try it. Four weeks on Clavamox twice a day dramatically reduced the phlegm expelled; whereas the supplements had decreased the sneezing from about twenty-five times a day to fifteen times a day, the long round of antibiotics diminished it further to about twice a day. I hoped this would help him be more adoptable.

I was able to increase Hero's territory into my bedroom as well giving him more space to run and play and explore. However, entering our fifth month together, he contracted a bad limping calicivirus. Under normal circumstances this virus is not deadly, but on occasion a bad strain spreads. It causes muscle weakness, fever, and often respiratory distress. The third day of this illness we went to the vet for pain meds. On about the fifth day of illness, he could no longer stand or walk due to intense muscle pain. I took him back into the vet. The veterinarian and I discussed the seriousness of the illness and the concern of the FeLV. The vet suggested we consider euthanizing him. I didn't want Hero to suffer unnecessarily, but I said, "Let's run some bloodwork, and if it is looking bad, we can put him down."

❀ *Hero just days before he got ill.*
(Photo credit Jim Grubb)

When the vet reported back, he said in a surprised way, "Well, Jessica, this kitty is very ill, but I have never seen bloodwork this good in any FeLV positive cat before." It was a testament to all of the efforts in using supplements, veterinary care, and a lot of love in a safe, clean environment. I did not put Hero down that day, but I did later on as the illness intensified, making Hero miserable. More on page 343.

Story Example: Using Muscle Testing to Clarify Needs

When Trixie and Beaux were still kittens and fosters, they got terrible diarrhea. Over several weeks I did fecal exams, dewormers, diet adjustments, probiotics, and more to no avail. Naturally, I could not interest adopters because I needed to disclose that the kittens had chronic diarrhea. I gave up when they were around 18-20 weeks old and signed the adoption paperwork to keep them.

Around this same time, I was studying the Emotion Code and learning how to use the Sway Test on myself to get yes or no responses to questions like, "Is this supplement good for me?" One day I went to the pet store to buy litter and food. I had used a wheat litter for years—since I had Stella. Stella, Prim, and Gigi all used it without problems. As Trixie and Beaux had gotten older, I allowed them to free roam the apartment, so they started using my forever cats' litterbox. They had been on a clay litter as younger kittens when kept in the big bathroom.

As I stood in the store to buy the litter, I suddenly had the thought to Sway Test litter on behalf of Trixie and Beaux. Sure enough, I got a big "no" response when testing the wheat litter for them. I switched to a clay clumping that day, and their diarrhea stopped. All of the previous efforts to heal them to no avail and a simple muscle test to discover an allergy did the trick.

Story Example: How to Learn More of Each Other's Communication Styles

Studies show that guardians can become adept at understanding the meows their cat expresses. They know by each utterance what the cat is telling them. These guardians are in tune with kitty and have paid attention to body language, vocal cues (other than meows), and the attitudes of the cat. In turn, cats try to learn more of our language. They do not have the physical capacity to speak words, but they understand quite a few. But more than words, they understand our inflection and energies around the words. Studies show that cats recognize mood changes and expression changes in the humans they live with, but do not recognize them in strangers. Your cat is trying his best to learn *you*.

At this point, I can tell by Gigi's meow if she needs to barf, feels playful, or wants a treat. With Honey and Trixie, they have both adopted a meow that encompasses jealousy, annoyance, and complaint when another cat they don't want near them gets too close. This especially happens when they are on my lap or sitting by me. Prim is chatty, and I know when she just wants to talk. Beaux has an obvious "don't" meow when I tease him. I've learned their voices over the years as I pay attention to what they try to communicate.

In turn, my cats have gotten good at understanding me via my tone and inflections. They know the word "no." They know their names. They recognize what I mean when I say, "Be nice," or "Are you ready for foods?" They are learning more than words, such as movements, smells, and energies that go along with words to help them see the patterns.

Story Example: Quality Over Quantity of Life

This means weighing the pros and cons on behalf of the cat. We can consider our own needs and desires here, too, but we should try not to make truly selfish choices on behalf of our cats. A selfish choice might look like insisting on kitty accepting the cheapest, lumpiest, stinkiest litter brand because we want to save a few dollars a month. It may look like refusing to address kitty's needs for a cat tree because we want to keep buying a $7 coffee every day. It may look like continuing to use strong chemical perfumes in the home when we know the cat hates it.

❀ *Honey in the front yard.*

Evaluating quality over quantity might include considering if the cat needs indoor-outdoor access. Some cats need more territory, access to nature, and higher activity levels than indoor life can provide. If kitty wants to go outside, how might we consider their quality of life over longevity of life? This can only be answered by each individual person, cat, and situation. There is not a true black-and-white answer here.

Of my six cats, two really do desire more freedom, alone time, exploration, and outdoor rejuvenation. The other four do not express any desire to go outside past our catio. I weighed the options overall and decided the two girls could do indoor-outdoor. I did my best to train them, set healthy boundaries on access, and give them added energetic protection.

Story Example: Seeking Personal Revelation from Spirit

Using our connection to Spirit and Universal Intelligence really can help us better understand each cat's needs. For me, I have used this frequently when asking about how best to care for and place foster cats. I had a group of four kittens in Spring of 2019. One was a disabled singleton, a kitten about a week old rejected from her mother cat because she had a deformed limb. The others were three solid black short-haired kittens about the same age. They became siblings by default.

I adopted out one of the black kittens, Pepper, when she was young, at about ten weeks of age, and that helped her get a home. Shorthaired black cats and shorthaired brown tabbies have the hardest time getting adopted, so finding a home for them when they are still small and cute, like ten to twelve weeks, improves their chances. However, right after that adoption event, the two remaining black kittens broke out with an unusual viral skin infection. It took about five weeks to heal up before they could go back to adoptions. Marvel, the calico amputee kitten, was ready at that time, too. She got adopted quickly by someone who had followed her story on the rescue's social media. But at sixteen weeks, the two black kittens struggled. Eventually Licorice found a home, but Poppy remained with me for over six months, the longest I've ever had a foster kitten. She was a very sweet and precious kitten with a gentle and caring personality.

In October of 2019, I prayed about keeping Poppy because Honey actually liked her. I got a "no" answer and felt that there was a family meant for her. Another month passed, and in mid-November I prayed again on whether I should just adopt her and got this answer—"I have given you an answer, but you are uncomfortable with that answer. Following my words will always lead you rightly. At this time, the answer is the same. Poppy will be happier in a home where she receives more individual care and attention. I will provide her with a safe and loving home where she will experience love."

A week later, a newly retired couple, who loved adopting black cats and had two at home, found Poppy at an adoption event and were happy to offer her a loving, safe home.

❀ *Poppy on the deck.*

Other Items to Ponder When Establishing a Holistic Home

Thoughts on Toxins

Ironic that the US culture emphasizes physique ideals while at the same time producing foods, clothing, furnishings, transportation, and more that are full of toxins. I have heard that we inhale more carcinogens with a single bus passing us by on the street than our ancestors of 150 years ago did in their entire lives. I previously brought up toxins to look out for on behalf of kitty in Chapter 10. Many more toxins, that we can't always avoid, bombard us all the time. These toxins add up over time, both in our bodies and in cats' small bodies, and can contribute to feeling unwell. My suggestion is to consider recurrently how can we reduce toxins in our lives. Wherever we can "go natural" with a product, we should choose to do so. For instance, with wanting to scent our homes—instead of buying perfumy products full of chemicals, use something natural like a pure essential oil and water in a diffuser. We can make these choices all the time—chemical cleaner or vinegar? Dry cat kibble with food colorings like toxic red number 40 or cat food with no colorants?

Higher Risk for Stress & Illness in Multi-Cat Homes

Opportunity for illness increases the more animals you have in the home. You can reduce possible transmissions of illnesses by housing fosters separate from forever pets, making sure your forever cats are vaccinated at least once against panleukopenia/FeLV/rabies, washing hands frequently if handling a sick animal, maintaining a clean home, utilizing crystals or essential oils to help cleanse the environment, using good supplements for immune support, and feeding the highest quality food you can afford.

Keep a Look Out for Aging Signs in Senior Years

Additionally, as the cat ages, his body will start to degrade. Most commonly arthritis sets in, creating daily pain. You may see changes in behaviors, some of which you may not like. The chance for urinating outside the litterbox can increase when harder for kitty to get in and out of said box; that, or the litter may hurt arthritic paws. Kitties who start to lose cognitive function may also have difficulties with the litterbox, simply because they become disoriented and forget where to find the box. They may yowl because they feel lost or confused. A cat that starts to go deaf may suddenly become louder when he meows. Show compassion for your aging friend. Offer whatever supportive care you can. Make adjustments in the living arrangements, as needed, to help him feel safer. Be patient. If you have a senior cat dealing with some chronic or terminal conditions, I suggest reading the book *Soul Cats* by Tamara Schenk to bring comfort and additional support.

VETERINARY VISITS

This section discusses ideas on how to select a quality veterinarian, prep for veterinary visits, afford the costs, advocate for your cat's overall wellness, study up on any diagnoses, and respect the value of early intervention.

Choosing a Quality Veterinarian

As your cat's guardian you must advocate for his wellness. A part of this means finding a great veterinarian you can trust. My best recommendation is to seek a holistic vet with high ratings. They are not easily found and often harder to get in to see because they can be in demand. If you cannot find a vet utilizing homeopathies, herbal remedies, energy medicine, essential oils, and the like, seek an open-minded vet. Slightly more veterinary practices are utilizing acupuncture, laser treatments, chiropractic care, and focus on quality nutrition. These vets will more likely be open to discussing safer, holistic options to care. A third-tier veterinarian practice would be finding one supportive of behavioral and training techniques as a valid treatment option and that will refer clients readily to professional trainers, consultants, and behaviorists. If you can't find any of the above in your area, pick a vet who truly listens to you.

Many doctors or vets get frustrated with people for researching ahead of a visit or self-diagnosing by looking up symptoms on the Internet and then presenting them to the doctor upon the exam. Now, there are many sides to this issue. It is *not* black-and-white. One of the biggest negative outcomes is that many medical professionals fully dismiss anything the patient or client brings up as a possibility or concern. This tends to be even more prominent between male veterinarians and female clients. I have personally been scolded by a few different male vets for suggesting the diagnosis (because what did I know?). Ironically, in both situations I was correct, but the veterinarian never apologized. This complete dismissal comes from a place of arrogance, judgement, sometimes sexism, and leads some professionals to assume the individual is more "nut job" over being in tune with the needs of their pet. These types of veterinarians often go out of their way to make clients feel foolish for listening to their intuition or pulling together legitimate ideas based on their experiences.

Now, on the other side of that coin, a few people *do* jump the gun or get amped up about possible worst-case scenarios when in fact the health situation proves more normal than dire. A small percentage of folks legitimately suffer from hypochondria on various levels and may project that onto their pets. This is an exception, not the rule.

Why am I bringing these things up? Because I want you to become savvier about your own health as well as the health of your pets. I want you to be observant, educated, open-minded, in tune with Spirit, so that you seek and find the necessary care for healing in all four energy bodies. I want you to find a veterinarian who values you as a person, trusts your observations, and gives real consideration to your suggestions.

Seek a veterinarian who:

- Makes enough time in consults to do a thorough exam and listens to you fully (if you are a big talker, prepare ahead with a document or practice saying bullet points to keep concise).

- Actually considers your opinion on what might be wrong or if the vet can rule your idea out, explains how or why *or* expresses why something else should be considered first.

- Treats you and your animals with kindness and respect. A "Fear Free" facility is best.

- Does not enforce yearly vaccination—vaccines remain viable within the immune system for *much* longer than the "annual recommendation."

- Has a clear love of animals, especially cats.

- Is open to alternative health care and how to pair it with western medicine practices.

- Has a great staff of knowledgeable and friendly people.

- Charges reasonable prices and works with you on expensive care needs.

- Works with animals on a volunteer basis when they can, offering free or discounted services to rescues, shelters, TNR groups OR who helps rescues by fostering animals with medical problems.

- Doesn't get upset with you for advocating for your cat's safety and emotional well-being (especially when you have an immune compromised cat).

- Keeps up on new scientific break throughs, procedures, and complimentary care.

Avoid a veterinarian who:

- Doesn't allow for your opinions or ignores your documentation of behaviors and symptoms.

- Talks down to or placates you.

- Is always unavailable to talk on the phone after a procedure or consultation if you have questions or concerns.

- Has unknowledgeable, short-tempered, or unhelpful staff.

- Does the bare minimum in a consultation exam because they are too busy to care about your pet.

- Refuses to accept, use, or consider any form of complementary, natural, or alternative pet care.

- Pushes upselling more than healing and charges higher rates than other vets (specialists are exempt from higher rate concerns).

- Readily offers euthanasia services for about any reason.

- Offers non-medically required, full-paw, toe amputation (declawing) services.

- Is incredibly difficult to get in to see last minute (as pets often require same-day or next-day visits).

Prep for Veterinary Trips

Depending on your kitty, veterinary trips can be very stressful. Some cats get so scared they pee or poop in the carrier on the way to the vet. Once at the vet's office, some vets do better than others to help cats in particular feel safer. So, what can we do to help the vet trips become less traumatizing?

Starting in kittenhood, make the carrier a safe and positive space and not the sign of bad things to come. In a previous chapter I spoke about helping to desensitize the carrier, associating it with treats, and making the result of trips only sometimes ending at the vet office. Another tip to make vet trips less traumatizing is to keep the carrier out all the time. Make it into a bed or an eating spot. Praise kitty for being inside of the carrier.

Spray pheromones like Comfort Zone inside carrier 30 minutes before departure time to help calm kitty. Place a towel or blanket that smells like home inside carrier. Give kitty some drops of Rescue Remedy for cats before travel. Place a rose quartz crystal in the carrier.

Making Veterinary Visits Better for Kitty

Once at the vet office, you can ask for (or seek out) Fear Free handling:

- A feline specific waiting area.

- Dedicated exam room for felines.

- Allows for five to fifteen minutes of time for cat to decompress before handling.

- Vet spends the time to help kitty feel safe and not jumping into exam—offers treats, kind words, or petting.

- The exam room has a pheromone or essential oil calming diffuser.

- Techs wrap a cat safely in a towel over scruffing or pinning to obtain any needed samples.

- Avoid where possible taking the kitty out of the exam room and into the back for things like blood draws or shots.

Advocating for Your Cat

You should not feel anxious about speaking up with the vet, asking questions, and getting the support you and your kitty require. This is why I suggest you seek out a like-minded vet when possible. It can be frustrating if a vet tells you that probiotics and vitamins have no healing value. Or that cats don't get UTIs and that it's "all in their head," meaning stress related. (While stress is the greatest culprit of urinary tract inflammation in cats, it doesn't mean that bacterial infections in the urinary tract *never* happens. I have literally seen and cleaned up a regular flow of pus coming from a cat's urethra which is a sure sign of infection.) It's likewise hard when a vet mocks you for speaking of energy medicine or other alternative treatments.

Ultimately, you have the final say in your cat's care. Yes, you need to seek wise counsel from medical professionals, but you have more options to explore than just standard western medicine. Don't be afraid to ask for what kitty needs or to seek out additional advice and alternative healing services.

Side Note: Over-Vaccinating

A responsible vet will only vaccinate three to five years apart, if that often. Outside of the legal requirements for rabies, no other vaccine is required by law. Indoor-only pets with little risk for exposure to other animals require very few vaccines in their lifetime. A single vaccine, without boosters, should create antibodies that last for years and years. A Titer Test will show which antibodies remain active in your cat's immune system, thus helping you know if he needs a booster or not. Even if not vaccinating, still keep an annual checkup with the vet.

While I am not "anti-vaccine," I am also not "pro-vaccine." I try to remain in a more neutral place, so I can make the right choices for each animal. I have seen many kittens receive vaccines between six to eight weeks old who then have mild reactions of low-grade fever and lethargy in the first 12-18 hours. They sometimes get a mild case of limping calicivirus after vaccination as well that lasts about 24 hours. A few times though, I have seen more drastic reactions to vaccines. Trixie almost died after receiving her first vaccine. She reacted with a full-blown case of panleukopenia but wasn't testing as such. I had another foster, Love Bug, for whom I gave a booster vaccine. I prayed that I delivered the vaccine safely and effectively but forgot to pray for her to be able to process the drug safely. She had a fever and lethargy reaction that day, which I never see on booster shots; worse than that, she had a personality change literally overnight. She shifted from a relaxed, purring lap cat to a cat who couldn't keep still, continuously pacing, not sleeping nearly as much as a cat should, and with a compulsive need to bite and pull at fabrics. She was about ten months old when I gave her that vaccine (almost all rescue groups require vaccines prior to adoption).

I researched and found that this reaction had happened in cats before. I found a holistic vet online who helped me figure out which homeopathic remedies to give to Love Bug. She said that she had treated the reaction my kitten had many times in other cats and dubbed it "brain on fire." We also gave detoxing supplements to Love Bug. Someone adopted her in the midst of the process, so I couldn't fully oversee the healing process, but the adoptive guardian was a nurse open

❀ *Love Bug on the screened porch.*

to holistic help and Love Bug did improve a bit: the biting and pulling reduced, but she remained really agitated. I was so sorry that she went from loving and snuggly to constantly in motion. I asked that the adopter never vaccinate her again because she clearly has a sensitivity to the adjuvants in vaccines.

Affording the Costs of Veterinary Healthcare

If you don't already, begin to view your cat as a family member. Providing needed and appropriate medical care is a sign of familial love and respect. Like everything else, the cost of veterinary care continually rises. Because of this, I suggest one of three strategies so guardians can always afford care.

- 🐾 Pay for pet insurance. Getting insurance coverage is easier with a young, healthy kitten. Make sure you have coverage for accidents, illness, hospitalization, surgeries, prescriptions, diagnostics, and more. Seek a lower deductible and co-pays.

- 🐾 Save money every month in a pet-health savings account. Depending on the number of animals you have, put away $25-$100 each month. Over time you should amass several thousands of dollars. This serves as emergency funds should kitty have an accident, require surgery, or need cancer treatments.

- 🐾 You could combine both strategies for additional security. $40/month for insurance and $40/month into a savings account.

Study Up on the Diagnosis

I advocate for everyone to research what other vet practices, holistic vets, guardians, and rescuers have to say about feline illnesses online. Educational pursuits should never be discouraged. *Sometimes* your veterinarian may give advice that isn't truly in the animal's best interest. I don't think they do so maliciously or even intentionally, but because they don't know better. For example, after diagnosing my cat Beaux with urinary crystals, the vet immediately recommended a popular prescription dry food to reduce crystals. This occurred years ago before I had learned as much as I know now, but something didn't sit right with me about feeding kibble as the path to better health. I read many blog posts from a variety of veterinary practices on the topic, most of whom touted the kibble. I finally stumbled into a research study a veterinarian had put together on which foods supported a reduction in crystals and which did not. And nowhere did she recommend dry prescription kibble, which incidentally contains about 40% carbohydrates and is too high in fat. I also found a company producing natural supplements for cats and dogs, and one of their formulas was for urinary tract health. I switched Beaux's diet to predominantly the wet foods the article recommended, added more attractive drinking options, and used the supplement monthly. I chose to use the specialized prescription kibble sparingly as treats or snacks. Beaux hasn't had crystal blocks or urinary pain again. So, always educate yourself on your kitty's diagnosis.

Respect the Value of Early Intervention

Earlier in my adult life, I made the mistake of waiting to get veterinary care for a cat because I didn't want to spend money and assumed she'd eventually get better. But my waiting led to her death. She needed immediate care. I hoped to save on money but wound up spending over a $1000 in a desperate and failed attempt to preserve her life. Had I taken her in two days earlier when I first noticed her symptoms, she may have survived.

I don't want this to happen to you. This is why I suggest a savings plan and insurance, so you will never feel like you can't pay for care. Emergencies frequently occur at night or on the weekend, and urgent-care vets usually charge higher rates. But if your cat swallowed something toxic on Saturday night, waiting until Monday afternoon to go to the regular vet may likely prove too late.

I have adopted a "when in doubt, just go" strategy with my forever and foster cats. It is better to pay for a clean bill of health than to have done nothing and kitty dies as a result. Felines have sensitive systems, so they need support quickly.

ALTERNATIVE HEALING TOOLS

Throughout this book I have brought up these tools. So I won't dive deeply again, but simply touch on them as a reminder that they could aid kitty when sick. All of the tools I will mention are not likely to be the solitary thing you will need to help an animal. On occasion, they only need a little support and a problem will resolve, but because cats are emotional, complex, and intelligent, they may need a variety of methods to actually shift into health or happiness— including standard medical care.

Acupuncture

Acupuncture can help with a variety of kitty health concerns like arthritis, chronic pain, neurological issues, urinary tract stress, cancers, inflammatory bowel disease, liver disease, kidney disease, trauma, and behavioral concerns.

Animal Communication

Getting a last-minute appointment with a skilled communicator may prove challenging unless you are a regular client. Still, when your cat becomes ill, it could be helpful to hear from the animal directly. I've mentioned this tool a few times but have yet to tell you of my favorite online video that features a gifted animal communicator. Google "how the leopard Diablo became Spirit."

What's more, you can train, especially if you feel you have gifts in this area, to communicate directly with your own cats.

Crystals

Let the cat choose crystals, meaning never force him into wearing or using them. Skippy is drawn to crystals and will play with them or sit on them or near them. When I want to put a crystal necklace on him to help him feel calmer or more confident (depending on the situation), I always hold it up for him to sniff.

If he backs away, I let it go, but he rarely does that. He mostly accepts it easily as I place it around his neck. I have done this without any treat association. I do, however, use verbal praise.

Energy Work

After a session of energy work, a human client will say things like, "I feel so much lighter and more relaxed." However, knowing if energy work on animals has had a positive impact can prove more difficult. These hints will help you recognize if an animal is processing or accepting the session while it is happening. That can look like relaxing and slow blinking, licking their lips, yawning, or even shedding a few tears. Of course, you can also look for behavior changes afterwards to see improvement in the issues you addressed in the session. *Energy work won't change the nature of a cat or the personality of an animal.* However, it can help reduce stress, increase healing, and work through abuse or trauma.

Story Example: Abused Dog

I had a client who adopted an older abused dog, Bubba, that was afraid of many things like leashes, feet, going outside, being petted, and even being in the living room. We did several sessions for him and he improved on accepting the leash, going on walks, being touched, but the living room remained a hold out. I could not energetically fix that for him. He had tiny breakthroughs but then would fall back into a place of stress over the room. The client previously had to put down a very sick dog and did so in the living room when this abused rescue dog was still fairly new to her home. But do you know what eventually did the trick? She adopted two puppies that looked like Bubba in size and color, and he now follows them gladly into the living room.

Essential Oils

Use these only when educated on how to appropriately administer to cats. Dog oil remedies are not automatically safe for cats. It is safest to use this support tool via aromatic diffusers or even by simply opening a bottle a few feet from the cat. Again, let the cat consent. If kitty's eyes blink rapidly and he runs away, it's a pretty clear "no" on that oil. If they stay and sniff a little at the air, they are accepting the oil aromatically. When diffusing, make sure kitty can leave the room if he chooses. Add just a few drops of oil with the required amount of water for the diffuser. When using topically, highly dilute: one or two drops of essential oil to about 100 drops of carrier oil (like food-grade almond, olive, or coconut). When applying topically, avoid sensitive areas like eyes, inside ears, or genitals. After checking the essential oil's safety for cats and diluting heavily, apply lightly by putting two to four drops in your hands, rubbing them together, and then petting the kitty. When the cat grooms, he will be ingesting a

safe amount of the oils to support his health and wellbeing. An important, nay, *crucial* point is to only use Pure Therapeutic Grade Oils from companies that provide third-party-certified oil integrity testing documentation. Companies I know of that do this are Young Living, DoTerra, and Revive. I use the book *The Animal Desk Reference: Essential Oils for Animals* by holistic veterinarian Melissa Shelton, DVM, the 2012 version.

Frequency Support

I have a device that emits frequencies. It is most impactful when I place the attached leads on my body and can feel the electrical frequencies. However, it also works sans leads, the way I always use it on animals. Like crystals, never force a cat to submit to a session with a device like this, so don't clip it to the collar. I have numerous photos of cats snuggling up to the device when they have felt unwell; they gladly use it when they need it.

Story Example: How Frequency Sessions Can Help

The first time I cared for a litter of kittens sick with panleukopenia, Skippy refused all food. He hadn't eaten on his own for over two days. I force-fed him Pedialyte and Gerber chicken meat and gave him sub-q fluids to keep his system running. The diarrhea and fever can be intense, so it's important that the kitten stay

❋ *Skippy during the frequency session and then right after. I was so relieved to see him eat.*

well hydrated and with food to process in the gut. After the second day of his refusal to eat, I remembered my frequency device and set it to run a cycle of a gastrointestinal frequency program. After about 20-30 minutes of using this program, Skippy got down out of my lap, walked over to the food bowl, and ate!

Homeopathy

Taking homeopathic remedies is really a form of energy medicine. It has been around for over 200 years and is a valid form of healing support. The medicinal formulas contain the energies of specific plants and minerals. Many critics of this modality say that the substance within the dose actually contains nothing. With this remedy, again, it is the *energy* of the item you want to access and not the actual item that you put into your body. This makes it pretty safe and very hard to mis-dose or overdose. A typical lab review of the tablets or tinctures would show "nothing" there, but a quantum physicist would tell you differently.

Light or Laser Therapy

Different light spectrums give off different colors. Several of the spectrums are associated with healing and reducing pain—blue, red, green, violet, and infrared. Lights are a gentle, if used appropriately, supportive tool. One litter of kittens I fostered had a bad viral skin infection, and I treated them with blue light every day for an hour to help support healing. They loved snuggling under the warm light pad. I performed this treatment along with applying topical diluted iodine several times a day.

🌸 *Skippy and Miss Kitty absorbing warm rays of sun on the road to recovery.*

Sunlight likewise offers healing support, especially for mental and emotional boosting. When Skippy and his sister started to heal after two weeks of serious illness, I immediately let them get some sunlight outdoors. The fall was mild with temps in the high 60s and low 70s, so for several days I intentionally placed them in that healing light. It perked them up—fresh air and sunlight.

SPIRITUAL GUIDANCE & MIRACLES

If you are open to it, with intention to receive from holy sources, you *will* receive help, answers, and miracles on your behalf or on the behalf of those you love, including kitty.

Earlier in the book, I reviewed a variety of spiritual tools that will help you heal, change, and grow (page 60). No need to overdo it here with a written repeat, but I do want to share two stories. One happened in my adult life where I allowed spiritual guidance to bring me peace in a tragic moment. The other I shared at the very beginning of this book and will briefly recap. The experience as a child shaped my life, helping me to know and appreciate the power of God.

Story Example: It's Not About Me

Skippyjon, who later became one of my forever cats, was incredibly ill with panleukopenia. I worked very hard, with sleepless days and nights, nursing this kitten and his sister. I asked for friends and family to fast and pray that the kittens would pull through. I sought help from healing Angels. I prayed that God would magnify all of my efforts to save them, as I knew they were imperfect efforts. I did my literal best. But one night, on day five of Skippy's illness, his fever spiked to over 106 degrees and his body went limp. I took him into urgent care in the wee hours of the morning. I had done all that I could (at least what I knew at that time).

Around 10 am, eight hours later, the rescue called to inform me that Skippy's condition had not changed. The vet recommended either longer hospitalization or euthanasia. A rescue must spend medical funds wisely, so they told me that Skippy needed to be put down (or I could bring him home until he passed). After having watched how his other sister suffered before her death two weeks before, I didn't want to do that to Skippy. So, I agreed to put him down but asked if I

❀ *Skippy the afternoon I brought him back home from the urgent care clinic.*

could be with him when it happened. The emergency vet made an exception (these were height of Covid-19 days) to allow me to enter the building to support Skippy when they put him to sleep.

I sobbed heavily for an hour before I left to go to the clinic. I cried and cried to God about why He didn't help me save this kitten's life. After all the prayers and fasting from everyone and all the work I put in, could He not save this kitten for me? Then I distinctly heard, "This isn't about you. This is about Skippy. This is about what he needs, and his life or his death is in My hands." I gulped down my last sob; my crying stopped. I was humbled and oddly stilled and comforted by these words. I instantly let my love for this kitten and *his* needs be my guide. If this was his fate, to die, I would go and show him all the love and support I could and take myself and my wants and needs completely out of the equation.

I arrived at the emergency clinic and employees ushered me into a room to wait. They told me his fever still hovered over 106 and that he wouldn't eat anything. Almost an hour later they brought me Skippy. I expected him to be weak and have that sad, lost look in his eyes, but he was totally excited to see me. He crawled all over me, head bonking my face, and purring up a storm! No way was I going to have this kitten put down when he was acting like this! I asked for them to take his temperature again, and it had decreased to 103, almost normal. At the same time, the rescue group leader called to tell me she'd remembered a supplemental tool that helped her save some panleuk kittens nearly a decade previously and wanted me to get it for the remaining two kittens. I told her how alert and happy Skippy was, and she agreed that I should take him home, get the supplements, and try again to save his life. And we *were* successful in saving Skippy's life *and* the other two kittens.

I was spiritually guided to remember to be there for Skippy, to let go of what I wanted and focus instead on what he needed. In the moment I accepted God's will, I received comfort and knew what to do. While this situation was meant to help teach me to accept God's will, everyone who fasted and prayed still ultimately received a miracle. This sweet kitten's life was spared. The miracle comprised of his fever breaking, his love for life radiating, and the Spirit helping the rescuer to recall what supplements could save his life all in the same moment. Though not out of the woods entirely, we were given the blessings and tools to move forward with hope for a happy outcome.

Story Example: Pepé

I share this story in the introduction of this book as it truly shaped my young heart. It taught me that God was real and powerful. If you recall, Pepé was on death row because of a full bladder blockage. I stayed home from church with him to spend our final hours together. After everyone had left the house, I went on the back deck to be with Pepé. He was relegated to the upper-level deck because he had pee accidents more often than my parents liked. This warm, sunny day, I lay down beside my buddy who clearly didn't feel good. I petted him and wept. At some point, I decided to pray to God and ask Him to heal my cat. I went a few paces away onto the screen porch and began my heartfelt prayer. The prayer of this little girl, desperate, longing to be heard by God, was lengthy. Eventually, I felt I should bargain with God. Maybe if I promised something in return, He would help me? I know God accepted that bargaining from my child self so He could give me a witness of His power and love. I told God I would read all of the scriptures if He would only heal my cat, to save his life. I needed Pepé; I loved him.

Well, I went back out to the deck and once again lay down with Pepé, crying some more. Then suddenly, urine flowed from him! I rushed into the kitchen for

paper towels. I was exuberant! I started singing children's church songs out of sheer joy. About that moment, my mother came home early from church and found me singing on the deck, gratefully mopping up pee. My mother felt so relieved because she did not want to put my kitty down. When she asked how this happened, I answered that I prayed for God to heal him. It was a miracle! There was no mistaking it for me, connecting my sincere prayer for help to the gush of urine mere moments later.

Pepé never got another urinary tract blockage. We continued to do our best to feed him a low-ash diet—and he continued to overeat—but he had been healed by God in answer to a heartbroken little girl's prayer. I did try to uphold my end of the bargain. As a twelve-year-old, I read about halfway through the scriptures before giving up. However, God upheld His end fully.

Looking back, I am grateful to God for not solely saving Pepé but also for taking time to teach me and establishing a pattern for me of believing that 1) God cares about all living creatures, 2) He cares about helping us amid our sorrows, 3) He wants us to believe in His very real power, and 4) miracles can happen for anyone. As an adult, I have continued asking for God's help in many things, but in particular for the care of my animals and fosters. I find that He helps me the most when I ask for Him to help someone else. Not that He hasn't or won't help us for ourselves, but that He values when we focus our hearts, minds, and wishes on the welfare of others. I have learned that miracles do happen when 1) we ask for them, 2) we believe they can happen, 3) we ask others with faith to join with us in asking, and 4) it is in the highest good for everyone involved including the animal. Sometimes we do not get what we hope or want, because greater purposes are at play. I have learned to take joy in the times the tender mercies and miracles do happen and take solace in the wisdom of God when they do not.

Prayer or communication with God is the key to receiving support. Sometimes the support comes as confirmation, like the story I shared about receiving the elephant sign when placing cats with a young couple. Sometimes the power of a group of voices raised up to Heaven invokes the miracle, such as my kittens cured of panleukopenia. Sometimes support arrives as a clear prompting to do something, like when I felt I should go into the garage and witnessed Honey lapping a toxic substance.

If you have a sick cat, your prayer might sound like, "God above, please help me find the right solution for my cat's illness. Please let the vet be wise and inspired when we visit. Send healing Angels to whisper the right solutions into the vet's heart and mind. If I need to do anything else to help my kitty, please inspire or lead me to the right answers. Help me to advocate for my cat and do my best to help him heal. Please, God, heal my kitty. I thank You now for this healing. Still, if not, I offer this prayer in love and gratitude for all that You are and for all You can do. Amen."

PURRRITO WRAP UP

No one else can advocate for our cats, so we need to take on the responsibility. We can start with focusing on healthy habits within our own homes. This may look like reducing toxicities, remembering the cats needs from a holistic body/mind/spirit perspective, or noticing signs of aging in our older cats.

It is important to find the right veterinarian, someone we feel concurs with all or most of our own values when it comes to medical and holistic care. We can plan ahead by saving money or getting pet insurance so that we always feel able and ready to afford veterinary care. Vet offices trained in Fear Free practices are most ideal because they understand how to make kitty as comfortable as possible in otherwise terrifying circumstances.

When kitty becomes ill, utilize our awareness of a myriad of holistic tools and modalities that can bring additional healing support. We can tap into the Spiritual realm as well, calling down from Heaven healing miracles and tender mercies. Ultimately, we can take comfort that God is in control and seek to align our wills with His.

CHAPTER 13

Terminally Ill Kitties, Learning to Say Goodbye

CARING FOR A VERY SICK KITTY

Discovering kitty is gravely sick can deal us an emotional blow. We expect it a little more when cats age, as their lives near an end. However, serious illness can strike at any time in a cat's life, and getting the news is never easy. This chapter, I hope, will help us better prepare for that outcome.

Cats hide their illnesses well. Often, those less experienced with cats will not even know the cat is sick or in pain until the cat has isolated herself away to die. Guardians may realize they haven't seen the cat all day and wonder if she escaped the house (sometimes that is the case). After frantically searching two or three times, they discover the kitty in a dark corner of a closet, underneath clothes or inside a box. Kitty's eyes will be full of that sorrow of sickness. She may hiss (if in a lot of pain) and resist coming out of hiding.

In the wild, cats must mask their illnesses well; otherwise, larger prey, or sometimes other cats in the colony, will target them. When they become so ill that they cannot hide it, they seek a concealed spot to wait out the illness, to either die or recover. This process is written in the small feline DNA.

Because of this talent for hiding disease, we as guardians must grow adept at reading signs of feline illness. It often starts with something simple like less energy, sleeping more, or eating less. Regular litterbox maintenance will help you to notice if kitty is peeing more or less. (This is harder in a multi-cat household.) You can tell if kitty has more constipated feces (a lot of small roundish, hard poop), diarrhea, or no poop. Watch food and water intake. If not eating *at all* for more than 24 hours, go to the vet. Drinking a lot of water may be a sign of kidney stress, urinary tract inflammation, diabetes, or other illnesses in kitty. If the cat stands by the water bowl, sadly hanging her head but not drinking, go to the vet immediately as kitty could be in organ failure or at the least *very* ill. Kitties pressing their heads against the wall or other surfaces also need a vet visit right away because it is a sign of neurological or nervous system distress.

Sometimes when kitty changes her behavior, humans often jump to a negative and incorrect conclusion that the cat is "being a jerk for no reason." Behavior changes can indicate illness or pain. If kitty unexpectedly won't allow petting and hisses and growls at you when you try to touch her, she is probably in pain. If kitty suddenly starts peeing outside of the box, something is likely wrong with her urinary tract. When cats urinate right in front of you, either in the litterbox or on your bed or clothing, and they have never done that before, they are trying to communicate that something hurts when they pee, so pay attention. Beaux did this to me a few years back. He never jumps into the box to urinate while I scoop it, but he suddenly did it three times in a row. The first day he did this, I didn't get the message, but the next day I realized he was trying to tell me something. So, I watched him go potty. He strained to pee. He crouched for 30-45 seconds trying to relieve himself and when he moved, I could see he barely got a small amount out. We went to the vet the next day and found that he had crystals in his urine that created pain and partial blockage.

If you have seen kitty eat a foreign object like part of a plant, paint, fluid from the car, deodorant, or the like, hop online immediately to check the item for potential toxicity. Double check your efforts, especially if kitty consumed a lot, by calling the ASPCA Poison Control Hotline or the Pet Poison Helpline. These services are not free, but worth the peace of mind or understanding the urgency of the situation. Program both of these numbers into your phone ahead of time. Keep food-grade activated charcoal on hand to administer to kitty in case of toxic consumptions. If you see that kitty consumed something like a sock, a lot of yarn, a chunk of plastic, make an immediate vet appointment. These types of solid items will not break down in the digestive tract and can cause serious blockages, so you want the vet to make a plan for kitty.

Side Note: How to Tell Kitty is in Pain

Cats hide pain as much as possible, but as it worsens, they will show visible signs. Favoring a paw or a particular part of the body when they move is a clear indicator. Reacting with hissing, growling, or snapping when you touch a certain area of the body is another signal of pain. You can also pick up on more subtle signs. The image below shows a good example of a cat's body language indicating signs of pain. The cat will often hang the head lower, ears increasingly turn askew, and the eyes close to a slit-like opening. Additional signs are underweight cats or dull fur not groomed as fastidiously as cats typically do.

When kitty is ill or had a major surgery, do your best to care for her. If you can afford hospitalization and you feel it's the right choice, especially if you don't believe you have the skill or ability to care for kitty at home, you can do that. I personally recommend that whenever possible, bring kitty home to nurse her there. Stress lowers the animal's immune system, just as it does our own. Staying at the vet hospital in a strange place with scary sounds, the sad yowls of other animals, and strong unfamiliar smells creates serious stress for cats. Furthermore, at home, you have the freedom to combine traditional veterinary care with alternative supportive healing care like a frequency device or supplements, crystals or energy work. At home, you likely feel more comfortable undertaking spiritual healing modalities as well, like praying over your animal, fasting for them, and asking for healing Angels to help kitty.

In a multiple-pet or busy household, keep a sick kitty in a quiet, safe place away from others. Kitty doesn't need pestering or stressing by a hyperactive puppy or growled at by a cat-mate because she smells different while sick and on meds. Choose a space you spend a lot of time. I usually choose my bedroom.

Story Example:
Enlist Help When Needed

If the cat requires around-the-clock care, I hope you find some help. I know from personal experience that when people become sleep-deprived for too long, they start to give up and just want the whole thing to be over, no matter the outcome.

While nursing sick kittens with panleukopenia, I spent about five sleepless nights before I found some amazing supplements to help. But those supplements required an hourly dose around the clock. On day eight or nine (day three or four of administering the supplements) the kittens were doing much better, so I said, "I'm

✿ *The miserable tenth night in this story.*

going to bed!" I slept for about six to seven hours, and the next morning the kittens had relapsed into high fevers and no appetites. I had to start over! On day ten, I was utterly exhausted, and at 3 am I bawled to God and said, "I can't do this anymore! Please God, You need to either heal them or take them back to You. I can't go another night with so little sleep. I just can't."

God answered my prayer, not in the way that I expected though. My then 16-year-old niece who knew what was happening came that afternoon and stayed the weekend, volunteering to take the night shifts so I could sleep. On day thirteen, we were all doing so much better (kittens and me) but not out of the woods. We still needed a few more days of hourly dosing, so my father who lived in my home volunteered to split the night shift with me. I would give meds until 2 am and then he would start the 3 am dose and continue until about 10 am when I woke up.

I hope your spouse, a reliable teenage child, a friend, or relative will help you. We don't do well without sleep, and with the added stress, it is easy to want to give up. When nursing my foster Hero, who I will talk more about in the next section, I was alone in the effort and after twelve days, I gave up, or at least my fatigue contributed to my choice to put him to sleep. And it haunted me that I let that be a contributing factor.

When you are nursing a sick animal at home you will likely need to learn about or do a lot of the following. You can have the vet office train you in much of it.

- Administer oral medications or topical meds
- Give B12 or insulin shots
- Tube feed
- Inject sub-q fluids
- Change bandages
- Take temperatures
- Hand-feed
- Give supplements or vitamins
- Keep things sterile and clean
- Check vital signs regularly (heart rate, breath rate, temperature)
- Cool fevers
- Warm kitty who has a low temperature
- Keep kitty comfortable
- Drain wounds or expel bladders
- Groom kitty (brush and a warm, damp cloth—not submerged baths)
- Perform or oversee alternative supportive care

Serious illnesses can last for weeks or months. I encourage you, if you feel reason to hope, try to save kitty. Take the vet's counsel into consideration. He or she may have seen many similar cases and can usually tell when the battle can or cannot be fought. Ponder what you know of yourself and your kitty. Consider what alternative care can offer. Not many vets utilize the potential help of holistic care in the process of healing a disease. For instance, with panleukopenia the vet offices will put cats on IV fluids, may offer some pain management, try to administer food, monitor, and that's it. A veterinarian would never have prescribed the supplements I used that saved the kittens' lives. If there is reason to hope, then hope! Make sure, though, that you do not let selfish feelings, fear, or sorrow factor into your decision. Confusing, right? What to choose in these situations is often hard to know on our own. I suggest ultimately to use prayer and meditation to help guide the choice to fight the illness or not. Ask Angels to direct you to the correct paths of healing or acceptance.

During these times of high stress, grief, and worry, utilize self-care. Do at least two or three of the most important things every day to keep you grounded and strong. For me, reading scriptures, listening to uplifting books, praying, doing energy work, getting sleep, wearing crystals, and soaking in hot baths are my best strengthening tools. I also benefit from avoiding sad TV and choosing shows that might make me laugh instead. Try to keep balance because when *you* are stronger, you make better decisions and can serve your beloved cat to the best of your abilities.

WHEN TO LET THEM GO

The process of death is often a scary one for us. Even when we believe in an afterlife, humans often fear the separation from a loved one in this life.

Animals cannot communicate to most of us to tell us what they want: to live or pass on. Certainly, you can work with a reputable animal communicator when your little furry friend is critically ill, and that process could bring you comfort. For most of us, in the crux of our feline friend's sickness or pain, we have to make the decision of life or death for them. Such decisions are always difficult. It is a terrible power to have over another creature, yet in these moments we must do our best to stay clear-minded, in tune with Spirit, and willing to take on the responsibility.

With my own forever cats, I have only had to make the choice once—my Stella when she ate lilies. I tried to keep her alive out of fear of being without her. I didn't make the best choices for her. Her kidneys were in failure, and she was so sick that the look from her eyes changed, as if she was no longer there or didn't want to suffer anymore. She didn't recognize me or want my companionship in the way that she had her whole life. After three or four days of trying to force her to stay alive, I succumbed to the reality that nothing would cure her and that the kindest and most loving act was to let her go.

In my cat fostering responsibilities I have had to make the choice between life and death many times. Those situations where I connect to Spirit, I make better decisions for the animal than the times when I am not in tune.

Though the following stories have unhappy endings, I share them to communicate the difference of what these life and death choices are like with no connection to Spirit and on the flip side, secure confidence in an answer received from Spirit.

Story Example: My Little Hero

I fostered a FeLV positive kitten with additional health complications. He came to me so fragile, so malnourished. I worked hard for months to nurse him back to health. The endeavor succeeded, and I fell in love with this little flame-point boy with big blue eyes. He was precious.

❀ Hero the day I got him and then four months later right before his final illness.

At this time, I also volunteered in a rescue leadership, and the work was grueling—fifty-hour weeks on top of my full-time paying job. The other leaders in the rescue were challenging for me in different ways. During this difficult time (which incidentally God told me not to get involved as a rescue director) I allowed these other leaders to pull me into conflict and stress with them. Moreover, the work itself depressed me—animals being surrendered, neglectful foster homes, decisions to euthanize, not finding enough

new foster homes. By the time this little flame-point, Hero, got sick with severe limping calicivirus, I wasn't even praying anymore. I completely neglected any daily support tools like meditation, reading religious or spiritual books, or doing energy work for myself. I couldn't feel the Spirit at all in my life.

Hero suffered for eleven days before I felt I could do no more on my own to heal him. I had taken him to the vet three times for medications, which I administered, but he refused food on the eleventh day and his eyes started looking really sad, getting that far-off look. I thought if I could get him on an IV through the night, maybe the fluids would help break his fever and he would feel better, so we went to the urgent vet clinic. But instead of turning the corner, he got much worse that night. The clinic did *not* give Hero the attention he would have received from me at home, so his face was covered in dried snot and eye goop. He still refused food. They had him on fentanyl, so he was either so high on the meds that he wasn't himself, or he had already given up on life, because he didn't really recognize me, and he just didn't seem to be there anymore.

🐾 *Hero, our last moments together.*

I was exhausted with no help at home. I worried (and had for months) about the FeLV virus spreading to my forever cats. I couldn't get a serious adopter interested in taking Hero on. I felt so hopeless in that moment. So, between how I felt and how Hero seemed to feel, I decided to put him to sleep. I didn't pray about it. I had no comfort from on High that I made the right choice for this sweet kitten. As a result, I was plagued for well over a year if I did the right thing or not. Did I give up a few days too soon? Could he have finally pulled through? Or if I waited, would he had suffered longer for no reason? I cried nearly every day for a year. I couldn't foster anymore, and I could not continue to work as a leader in that rescue. I had to walk away from all of it.

This hard experience is one reason why I am trying to convey to you readers how important spiritual connection can be when caring for your kitty. Having an all-knowing source to tap into for help is beyond comforting. It is affirming.

This is the final story I will share on making decisions involving euthanasia, but I want to share because it helped me make the right choice for the foster animals in my care at the time, even when on the outside it seemed to the veterinarian that I was not. Despite the vet's feelings, and I do feel so profoundly sorry for vets who must euthanize so many animals in their careers, I know I made the correct choice for the sick kitten and for the other kittens at home.

Story Example: Sweet Baby Girl

Because of the panleukopenia in my home fall of 2020, I could not safely foster unvaccinated kittens for a while. Some experts recommend waiting a year; some say closer to two years as this incredibly hardy virus can live on surfaces for a long time. Well, in the summer of 2021, I was barely starting to work with a rescue as a leader, and we had taken in more kittens than we had foster homes for. As a result, I would act as a temporary foster for bottle babies and keep them in a small, sanitized area like a laundry basket. I was very careful about being clean when handling the babies. I then passed them on to permanent fosters as soon as the group secured them, which isn't easy because of the amount of work and dedication it requires.

In late August I temporarily took in a mama cat with her three babies. I sanitized my bathroom thoroughly before bringing them home—everything in their space was new and not used in the past for other fosters. I went in the room shoeless, always washed up, and wore an apron. I sat on a towel that I then removed when I left. At this time, the rescue organization also asked me to take on a one-day-old kitten found alone outside. I had an incubator that I had sanitized several times since the last occupants. I placed this teeny, little girl neonate in there to keep her warm and safe. I remained vigilant about sanitizing myself between the two separate groups of kittens to care for them.

My tiny little girl did well. She was growing and so sweet. At almost two weeks old, she started some diarrhea. This is normal for most bottle-fed kittens (but still a serious concern to address). I worked on it via the normal at-home remedies for a few days. I wasn't worried because she was still growing, eating, and healthy in every other way. I did get her into the vet because the diarrhea didn't resolve. I thought maybe she needed an antibiotic. The call from the vet saying that she was panleukopenia-positive shocked me. I had no inclination that she had that kind of illness. I brought her home. And I prayed a lot for an answer of what to do for her. I likewise worried about the mama and babies in the other room. I couldn't risk them being exposed, and we couldn't pass them to a new foster home now for fear they were already exposed, and the rescue couldn't afford to lose another foster home if they did wind up with panleuk. Those babies were just three weeks old themselves.

With the kittens in 2020 with panleuk, I saved them with supplements, but those supplements contained alcohol and could not safely be given to kittens younger than 6 weeks as it would likely cause liver damage. Before I had those tools to help my last batch with panleukopenia, I was limited to sub-q fluids, B12 shots, fiber, antibiotics, probiotics, and vitamins. And the kittens still were very sick with that supportive care.

As I sat with this tiny kitten, barely two weeks old, at the beginning of a very serious illness, it was hard to know what to do. She seemed pretty good other than bad diarrhea. She still wanted to eat, and she only had a low-grade fever. But should I ask her to suffer through a long illness until she was sick enough to justify euthanasia? And while caring for this sick little singleton, how much more likely would the mama and babies be to contract it too?

I stayed up with tiny girl that whole night after her diagnosis. In the early hours of the morning, I finally received an answer to prayer on what to do. These words came to me, "It is wisdom in Me that this little one should come home to Me. You have done your best. Your focus now needs to be on the other kittens. Help them." I felt in the subtext of the words that God had intended her to pass sooner, maybe not even meant to survive day one. But because I had taken such good care of her, she had lived longer. I cried a few tears as I looked at this little creature. So helpless. I took her back to the vet the next morning to be euthanized. A part of me felt like, "But she looks like she might make it! What are you doing?" a part of me that thought, "It is a matter of a day or two before she is really suffering. Remember how awful dying was for Sadie-Lynn and she was five weeks old," and another part of me—"God has said she is meant to come home to Him. I can take comfort in this choice and turn my attention to making sure I do my best for the other three kittens and their mama."

❀ *Last moments with my tiny baby girl.*

I share these stories, not to depress (I hope you aren't depressed!) but to illustrate the differences in situations and how feeling spiritually affirmed in your choice, when and if you must face euthanizing your sweet kitty, can bring so much clarity and peace to the situation.

When you are nursing a terminally ill kitty, you might have some time to plan ahead. An animal communicator may help you know what the cat might prefer in planning her departure from this life. Ask about and seek answers to very specific questions via prayer or meditation. Have clear intentions in mind for the animal. Your prayer might be phrased like, "Dear God in Heaven, my kitty is very sick with her kidneys failing. I am very heartbroken, but I truly want to do what is best for her. Thank You for helping me now, to receive correct answers to my questions on how to plan out her remaining time on this earth. Please, only allow me to be influenced by Angels and energies that have her highest good and my highest good in mind." Then you can ask for details involving her treatment plan, whether to separate her from other pets or not, what might bring kitty joy in her remaining time, how she prefers to die (naturally at home, at home with vet help), if she might like to say goodbye to others and who she wants to say goodbye to, and more.

If you plan to put the kitty down with vet support at home, be mindful of where in the home you do this and where the other animals in the home are during the procedure. Pray about what is best to do, and ask your Angels to inspire you. Remember the story about a client who had her very sick senior dog put to sleep in the living room and the other dogs were wandering around? She had a newer one to her home with an abuse and neglect background who was likely traumatized by this event. In his case, it may have been better to have him closed in a room until afterward. Be mindful and prayerful of how this event will impact the others. I do not discourage the practice of putting kitty down at home. On the contrary, it is a very loving and gentle way to let the sick kitty pass—in her own home with her people around her.

With a cat suffering greatly or in organ failure, you may have to make an immediate choice. If unsure of what to do or afraid of making the choice, seek that affirmation from on High. Ask for Angels to attend you and influence you or to bring you comfort as needed.

Whatever you do, be brave and have courage. Remember to be there for your kitty if you go into the veterinary office for the procedure. Stay with the kitty in this process. Offer comforting words and gentle loving strokes. Remember as hard as it is on you, this is her death, and having her loved one near is important for her as she transitions. Surely, or at least I believe, loving Angels await your kitty's spirit to carry her to a state of peace and love.

GRIEF OFTEN RESULTS IN QUESTIONING OURSELVES

Some say animals are soulless; some say they have souls. Some define souls as having a piece of God within them. Some define a soul as the spirit and body together. What I do know for sure is that every living thing has an individual spirit. We see that each pet has a personality, pleasures, and fears unique unto themselves. They have distinctive opinions and feelings. God is a God of love. I know He loves the creatures as well as the humans He created and placed on this earth. While I may not have a full understanding of what happens to animal spirits after this life, I feel sure they live on. I have felt the presence of some of my kitties after they passed. I hope you have a similar belief that your furry friend's spirit goes beyond this life in some way, that they have something next in their journey full of peace, joy, and love.

Having a hope in this beautiful afterlife and trusting in the love of God will help you process your grief. If you had a confirmation from Spirit that it was the right time to let your furry friend go, you will have additional strength from that knowledge.

If you lost your kitty suddenly to an accident, and you had no chance to say goodbye, prepare, or pray for help—this has its own potential set of challenges. You may be a strong, emotionally balanced person who can see the big picture of life and death and take comfort in this natural process, or you may not be in a place right now to see that, and that is okay. You may understandably feel shock, panic, and anger. You might question yourself, wondering if you had just done something differently,

❀ *My memorial for Hero. I planted a white rose above his body.*

would kitty still be with you? This feeling is normal, but not healthy when it goes on and on the way it did with me in regard to Hero. I second guessed so much about what I did or didn't do that led to his sickness. I questioned myself heavily on if I made the right choice, or if I did it selfishly because of my exhaustion from twelve sleepless days and nights combined with the fear of not finding him a forever home with his medical setbacks. It took months of grieving before I could hear any reply from Spirit. I did eventually receive, "Be open to counsel. The Lord is sorry your heart breaks for Hero. Have faith that his precious spirit is being tended to by the Lord. You did not sin in taking his life. He was gravely ill and in pain. Take counsel in knowing he is fine." That was important to hear, but I didn't fully accept it, doubting repeatedly for many subsequent months. Eventually, I felt Hero come to me a few times—I could see him in my mind's eye rubbing his little body around the furnishings, around my legs. Gratefully, I began to feel peace.

How might you gain peace or perspective if you feel stuck wondering if you could have done something differently to save your cat or if you made the right choice to let the kitty go? For myself, I have learned that sometimes Spirit warns us ahead of time before an accident and sometimes Spirit does not. In those times when you were warned, you may recall you had a feeling to do something, but you ignored it. And then a chain of events led to kitty dying or becoming really ill or getting seriously injured. I've had this happen to me numerous times. I believe that many cat spirits agreed to sacrifice themselves to help me learn the all-important lesson to heed the promptings Spirit gives me.

Throughout the book, I shared a few stories that illustrate this. With Stella, Spirit distinctly told me not to buy that Easter lily, and I ignored it. With my niece's cat Tat Tat, who I fostered for a few months while she sold her home and moved, Spirit absolutely warned me that if he came to my home he would die, and I ignored it. He died merely days before he was to go back to his family from a bizarre accident.

If this happened to you—you received a warning you ignored—I hope you forgive yourself. Many before you have made the same mistakes and regretted them, too. Myself, too frequently. I wish I had learned more quickly. I hope you can learn from me and do better than I did.

If you have experienced promptings, but you did not receive any warning or sign in this instance and what happened with your kitty came completely out of the blue, it may be nothing you could have done would have made it different. Her life ending was likely a planned exit. You will still grieve, learn from this incident, and inevitably do better for a future cat. Turn to prayer or meditation for comfort. Ask the Angels to send a sign that your kitty is okay. Ask for the ability to feel the presence of your kitty to gain peace.

If you have not yet had the experience of getting these kinds of warnings, signs, or promptings I have talked about, but you want to be able to "hear" the messages from above moving forward and follow them in confidence, you can try different methods to be more open to receiving them. Here are ideas to help.

- **Believe that we can get these messages**, that a higher, loving power wants to guide us. If unsure about the idea of Angels all around us willing to help, ask for a way to confirm their presence. Remember, God gives us agency in this life to help us learn, so Angels and Spirit need us to *ask* for help.

- **Clean up and clear out our hearts and minds from negative influences.** All of us need to do this, usually *many* times in our lives, so this is not an accusation. We do this in countless different ways, which I will list in #3, but it starts with the ability to identify those things in our lives that make us less sensitive to spiritual matters. Are we struggling with any addictions? Do we feel a lot of anger? Do we have a lot of noise or chaos in our life? Do we listen to, watch, dwell on, laugh at, read, talk, or think about really negative things? Do we have traumas to heal? Are we in physical pain? Are we afraid for our own safety? Do we struggle to believe in God or believe He loves us? Do we carry intense shame or guilt for things we have done to others? There could be other blocks as well. We need to identify the ones most impacting our lives right now and start removing them.

- **Find the ways to heal that are right for us.** So many paths offer help to lighten our load and find emotional, physical, mental, and spiritual healing. Some of the more traditional routes might include medical doctors, therapists, nutritional changes, recovery centers, or 12-step groups. We might seek out an ecclesiastical leader to help us, get a life coach, or a spiritual mentor. We can journal, ask forgiveness from those we've hurt, repent to God for the mistakes in our lives. Seek out one of many alternative healing modalities like energy work, frequency devices, crystals, acupuncture, and so much more. We might change our lifestyle to one with less social media use, TV or movie-watching, gaming, loud music, and news consumption. Consider this seriously, as much of this content is of a low vibration, or if not that, too much of it wastes our time and creates constant background noise, causing us to lose sensitivity to the spiritual realm.

- **As we heal, seek to know the ways Spirit and Angels can get through to us.** Everyone is unique. Some people get answers hearing an audible voice, some have dreams that teach them what to do, some channel the words of Spirit as they write in a journal, some feel warmth and peace about a decision, some "hear" distinctive words in their minds, some see messages and signs in the world around them, some meditate and see a clear path of what to do, some find answers popping out at them in books, music lyrics, or in the words of people around them, and some have amazing gifts of seeing and speaking with Angels. Discover the ways we receive. Most likely we have several ways to receive. For myself, I "hear" or "see" words and images in my mind's eye, I channel Spirit when journaling, and I see or receive signs in the world at large.

- **Ask for help and guidance.** Be open to following it. The more we invite, accept, and follow through with the messages, the more we receive. The more we resist the messages, the quieter they become until they stop all together.

- **Be aware that evil can send messages or signs too.** If there is a loving God, there is surely His opposite to contend with. When asking for help, ask for protection from any evil influence. It can be challenging, but it is possible to learn to decipher between messages from God/Spirit, your own thoughts, and the intrusive or negative influence of evil. I have been taught and believe that messages from a spiritual realm of love typically come as clear, and often concise, statements. Your own thoughts tend to have a tone of insecurity or questioning to them. Evil often justifies itself to you, persuading you. Examples? A spiritual prompting would be like this: "Call your sister today." If it's your own thoughts it would appear more like this: "I haven't talked with my sister in a while, I wonder how she is doing? Maybe I should call to talk with her? I'll try to remember to do that after work." An evil influence might sound more like this: "Family is so difficult to deal with. I don't have to associate with my sister if I don't want to. She was rude to me last time we spoke. I don't deserve that. She can call *me* if she really cares."

I pray that these suggestions help you start recognizing or receiving promptings and messages from enlightened sources, that in doing so you will feel peace.

PETS LEFT BEHIND MAY GRIEVE TOO

Story Example: Grieving Cats

My sister, Ellie, had four cats back in 2019. Octapussy was a senior she rescued as a tiny kitten and bottle-fed, Fluffy was a middle-aged kitty with lots of catitude, and Yuki and Toto were younger sibling Japanese Bobtails from a breeder that Ellie knew from church.

In a six-month span, both Fluffy and Octapussy quickly grew very ill, and both were put to sleep—Fluffy at the vet's office with a diagnosis of cancer and a collapsed lung, and Octapussy at home from extreme old age. After this happened, Toto started attacking his sister numerous times a day. Yuki took to hiding and overgrooming to deal with her stress. Both cats avoided Ellie.

Ellie told me about these new issues, and we decided to try Body Code work on the two cats. I discovered in the sessions that in their grief and confusion, both cats saw Ellie as the person who "disappeared" their cat-mates. Toto felt perplexed by the sudden shift in environment and power balance, and he wasn't very good at handling the changes. Yuki felt distressed at losing her cat-mates, but also at suddenly being targeted by her brother who used to be totally fine with her.

❀ *Toto snuggling with Octapussy, the calico, the day she died.*

These animals were grieving. Cats will display their grief in different ways; no two situations will be exactly alike. Know that in a multi-pet or multi-cat household, if one of them passes, this will impact the others. Some cats may obviously grieve the loss, some may grieve because you are grieving, or they may go on as if nothing affected them. Behaviors may change. Some may become depressed, some more aggressive. Some may lose weight; some might gain. Where possible, whether the deceased cat was put down at the vet office or home, it helps to let the others have a chance to recognize what happened by giving them access to the body. They may hiss at the departed body because of changes in the odor, but this practice still has value for helping the animals left behind process. If you do not have a place to bury your furry baby and you need the vet's cremation services, ask if they will let you bring kitty home for a few hours so that the other animals can cope with the event. Then take the deceased kitty back for cremation.

After the loss, take extra good care of other pets in the weeks that follow.

Here are suggestions for helping cats handle the change:

- The stress of the situation may lead to a drop in the immune system. It's a good idea to administer vitamins, probiotics, or other immune strengthening supplements for several weeks or months.

- Make sure they stay hydrated. Maybe offer more broths as treats during this transition time (low sodium/no spices if canned human broth).

- Give more verbal and affectionate assurances to comfort kitties.

- Offer patience as they work through their grief.

- Try to keep up routines of feeding times, litterbox maintenance, and play time. This will help reduce some of the environmental and emotional stress after the loss.

- Buy cats a new sensory toy, catnip toy, or some new cat furniture to focus on.

- Offer good exercise via playtime, new toys, going outside on walks with you (only if that was a previously known activity; don't introduce a new stressful activity to kitties at this time).

- Have crystals ready to set near cats or have a crystal necklace for them to wear on occasion during the grieving period. Healing crystals good for processing grief include amethyst, rose quartz, smokey quartz, clear quartz, moonstone, amazonite, Apache tears, malachite, and rhodonite.

- Have a calming environment where possible. Especially avoid chaos, loud noises, construction, yelling, and violent TV during these times. Play peaceful, healing music on low volume. Try to bring loving or joyful laughter back into the home.

- Talk to your cats about what happened. Don't keep the sad truth from them. Ask for Angels to help your cats understand what happened, to translate as needed, and bring comfort to them.

- Reach out to an animal communicator and set an appointment. They can likely give you valuable insight into how the animals are coping.

- After a few weeks, do energy work for the cats to help remove any lingering emotional trauma.

If a guardian or other human loved one in the home passes, kitties will also display grief and potential behavioral changes. They need the same space to grieve and react to the change. If *you* are grieving the loss of someone you love, whether they lived in the home or not, kitties will pick up on your grief, particularly if you are the primary person they are attached to. Cats can be little sponges for our energies and can reflect back to us our own stress via their behaviors. In times of loss, sorrow, or change, be gentle with yourself and your kitty companions. Turn to the list above if your personal sorrow impacts your kitties. Tending closely to their needs may help reduce your own suffering.

The signs of grief in your cats may last a short time, or they may persist a long time. In a multi-cat household of three or more, understand that the dynamics between the remaining two cats (or however many) may shift and create permanent changes in interpersonal animal dynamics.

If kitties have big behavioral changes negative for themselves or the household, work toward addressing them sooner rather than later. Cats can create new habits quickly. Having books like this can help you, but consider hiring a professional cat behavior consultant to review the uniqueness in your situation and help pinpoint triggers that this book might not cover.

SPIRITUALLY PROCESSING OUR GRIEF

The pain of losing a loved one is intense, including our furry friends. Like our companion animals, we process this loss in different ways. None of us are exactly alike in temperament, situation, and past experiences which have shaped us. For some like me, who rely heavily on my companion animals for company, connection, and purpose, losing a pet can be particularly devastating. For those who have an abundance of human love, connection, devotion, and support in their lives, losing a pet will hurt, but maybe not as deeply. Again, it all depends on the details of our individual lives with how intensely the pain may manifest.

Because we are individual in our emotional processes and reactions, having God, an all-knowing and all-powerful Guide, to help us understand our own individual needs for healing, is a beautiful blessing. Using prayer, meditation, Angelic guidance, and spiritual study helps us find a path to wholeness more readily and peacefully. We will still have tears, depression, confusion, questioning, and heartache, but these will be moments we experience and then release with the help of this Higher Power.

Understanding the normal human processes of grief is helpful for us, too. Scientists and therapists have identified an emotional path, or stages, we often take as humans when struck with a loss or a shocking event. These stages of grief often include feeling 1) Denial, 2) Anger, 3) Bargaining, 4) Depression, and 5) Acceptance. Some people may not need one of the stages and skip over them. Some move through to acceptance fairly smoothly, and others take a while to arrive there. There isn't a correct way to grieve. However, when we get stuck for a long time in one of these stages before acceptance, we are not really living our lives in a full or healthy way. I believe strongly that our loved ones who have left this life, particularly the pure hearts of pets, simply desire for us to be happy and continue on. They don't want us lost in anger or depression for long stretches. They want us to feel joy, peace, love, and hope.

We often experience steps two and three, our anger and bargaining, with God in mind. We may feel like He didn't answer our prayers to save our cat and then we can become resentful or distrusting. Or when an animal is very sick, we may try to bargain with God to save them. I did that as a child, and God did have mercy on me in that situation. In a few desperate

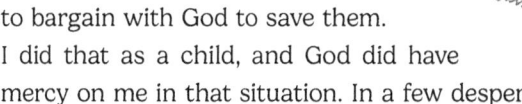

moments as an adult I have found myself trying to bargain with God, but I know now that this isn't always affective. God wants us to trust in His plans, purposes, and will. Then, sometimes, God doesn't control a situation *in that* He allows other people their agency. Some people may use that agency for ill—for example, a cranky and compassionless neighbor who poisons neighborhood cats. God *can* intervene—and He may have tried by sending inspired thoughts to us that we ignored—but God also allows hardships to happen because of a person's agency or because it is for our highest good or the highest good of others.

We can get blinders on about this life; we focus so much on this moment, we forget that from God's view that there is *so much* more. I believe in a before life and in an eternal afterlife. This life is but an experience. If we can look at life from this view, we can more readily understand why God might allow difficult situations to come to us, so that we experience more fully the good and evil, happy and sad, right and wrong.

What does that even mean, "our highest good?" How can something awful, painful, negative be for our good? It can be difficult in the midst of adversity to see *anything* positive. Still, I think most of us, especially when we try to live a spiritual life, can look back at previously challenging times and see that there were positive purposes: like how much we grew in empathy or how we learned something valuable that we can now share with others. I love the Bible verse from the ancient prophet Isaiah about God turning our ashes into beauty. Sorrow into gladness. Some of this life's most beautiful examples of that can be seen when addicts finally get clean and then help others get clean. When we see criminals truly repentant and turn their lives around to serve others in meaningful ways. Victims of sexual trauma who heal their wounds and then turn back into that darkness to rescue and save as many others as they can.

You and I can give back in the same kind of way, turning our sorrows from our past losses of beloved pets into empathy when others in our path go through it, too. We have the capacity to be gentler and less judgmental with someone's sorrow over a lost kitty. Often, we can comfort with the right words or offer the right tool to recover because we know what helped us when we felt something similar.

However, there is a time and place for advice and tools, and it isn't often in the height of someone else's fresh grief. Having Spirit as a guide, being in tune, will help us know when to offer counsel or when to just put our arms around someone and tell them we love them or support them. For someone like me, who feels called to help others learn the tools, this book is my way to help—to prepare individuals ahead of time where possible.

Have patience and compassion for others going through the grief process. Do your best to be supportive with simple phrases like "I'm sorry" or "I'd like to do something to help you; what do you need me to do?" If you see an obvious need, don't ask, just do. Like helping an elderly woman dig a grave for her kitty that was hit by a car or making a dinner for your friend who had to put down her sick cat that day. Try not to tell people how they *should* feel or that the loss of a pet isn't that big of a deal. Don't make their current sorrow about your past sorrow and monopolize their time with your story. No judging comments either; it *never* helps. For instance, a person who chose to let their cat outdoors and kitty died because of something outside doesn't need scolding that it could have been prevented if the cat remained inside. They will most likely be beating themselves up and don't need reprimands, but they could really use kindness.

If our own grief feels really overwhelming, please consider self-care strategies to find the way back to peace. Here are some ideas:

- Use Body Code, RET, or Reiki to shift out the most intense feelings we might struggle to let go of. Tapping (EFT) can help a great deal with releasing grief.

- Create a crystal grid for peace or emotional healing.

- Take a two-to-three-day retreat trip to the beach, lake, or mountains for renewal.

- Volunteer at an organization with a meaningful mission to lift our spirits.

- Blog or journal about our feelings and experiences as it can be therapeutic.

- Learn a new hobby we have been meaning to develop—making homemade bread, gardening, or knitting. Find joy in creativity.

- Ask our guardian Angel for inspiration or signs—to know we are loved, for healing, for guidance on what is next.

- Let go and forgive ourselves or others involved in the situation.

- Heal any rifts in our relationship with God because of the loss.

- Adopt a new pet for healing but be prayerful about when the timing is right for ourselves, family, or other pets.

Side Note: "No More Pets"

Sometimes when we struggle to process grief healthily, we proclaim we will never get another pet again because the pain of the loss was too great. Please don't let this happen to you. If you loved your kitty so well as that, think of all the other cats out there in need of a safe, loving home. Grieve, heal, and then adopt again. Quality pet guardians are not easy to come by for all pets; don't let them down by choosing to protect your own heart over offering love to another. Really, in the end, genuine love is all we have of worth so create more of it; share more of it.

PURRRITO WRAP UP

Many challenges come to us when we face terminal illnesses and loss of a cherished kitty friend. We can be strong and offer the loving support our pet needs during this time, especially if we are in tune with Spirit. The confidence we receive when we have answers to prayers in these matters can really comfort us.

I allowed myself to become stuck after Hero died. I felt like I needed to punish myself for about a year by feeling guilt and sorrow just in case I made the wrong choice. I didn't seek to repair my relationship with God and Spirit like I should have to work through the pain more gracefully and peacefully. I wish I had done things differently for myself and for my remaining cats. I hope if you have to face similar circumstances of loss or choices around euthanizing a beloved pet, that the thoughts in this chapter will help you move through the heartache in healthy and hopeful ways.

Cat Guardians

"You will always be lucky if you know how to make friends with strange cats."

— Colonial Proverb

A strange dichotomy has always existed between the small domestic cat and humans. You and I love them, doing our best to understand and care for them. Other people, however, have greatly traumatized cats throughout the centuries. They slaughtered cats in great numbers. We think of the Egyptians who so loved the cat that they created a cat Goddess, Bastet. Crazy then, to me, that they raised, traded, and sold hundreds of thousands, if not millions, of cats for the sole purpose of sacrifice. In the Middle Ages the Christian faith targeted cats as evil, an instrument of the devil causing the black plague, and therefore massacred them. Ironically, killing cats increased the spread of this disease carried by rodents. In our recent family histories, great-great grandparents and great grandparents, while they may have owned pet cats, they did not have the means to fix their pets, so they frequently drowned kittens or took them deep into the woods and dropped them. In our modern world, we still kill cats as the greatest means of population control. Animal advocates in "no kill" shelters can claim a significant decrease in feline euthanasia. Around five years ago, the annual numbers of cats killed in shelters dropped from 1.2-1.5 million a year to a high eight hundred thousand each year in the US. While this downward movement is in the right direction, can we even fathom the annual global feline euthanasia rate?

Dogs do not have this same kind of traumatic history with humans. While we do euthanize dogs in our modern world of shelters, people surrender and kill cats at two to three times the rate of dogs. I have wondered if our current culture

values dogs more highly because in the US almost 40% of them are purchased from breeders, whereas less than 5% of cats are purchased. Are dogs seen as a financial investment and worth more than cats? Is it any wonder then that it doesn't take much upset for our pet cats to go into survival mode with humans or that in a single generation cats can revert back to being fully wild?

My vision when I started this book was, "How can I help people and cats live together more harmoniously?" What can I do to reduce the number of cats surrendered? How can I teach cat owners to understand that cats, like dogs, deserve professional behavioral intervention and training? Why do people so readily cast aside the cat? My personal dive into the details of these questions revealed to me that spiritual, happy, mature, open, and healthy people make significantly better pet owners than those who are not. So, I sought with this book to bridge the gap for both felines and humans. It was undoubtably more than simply talking about cat behavior and scientific evidence on how to meet feline needs. Others have done that before me, and more profoundly. The work of becoming a wonderful cat guardian is about healing self, developing spiritually, and utilizing more unique tools for both cat and human wellness, in addition to learning about cat's needs.

Generations upon generations of humans have allowed cats into their lives. Why? At first it appears to have resulted from a symbiotic coexistence. Humans need grain, mice need grain, and cats need mice. Fewer mice equals more grain for humans. Farmers valued cats for rodent control. Eventually cats moved with humans across oceans and into cities, most likely again for rodent control.

In our world today, rodent control is a plus, but the majority of pet cats do not earn their keep in this way. So why do we invite them in? Somewhere along the line, someone loved a cat. A cat returned that love to the human. They had a bond. The connection, companionship, and friendship blossomed.

Cats are lovable to me because they are so distinctly unique in personality. Some are sassy, some gentle, some shy, some bold, and everything in between. They have humor, opinions, and great curiosity, which make them interesting.

"Happy is the home with at least one cat." — Italian Proverb

You may or may not have picked up on the two main terms used throughout this book to describe people who have cats: Owners and Guardians. Some animal people cringe at the word "owner" because if the animal is truly loved and cared for it can't be "owned" like one owns a house or a car. I'm not adverse to the word "owner" in that way, but to me it does imply a "less-than" type of relationship with kitty, but guardian  implies a better, "more-than" connection between human and cat. When I used the word owner, the context leaned more basic or negative, whereas when I used the word guardian, it always tended toward a positive or hopeful context.

Anyone can "own" a cat, but the beauty of the relationship comes when the cat "owns" a piece of our heart and soul. Their life becomes more to us. They enrich us. Laughter, sweetness, comfort, playfulness, and love encircle us when we encircle them.

"Beware of people who dislike cats." — Irish Proverb

As a society, we can surely do better for the domestic cat. Now that we've become educated, enlightened, and are in love with a cat, how can we help the broader world to treat felines with more respect? What can we contribute outside of our homes to end the cycles of abuse and slaughter?

One simple and quiet way to support cats is not perpetuating negative ideas and words about them. While it is good to embrace that cats are funny and quirky, so commonly in our society today people mock and exploit the reputation of cats via social media, spreading incorrect ideas about them. As cat advocates, we must help others strike the correct balance between appreciating the humor in these furry companions without taking it into a negative space. Think of how people still often label the black cat as unlucky or a bad omen. This has carried over in literature and media for centuries from the Middle Ages! It is completely untrue. There is nothing inherently evil about a cat who happens to have all black fur. Today, what other untruths does society perpetuate about cats?

"Fat cats are funny and cute." In reality, as an owner, allowing our cat to get obese is on us. The common diseases and ailments that arise from obesity shorten cats' lives, as well as their quality of life when they can't play readily, groom themselves properly, or run and jump easily.

"Cats are tiny psychopaths." Because so many people do not understand cats and don't know how to integrate them into their homes, some humans think cats are crazy and scary, wielding knives and plotting to kill them. There is zero truth in cats planning to harm or murder the family. If cats are unpredictable and lash out, it most often results from the family's failure to properly socialize the cat.

"People who like cats are *crazy*." There is no such negative word that I am aware of applied to dog lovers. So why cats? My father once bought me a "crazy cat lady" mug, and I informed him, "I *am* a cat lady, yes, but I am in no way crazy." Along with this "crazy" term, men often still get mocked by other men if they say they like cats. Somehow, it's unmanly to like cats?

Let's not participate in these false ideas. Don't buy that "funny" knife-wielding cat t-shirt. Don't repost the fat-cat meme. Don't agree with others when they say negative things about their cats. Instead, do your part to add positive information about cats to the world. Share your love for them. Create messages of respect around kitties. Embrace wholesome cat humor. Encourage men to openly adore cats.

Help cats beyond your homes by donating to good causes, rescues, or shelters that support the positive and healthy care of cats. Find an organization that helps low-income families with pet food or medical costs and promote them on social media or in email to your friends and family. Support rescues that foster pet cats temporarily for families when they fall on hard times like homelessness, imprisonment, or spells in rehab—the goal being to reunite the family and pet within 3-12 months. Check in on the permanent no-kill sanctuary for unwanted cats in your area, if there is one, and make sure they are caring for the cats well.

Sometimes sanctuaries take on too many cats and may need help expanding their facilities, caring for cats with disabilities, or deep cleaning the shelter.

An enjoyable way to help cats is to become a foster home within the rescue or shelter system. It's super fun and fairly easy to care for older kittens or a mama cat with kittens. Neonatal orphaned kittens need quality foster homes, willing to devote the time and attention to raise them. There is a great need for people to specialize in fostering adult cats who require rehabilitation in either behavioral concerns or from trauma. If you have a medical background, you might look after cats or kittens with physical recovery needs.

Or simply advocate for cats with everyone you meet. Through conversation, help them know what you have learned. Raise their level of cat care by being a good example and resource.

"In a cat's eye, all things belong to cats." — English Proverb

This book is a great reference tool for you in the future, when you or a friend run into some concerns with a kitty. However, I want our final parting thoughts to focus on the major points that I hope are committed now in your mind and heart.

It's a Journey

Everyone is at a different place in their life and on the journey with their pet cats. Regardless of where you are, as long as you are facing and moving in the direction of healing and love, allow yourself some compassion. We don't want to get complacent. Staying longer in a neutral zone makes it easier to turn back and revert to old patterns, habits, feelings, and beliefs. The journey forward takes consistency of effort. Even if you only move a few steps forward at a time, it's progress. *Enjoy* the journeying and growing—becoming a better person and a skilled cat guardian.

Not Perfect, But Purrrfect

On your journey you are not likely to do things perfectly, every time, every day. Your kitty will likewise have imperfect spells, too. Show love

❀ *A "purrrfect day" to smell roses.*

for yourself and for kitty as you both grow and change and help each other. "Purrrfect" represents progress in your connection and not actual perfection.

BOND

Everything I have taught in regard to taking good care of your cat can boil down into this: **Be O**bservant, **N**urturing, **D**edicated. We need to *observe* carefully how our cats communicate with us, and how their bodies are doing, how our environments shift, how others in the home interact with each kitty. We *nurture* by offering patience, compassion, affection, empathy, support, and healing. Our *dedication* comes in the form of not giving up. We go all the way *and* the extra mile.

❀ *Minnie right after her first adopter surrendered her back to me.*

Spiritual Growth is Vital

Becoming aligned with God and Spirit, with Universal Intelligence, with Angels, and the signs they send us is the one true and lasting way to find joy and peace. When we put our spiritual health and vitality first, our emotional, mental, and physical health will all automatically improve. Alignment with God allows us to become open to receiving messages, instructions, and inspiration that can literally save lives, including our beloved kitties. Miracles are possible. Signs are given. Spirit gently whispers and guides. Angels can only help us if we ask.

Holistic Helps

We have many alternative tools to consider in both our own care and for the care of our cats. Wherever we can, let's reduce toxicity in our lives and promote cleaner living and eating. When we take better care of ourselves, we are more equipped to help others, like our pets. There is much to explore, and it requires self-education and research to make wise choices. When it comes to medical care, work with a holistic veterinarian or one open to exploring holistic remedies with you. It's okay to think outside the box in health care while respecting the value and place of traditional medicine.

Energy Healing is Amazing!

There are so many modalities to try out. All are helpful in shifting energies, releasing the negative and encouraging the positive within all the energy bodies. I recommend Emotion Code, Body Code, Belief Code, EFT, and RET, as these tools have made a positive impact in my own life and health. Other aspects to energy healing might include utilizing crystals, healing sounds, or frequencies.

Hire a Cat Behavior Professional

Just like with dogs, cats and people need help understanding each other. This book does exactly that. But it isn't possible to put *everything* in one book. Each situation will have its individual nuances, and a professional will be able to figure out what your specific situation requires.

Lap Cats Should Not Be Rare

Well-socialized cats want to live with a human they love and trust. Happy cats follow their people from room to room, ask to be petted and picked up, snuggle against them or on laps. If we build trust and make the environment safe for kitty, he will show affection. We can help shift the perception that cats are aloof by becoming the guardians with whom they want to love and cuddle.

Spread Purrrfection Everywhere

Wherever you can, help spread the good words you have learned here so that cats everywhere will have better lives. As you become a wonderful cat *guardian*, help others around you to do the same. Cats world-wide deserve better home lives, as we all do.

I recall years ago chatting with a man online via a dating website. He was interesting, but I quickly sensed red flags and decided to discontinue communication. One of the flags for me was that he said in a very authoritative way that God (in the Old Testament) stated animals were unclean and not to be allowed into our homes. I never did find that reference within the Bible and would not have been swayed by it anyway. While animals do of course bring dirt into our homes, *they bring so much potential for joy*! The purring and head bonking of the cat when you come home, the excitedly thumping doggie tail when he sees your car drive up, the crazy funny antics of all pets that bring laughter into our lives, the sweet snuggles when we are ill or sobbing from a heartache. I cannot imagine a God of love, my God, creating these creatures for us and then barring them from our homes. He created these animals in particular, knowing they would become companions for millions upon millions of his children throughout time. He *wanted* them for us—to bring joy, friendship, lessons in love and loss, experiences of sacrifice and service, and so much more. I know God has and will continue to use animals to teach His children gentleness, kindness, and acceptance. We can develop, progress, and draw closer to Him because of our associations with His lovely, adorable critters—for me most particularly, the cat.

"The dog may be wonderful prose, but only the cat is poetry."

– French Proverb

ANSWER KEY FOR CHAPTER 1 QUIZ

1. How frequently do you yell at your cat?

a. 1 point   b. 2 points
c. 3 points   d. 4 points

2. Do you find yourself complaining about your cat to others?

a. 4 points   b. 2 points
c. 3 points   d. 1 point

3. Have you ever used corporal punishments with your cat like spanking, slapping, nose bopping, shoving, flicking, or kicking?

a. 2 points   b. 4 points
c. 3 points   d. 1 point

4. Do you use punishments like water spraying, yelling, hand clapping, scolding?

a. 4 points   b. 3 points
c. 2 points   d. 1 point

5. Does your cat spend the day mostly hiding away from everyone?

a. 4 points   b. 1 point

6. Does your cat lash out at you when being picked up, petted, or played with?

a. 3 points   b. 2 points
c. 4 points   d. 1 point

7. Does your cat follow you around the house from room to room?

a. 1 point   b. 3 points

8. Does your cat ever seek you out for snuggles, petting, or lap sitting?

a. 1 point   b. 2 points   c. 3 points

9. Is your cat curious, exploring, playful?

a. 1 point   b. 2 points   c. 3 points

10. Was your cat fully socialized during the critical period of age two weeks to nine weeks with humans prior to adopting her?

a. 1 point   b. 3 points   c. 2 points

11. Do you have behavioral concerns with litterbox, spraying, aggression, destroying furniture/home, yowling, fear of people, or overgrooming?

a. 5 points   b. 4 points   c. 3 points
d. 2 points   e. 1 point

12. Is your cat spayed/neutered and vaccinated?

a. 1 point   b. 2 points
c. 3 points   d. 4 points

13. When did you last go to the veterinarian with kitty?

a. 1 point   b. 2 points   c. 3 points
d. 4 points   e. 5 points

14. Do you ever swear at the cat?

a. 3 points   b. 2 points   c. 1 point

15. Did you give kitty a negative sounding name or nicknames?

a. 2 points   b. 3 points   c. 1 point

16. Do you love your cat?

a. 3 points   b. 2 points
c. 1 point   d. 4 points

Index

Acknowledgments

To my dad who sparked this cat book writing idea and to my mom for encouraging me on this creative endeavor. Thanks to Ellie Whitney, my sister, writing buddy, sounding board, and grammar guru. Thank you to these women who helped in different ways to produce this book—Beth Wareham, Anna K. Mockett, Connie J. Mableson, Esq., Anna Krusinski, Megan Sheer, Heather Wallace, Lara Abramson, and Dr. Eleanor Jenson, DVM. To God for inspiration on what to add and what to remove.

Author Bio

During Jessica's college years, a fellow student once predicted, "You're going to become an old maid with five cats!"

He was so wrong. She actually has six cats.

Jessica lives with her family of cats in northern Utah where she longs to have a beautiful farm. But, until that dream comes true, she gardens, preserves food, bakes bread, and crochets a lot of blankets. She values all things holistic and desires to continue to improve her own life through green, organic, self-sufficient living.

After seventeen years working as a producer, director, and creative project manager in the video and marketing realms, Jessica felt a calling to switch career paths. Now, she loves her work even more because she finds so much fulfillment helping her cat and human clients via energy healing and spiritual mentoring so that they can heal their rifts and come together in healthy bonding.

In addition to her personalized consultations, with the release of *Purrrfecting Your Bond*, Jessica looks to offer practical cat care tips, coupled with spiritual practices, to foster a harmonious human-feline relationship.

Visit jessicamockett.com to learn more about her one-on-one consultations.

www.ingramcontent.com/pod-product-compliance
Lightning Source LLC
Chambersburg PA
CBHW051606120626
46551CB00014B/1695